ALLEGORIES OF TRANSGRESSION AND TRANSFORMATION

ALLEGORIES OF TRANSGRESSION AND TRANSFORMATION

Experimental Fiction by Women Writing Under Dictatorship

MARY BETH TIERNEY-TELLO

STATE UNIVERSITY OF NEW YORK PRESS

Published by
State University of New York Press, Albany

© 1996 State University of New York

All rights reserved

Printed in the United States of America

For information, address State University of New York Press,
State University Plaza, Albany, N.Y. 12246

Production by M. R. Mulholland
Marketing by Theresa A. Swierzowski

Library of Congress Cataloging-in-Publication Data

Tierney-Tello, Mary Beth, 1961-
    Allegories of transgression and transformation : experimental
fiction by women writing under dictatorship / Mary Beth Tierney
-Tello.
        p.   cm.
    Includes bibliographical references and index.
    ISBN 0-7914-3035-9 (hc : alk. paper). — ISBN 0-7914-3036-7 (pb :
alk. paper)
    1. Latin American fiction—20th century—History and criticism.
2. Latin American fiction—Women authors—History and criticism.
3. Experimental fiction, Latin American—History and criticism.
4. Women and literature—Latin America. 5. Dictatorship in
literature. 6. Allegory. 7. Piñon, Nélida. Casa da paixão.
8. Eltit, Diamela, 1949-   Por la patria. 9. Roffé, Reina, 1951-
Rompiente. 10. Peri Rossi, Cristina, 1941-   Nave de los locos.
I. Title.
PQ7082.N7T46 1996
863—dc20   95-41407
                                                                              CIP

FOR GUILLERMO AND NICOLAS

CONTENTS

ACKNOWLEDGMENTS

I am grateful to many people for support while writing and revising this book. I would first like to thank the many friends and colleagues at Brown University who provided intellectual stimulation, guidance, and various kinds of sustenance during my years there. My deepest thanks go to Stephanie Merrim, Nelson Vieira, Dorothy Escribano, and Pilar Tirado for reading early drafts of each chapter and for their encouragement during the most difficult phases of this project. Special thanks go to Beth Bauer who, on short notice, gave me invaluable feedback on the introduction. Thanks also to Julio Ortega for his generosity with materials. At Wheaton College I would like to thank all of my colleagues in the Department of Hispanic and Italian Studies, especially Héctor Medina for his unstinting support and Tommasina Gabriele for her friendship and sound advice. I am also grateful to Wheaton for release time from teaching which allowed me to complete the book. For clerical assistance, computer rescues, and good cheer, thanks to Marie Roderick (at Brown) and Marilyn Todesco (at Wheaton). And I am eternally grateful to the library staffs at both Wheaton College and Brown University, especially in the interlibrary loan offices.

I am particularly indebted to the readers for SUNY Press—Amy Kaminsky, Marjorie Agosín as well as another reader who chose to remain anonymous—for their wonderfully detailed readings and insightful suggestions which helped immensely as I revised the manuscript. Very special thanks go to Diamela Eltit and Reina Roffé for taking the time to respond to my queries about their work. I also extend my thanks to Patricia Sobral for proofing my translations from the Portuguese with great care, insight, and enthusiasm. Marguerite Harrison and Ellen Douglass were sources of inspirational "conversa portuguesa" and insight into Brazilian culture; my warmest thanks to them and especially to Ellen for her generosity with materials on Nélida Piñon. For the past two years I have relied heavily on the expert child care provided by Cheryl Goupil, Barbara Tierney, and Nancy Hobson. Without them this book would have taken many more years to complete. I thank my parents for all their support. For friendship, ideas, encouragement, and humor over the years, my most heartfelt thanks to Laura Pirott-Quintero, Marje Salvodon, Sylvia Santaballa, Lisa Maurizio, Annie Smart, and Brad Epps.

Finally, my deepest gratitude goes to Guillermo Tello whose generosity of heart, unwavering faith in my abilities, and sense of perspective have been a blessing in many ways. And to little Nicolas, for bringing me so much joy.

I gratefully acknowledge permission to reprint material from chapter two that originally appeared in *Monographic Review/Revista Monográfica*, volume VIII, 1992. Parts of chapter three originally appeared in *Latin American Literary Review*, volume XXI, number 42, 1993, Pittsburgh, Pennsylvania; reprinted by permission of the publisher. I also gratefully acknowledge permission to reprint material from the following: from *Por la patria*, Copyright 1986 by Diamela Eltit, reprinted by permission of the author; from *La nave de los locos*, Copyright 1984 by Cristina Peri Rossi, reprinted by permission of Seix Barral, S.A. and the author; from *The Ship of Fools*, Copyright 1984 by Cristina Peri Rossi, translated by Psiche Hughes, reprinted by permission of Readers International, Inc.; from *La rompiente*, Copyright 1987 by Reina Roffé, reprinted by permission of the author; from *A Casa da Paixão*, Copyright 1972 by Nélida Piñon, reprinted by permission of the author; from *Zones of Pain/Las zonas del dolor*, Copyright 1988 by Marjorie Agosín, translations by Cola Franzen, reprinted by permission of White Pine Press; from *Descomposición*, Copyright 1986 by Liliana Lukin, reprinted by permission of Ediciones de la Flor, S.R.L.; from "El discurso público de Pinochet (1973–1976)," by Giselle Munizaga and Carlos Ochensius, Copyright 1983 by Hernán Vidal, reprinted by permission of the Institute for the Study of Ideologies and Literature; from "Política, ideología y figuración literaria," by Beatriz Sarlo, Copyright 1987 by the Institute for the Study of Ideologies and Literature, reprinted by permission of the Institute; from "Apuntes sobre la crítica feminista y la literatura hispanoamericana," Copyright 1986 by Jean Franco, reprinted by permission of *Hispamérica* and the author; from "Third-World Literature in the Era of Multinational Capital," by Fredric Jameson, *Social Text.*, 15:3 (Fall 1986), pp. 65–88, Copyright Duke University Press, reprinted with permission.

INTRODUCTION

WOMEN WRITING THROUGH AND AGAINST DICTATORSHIP: AUTHORITY, AUTHORSHIP, AND THE AUTHORITARIAN STATE

La experiencia cotidiana concreta de
las mujeres es el autoritarismo.

[The concrete everyday experience
of women is authoritarianism.]

—Julieta Kirkwood

Tell all the Truth but tell it slant—

—Emily Dickinson

Conventional wars are most often fought against enemies outside the social fabric of a particular culture or country. Yet in Brazil, Chile, Argentina, and Uruguay during the 1970s and 80s, "dirty wars" were fought against an enemy within the very tissue of those societies. As more and more groups (radical student and labor organizations, leftist movements) in these countries demanded representation and social change during the 60s and 70s, there were corresponding *golpes* by the military apparatuses in those countries, whose main goal was to wipe out the burgeoning revolutionary forces. The military governments went far beyond their initial task of annihilating the subversive movements in their respective countries, however. Implementing a so-called doctrine of National Security, these regimes virtually waged war on their own populace, which they considered to be dangerously contaminated by Marxist ideology.[1] Because of the nature of this "internal" threat, culture (in all its manifestations) and education were prime battlegrounds for what the military regimes viewed as a virtual ideological war. In order to eradicate what they saw as "the marxist cancer,"[2] they coerced and brutalized their own citizens (including women, men, and children) into a state of abject terror, using such techniques as censorship, kidnapping, torture, and murder.[3] The most obviously and directly affected by the brutality of these regimes were the "disappeared," whose numbers are estimated in the thousands, and their families. The stories of those who survived their ordeals are recorded in volumes such as *Nunca Más* (Argentina) and *Brasil, Nunca Mais.* But, in many ways, the testimonies of the "disappeared" as well as of intellectuals and dissidents who, also in great numbers, fled into exile, constitute only the more formal documentation of a society at war with itself. The collective consequences of such silencing, of such fear and institutionalized violence, are perhaps less easily documented and only beginning to be witnessed. Indeed, the effect of these "dirty wars"—where the enemy was located as internal (that is, both within the borders of the country as well as within the minds and hearts of its citizens)—was a correspondent interiorization of censorship, exile, and violence. Furthermore, in the aftermath of such horror, when the refrain "algo habrán hecho" ["they must have done something"] could no longer defer the horror of the regime from the national consciousness, when it was no longer possible to believe in the "guilt" of all of the disappeared and tortured, the populace was forced to confront the fact that the enemy was indeed within: their neighbors and relatives had been kidnapped, tortured, raped, and murdered by their own fellow citizens and, moreover, not by "criminals" but by the very forces supposedly assigned to protect the civilian population.[4] It is perhaps this aspect of the authoritarian regimes that proved the most chilling, producing a silence pregnant with pain, loss, and guilt, a silence that Argentine poet Liliana Lukin characterizes as "like looking into the eyes of the murderer / while remembering the eyes of the murdered" ("proceso" in *Descomposición*). Chilean poet Marjorie Agosín's words also convey the sense of incredulity, complicity, and shock caused by the realization of this enemy within, of these torturers who are "padres de familia / abuelos / tíos y compadres":

> Y lo más increíble
> era gente
> como Usted
> como yo
> sí, gente fina
> como nosotros.

[And the most unbelievable part
they were people
like you
like me
yes, nice people
just like us.]

(*Zones of Pain* / *Las zonas del dolor* 11–12)

The horror and violence is thus very much within the borders of the nation, within the citizens who form that nation. Indeed, that such a horrible violence could thrive within the very institutions of "justice," of the "law," all in the name of democracy, the family, and national security, ultimately points to a radical failure of such institutions and social structures. In the face of such failure, and with the recognition that a change of consciousness cannot be legislated, it becomes even more clear that profound, internal transformations are needed. Literature is perhaps the place where these internal horrors and transformations can be most cogently glimpsed, represented, and addressed. Raymond Williams has described how literature is uniquely situated to take stock of what he calls "structures of feeling," that is, those "social experiences in solution" that have not yet been crystallized in rational or expository discourses, but which are nonetheless part of the experience of the social subject (132–34). Uruguayan poet and novelist Cristina Peri Rossi would perhaps characterize such raw and, as yet, unarticulated experiences as "indicios" / "indications": "actions or signs that reveal what is hidden" (*Indicios* 9). She chooses to "read" and textualize these "indicios" in the short stories, poems and prose pieces that make up her volume *Indicios pánicos*, written before the military formally assumed power in Uruguay and yet presaging that course of events that would later drive her into exile. As Peri Rossi makes clear in this text, literature is, for her, where the multiplicity and contradictory nature of these "indicios" can be read and written into some sort of coherence:

Leer (y nunca sabremos si una lectura ha sido correcta, entre todas las posibles) esos indicios, descubrirlos, desentrañarlos, significa poseer una visión del mundo, sin la cual el caleidoscopio es desconcertante, a menudo contradictorio, siempre azaroso. No hay *una* lectura, pues, y los indicios son múltiples, infinitos, inabarcables. Lo cual permite, además la pluralidad de libros, de cuadros, de poemas. Un mundo regido por una sola lectura, sería insoportable, y eso es lo que a veces no comprenden los políticos, los propios visionarios, los místicos (*Indicios* 10).

[To read (and we will never know if a reading has been correct, among all the possible ones) those indications, to discover them, to disentangle them, means possessing a vision of the world, without which the kaleidoscope is disconcerting, frequently contradictory, always chancy. There is not one reading, then, and the indications are multiple, infinite, ungraspable. This permits, furthermore, the plurality of books, of paintings, of poems. A world governed by *one* single reading would be unbearable, and that is what politicians, mystics, even visionaries sometimes do not understand.]

In this way, the multifarious coherence of art and literature, always provisional and never final, is nothing like the type of coherence sought after by authoritarian regimes that attempt to impose a singular "reading" of the human condition. Literature is thus where this authoritarian single-mindedness can be perhaps most effectively confronted and dismantled.

The univocality of authoritarianism has been noted by many scholars who describe how the regimes typically monopolized public discourse (the press, publications, television) such that dialogue was eliminated, driven underground, muted, or completely silenced.[5] In a similar vein, Argentine writer and critic Ricardo Piglia shows how the military regime tries to be the source of all meaning, producing its own criminal "fiction" in order to "cover up reality" (97). But, as Piglia points out, narrative picks up such social fictions and reworks them: "the novel in reality reproduces, interiorizes and transforms—and, I would say, preserves—these social fictions. I think that this is the way literature is connected to the social and the political" ("Ficción y política" 97–98). Literature, thus, working at the intersection of personal biography and social discourses and fictions, both incorporates and transforms systems of signification. Even further, literature and other cultural production can resist the univocality imposed by what has been called the discourse of authoritarianism. Beatriz Sarlo eloquently sums up the relationship between such a discourse and literature:

Si el discurso del régimen se caracterizaba por cerrar el flujo de los significados y, en consecuencia, indicar líneas obligadas de construcción de sentido, proporcionando un modelo comunicacional pobre y unidireccional, en el cual un elenco muy reducido de figuras agotaban las representaciones de lo social y lo individual, de lo público y lo privado, del presente y de la historia, los discursos de la literatura podían proponer una práctica justamente de sentidos abiertos, de cadena que no cierra, de figuraciones abundantes ("Política, ideología y figuración literaria 40).

[If the discourse of the regime was characterized by closing off the flow of meaning and, in consequence, indicating obligatory lines of the construction of meaning, thus providing an impoverished and unidirectional communicational model in which a very reduced list of figures depleted the representations of the social and the individual, of the public and the private, of the present and of history, the discourses of literature could propose precisely a practice of open meanings, of an unclosed chain, of abundant imaginings.]

In fact, Sarlo's article (specifically focused on Argentina) provides much insight on how literature in general manages to narrate and/or critique what authoritarian discourse works to hide or naturalize. Indeed, her observations on narrative structures can be fruitfully read with regard to many works written under similar circumstances. She ends her essay with the following summary: "[these texts] spoke of what the voice of power concealed or naturalized; they . . . showed up the fissures through which one could see, as Adorno would say, 'that which ideology conceals,' that is, also, what it is possible to suffer, but difficult to turn into discourse" ("Política, ideología y figuración literaria" 58). While Sarlo deals exclusively with Argentine narrative by male writers (of the thirty-two works she mentions, none is by a woman novelist), I would suggest that such narrative techniques are complicated and enriched as women writers confront not only what is obscured by authoritarian discourse but by patriarchal discourse as well.[6]

Just as authoritarian discourse works to conceal as well as to naturalize certain social phenomena (as Sarlo points out), so too does patriarchal discourse work to hide, obscure, and/or naturalize aspects of sexuality and gender. Feminist scholarship of the past several decades suggests that what patriarchal discourse most works to naturalize, to render "clear" and beyond interrogation, is women's roles, the family structure, and sexual relations—in other words, the sex/gender system.[7] The flipside of this "clarity," of course, is that what the patriarchal sexual order most obscures is feminine desire. Many feminists have shown how, in patriarchal discourse, woman is projected as man's "other," seen to be his reflection, that is, everything he is not, thus cutting her off from any desire of her own.[8] Together this organization of sexuality and desire constitute what is generally known as the patriarchal sexual economy. Such an organization of sexuality and gender is certainly not discordant with the authoritarian worldview; indeed, the authoritarian system could be seen as an intensification of the patriarchal order.[9] In the authoritarian regimes under discussion, the official discourse indeed gives a singular and highly traditional "reading" or interpretation to the sex/gender system, attempting to make its function appear natural and beyond question: women's role is maternal self-sacrifice for the good of the future of the nation (their children), the family sphere is a sanctum where clearly denominated sex roles prevail thus preserving the nation's moral fiber, and sexual relations, needless to say, are confined to matrimonial heterosexuality.[10] Likewise, with regard to desire, in attempting to be the source of all meanings and to shut down figurative possibilities, the authoritarian regime tries to limit the populace's own libidinal reproductions, causing a general alienation that is not unlike what women experience in the face of patriarchal representations of Woman.

Such a relationship between the patriarchal sexual economy and authoritarian practices has become increasingly clear to women of the Southern Cone; indeed, an important aspect of the political mobilization that led to the transition to democracy was a surge in women's movements which ultimately came to see authoritarianism as an expression and outgrowth of patriarchal oppression.[11] As Sonia Alvarez points out: "Mainstream analysts overlooked this gender-based dimension of the military authoritarian State. *South American feminist scholars and activists, however, insisted that militarism and institutionalized violence rest on patriarchal foundations*" (7; emphasis added). Indeed, the fact that feminist theorists and writers of the countries under consideration perceive a clear correlation between authoritarianism and gender politics could actually be seen as an inadvertent by-product of the state policies of the regimes themselves. Alvarez, for example, explains how policies that attempted to mark a strict (and traditional) division between public and private actually caused women to bear the brunt of conservative economic policies that increasingly impoverished the working classes.[12] It was, therefore, women (especially of the working classes) who began organizing, protesting, and demonstrating *first*, and marching, furthermore, *as mothers*, a phenomenon Alvarez calls the "politicization of motherhood" (43–51). In addition, the violence enacted by the military was often directed against women in particularly brutal ways, which included the systematic sexual assault on women prisoners, the rape of mothers in the presence of their families, and the abduction of pregnant women who were then either tortured until miscarrying or who were allowed to give birth only to be permanently separated from their newborns.[13] Such actions, as Jean Franco points out, constitute vicious attacks on the very institutions (e.g., the traditional family) invoked and extolled by the military.[14] Indeed, as Franco and others have pointed out, the Madres de la Plaza de Mayo constitute one example of how women—after being forced out of their traditionally private sphere by authoritarian practices and policies—have redefined their roles as mothers in the public sphere, thus revealing the hypocrisy of a government that sought to glorify maternity and yet took their children from them.[15]

Just as many Latin American feminists working on social issues inevitably began to see gender issues and politics as interrelated, literature by women writing under dictatorship is also often concerned with the politics of sexuality. Extrapolating in a way from Sarlo's formulations to include generic concerns, we can say that where patriarchal, authoritarian discourses obscure feminine desire, reducing female sexuality to reproduction and maternity, literature by women can uncover the power relations at work in the conventional sex/gender system, multiplying the possible paths of desire and broadening the female sexual imaginary. Where authoritarian, patriarchal discourses constitute a particular sociosexual script for women, providing and reinforcing normative representations of Woman, writing by women can work to delegitimate and undo such scripts and to rewrite female sexuality.[16] Certainly, male writers also used sexuality, the body, and gender differences in order to refer to and denounce the power relations at work under authoritarianism.[17] I am more interested, however, in exploring in depth how several selected women writers confront and respond to patriarchal, authoritarian discourses and representations, how processes of gendering come under attack in their texts, and how they manage to open new imaginary repertoires for women writers and create new possibilities for female subjectivity.[18] For this task, I have selected several works by four South American women authors who were writing during or in the aftermath of the authoritarian regimes in their respective countries: *A Casa da Paixão* [The House of Passion] (1972) by Brazilian Nélida Piñon, *Por la patria* [For the Fatherland] (1986) by Diamela Eltit of Chile, *La rompiente* [The Breakwater] (1987) by Reina Roffé of Argentina, and *La nave de los locos* [*The Ship of Fools*] (1984) by Uruguayan Cristina Peri Rossi.[19] As we shall see in subsequent chapters, these narratives were written at different moments under authoritarian regimes and their authors maintained a distinct relationship to their sociopolitical and literary context. In fact, two of the authors—Roffé and Peri Rossi—went into exile in response to the oppression in their homelands. Similarly, just as each writer's personal situation was different, the texts I have chosen do not represent a singular response to authoritarianism. Rather, each text addresses different aspects of the effects of dictatorship, while also striving—each in a different way—to develop new means of articulating gender and feminine sexuality. Common to these narratives is an element of resistance to authoritarianism that is articulated in particularly sexual terms. Indeed, in each case there is a particular combination and conflation of the sexual and the political, realms traditionally held separate and whose boundaries the authoritarian regimes tried to strengthen and reaffirm. As we shall see, sexuality is not portrayed as a personal and intimate sphere of interaction, but rather as a highly political, social process where issues of power and control are foregrounded.

Resistance to authoritarianism in these novels is thus seen as having everything to do with psychosexual transformations, with the supposedly "personal" sphere of the body and sexuality. Taken as a whole, these texts suggest that resistance and transformation must occur on a sexual as well as a social level. That sexuality and politics are drawn together in this way can be seen as both a response to and an outgrowth of authoritarianism since, indeed, the authoritarian regime wages part of its ideological battle on the turf of sociosexual roles.[20] But such a correlation between generic concerns and political issues is obviously complex and realized differently in each social subject. *How* each of the texts I have chosen draws the political and sexual together is the focus of my readings. Yet, this focus is not merely thematic but rather allows for the examination of how these texts confront and critique the intertwined power structures of patriarchy and authoritarianism. Such a confrontation necessarily takes place in the realm of language and discourse. Indeed, in each text, language and literary practice are inscribed as of prime importance, as a site of a battle for meaning, as a simultaneously personal and social sphere where both complicity and resistance are engendered.[21] It is this web of authority, gender, and writing to which I will now turn.

Resistance to Authorities: Politics, Gender, and Women's Writing

Jean Franco has pointed out that, when asked, most Latin American women writers deny that anything such as "women's writing" exists.[22] She goes on to suggest, however, that the question is poorly formulated and proposes instead that the focus should be on power relations, on the historic marginalization of women, and on the consequentially problematic position vis-à-vis authority faced by women who write. Her observations are worth quoting in full:

> No se trata de averiguar si las escritoras tienen temas específicos o un estilo diferente a los hombres, sino de explorar las relaciones del poder. Todo escritor, tanto hombre como mujer, enfrenta el problema de la autoridad textual o de la voz poética ya que, desde el momento en que empieza a escribir, establece relaciones de afiliación o de diferencia para con los "maestros" del pasado. Esta confrontación tiene un interés especial cuando se trata de una mujer escribiendo "contra" el poder asfixiante de una voz patriarcal ("Apuntes" 41).

> [It is not a question of investigating whether women writers have specific themes or a different style from men, but rather of exploring power relations. Every writer, man or woman, confronts the problem of textual authority or of poetic voice since, from the moment he or she begins to write, he or she establishes relationships of affiliation or difference with the "masters" of the past. This confrontation is of special interest when it is a question of a woman writing "against" the asphyxiating power of a patriarchal voice.]

Indeed, in the context I am dealing with in this study, the "voice of authority" is a many faceted entity, whose complex and multiple aspects the social subject necessarily experiences in a conjugated way. First of all, as writers of contemporary Latin American narrative, each of the authors included in this study inevitably confronts the authorial authority of their literary traditions, the most resonant being, in this case, the canonical "Boom" writers.[23] Secondly, the fact that all of the writers ever included in the "Boom" are men only illustrates Franco's point: women writers face an additional confrontation with the authority of a patriarchal order, an organization of the gender system whereby one gender undeniably has a privileged relationship to the production of meaning and whereby Woman is a normative representation that inhibits rather than enables women's subjectivity. But not only do these particular women writers confront an authority that has traditionally marginalized them, they also write against another gen(d)eric authority of literary history, which, as Debra Castillo explains, holds that if women write at all, they "certainly do not write narrative" (26). We can add another authoritative "expectation," which each of these writers confronts and works against—that is, that if women *do* write narrative, it is subjective and *intimista*, concerned with domestic issues, disengaged from history and politics, and most certainly not experimental.[24] Finally and perhaps most importantly, the authorities of a (patriarchal) literary tradition are, of course, further intensified and complicated by the univocal mandates of the authoritarian state, which advocates traditional gender roles and which polices *any* cultural production through censorship.

Each of the texts under consideration here works to challenge these authorities to various degrees and in different ways. My conceptualization of a women's writing thus has less to do with a specificity in language and more to do with women's historical marginalization from the production of meaning, with their specific relationship to the process of author-ization. In this regard, Sylvia Molloy's comments on women's writing are elucidating. In response to an interviewer's postulation that "phallocentric language excludes women" (146), Molloy stresses marginalization rather than outright exclusion: "It doesn't seem to me that it is a question of exclusion. More than exclude the woman, that language relegates the woman to a subaltern place and *through its authority it deauthorizes the feminine word.* That is to say it includes her, but in a position of weakness" (146; emphasis added). Authority is thus the central issue: women are always differently invested in power structures because they are women (which is not to deny that social class, race, and cultural conventions also determine the nature of that difference, creating profound differences among women themselves). The specificity of women's condition and of women's writing is primarily a function of this different relationship to authority. For Molloy, for example, women's writing has less to do with language itself and more to do with how women deploy their given language:

"establishing a new practice, subverting authoritarian language that puts women 'in their place,' dis-placing themselves through what Josefina Ludmer calls 'the tricks of the weak'. That is where their specificity lies, manifested in different ways in each period" (147). Women's writing, indeed that women assume authorship at all, can thus be conceived as an act of resistance. Debra Castillo points out that female defiance and resistance in literature—in many ways the subject of her book *Talking Back*—necessarily involve a double agenda of both literary and practical concerns: "The refusal to abide by old discursive traditions is . . . both poetic and political, involving the careful critique of conventions that are both literary/rhetorical and ideological" (11). Likewise, in addressing the narrative texts chosen for this study I direct my attention to the various ways they defy conventions: textual, sexual, and political. First, in terms of an ideological critique, each of these texts challenges both the authority of gender codes as well as the more sociopolitical authority of the authoritarian state, in such a way that resistance to authority is enacted on both a sexual and political level.[25] Second, on a "literary/rhetorical" level, as we shall see, these narratives manage their ideological critique through the use of experimental narrative techniques, one of which is the use of allegorical gestures.[26]

Turning first to the ideological critique, each of the texts I have chosen represents a power struggle that enacts a double social critique: of the patriarchal sexual economy as well as authoritarianism. First of all, if we consider, as Sally Robinson suggests, that gender "can be conceived as a system of meaning, rather than a quality 'owned' by individuals,"[27] each of the texts included in this study (re)produces gender in particular ways, suggesting specific manners of understanding gender differences and sexuality. My hope is to give these postulations their due, in all their complexity and contradiction, in order to try to respond to Sara Castro-Klarén's call for theorizing *from* Latin American women's literature. As this critic asserts: "There now exists a good number of texts written by Latin American women, but we still have not elaborated theoretical positions derived from the reading of *those* texts" (43; emphasis in the original). Likewise, my working hypothesis as I approach each of my selected texts is that we can learn a great deal about theories of gender *from* their fictions. The ways gender is (re)produced in these texts provide different views on previous formulations as well as new postulations of their own. What these texts share—and causes me to consider them as a group for this study—is a decidedly critical view of past or current forms of gendering. Each narrative in some way suggests that gender and sexuality are places of (political) contention, effectively denaturalizing the patriarchal ideology that would forever confuse nature and culture, females and the feminine, women and Woman, so as to perpetuate the status quo. So, while the contentious view of gender takes different forms in each text, resistance to authority and transgression of norms are a common thread. For example, in Piñon's *A Casa da Paixão*, the bulk of the narrative involves a daughter's struggle against her father's law and the traditional process of gendering. In Eltit's *Por la patria*, the family sphere is not a place of acceptance and implementation of sexual law but rather an embattled scene of incest, sexual confusion, and disidentity. Sexually inflected struggle is also key to Roffé's text, *La rompiente*, which strives to break down censorships pertaining to feminine desire and sexuality. And finally Peri Rossi's *La nave de los locos* critiques traditionally binary gender identities as rigid and oppressive. In this way, each text engages in a resistance to authority of a sexual/genderic sort. This resistance often involves overt transgressions of sexual norms, ranging from a parody of the typical heterosexual love story in *La rompiente* to representations of a sexual liaison with the sun in *A Casa da Paixão*, of homosexual and lesbian eroticism in *La nave de los locos*, and of incestuous relations in Eltit's text.

Furthermore, while the struggles in these texts blatantly work to resist authority on a genderic level, they also suggest a relationship between their defiance and the authoritarian context. The relationship between the genderic power relations and the sociopolitical situation is perhaps most oblique in Piñon's *A Casa da Paixão*. Given that the text was published at the most oppressive moment of Brazil's dictatorship, I read the power struggle against the authoritarian father as obliquely figuring a struggle against the oppressive, dictatorial state. Yet, such a relationship is primarily brought to the text through reading in context. On the other hand, the bringing together of sexual and political critiques is most explicit in Eltit's text where acts of sexual treason question the "law of the father" as both sexual prohibition and authoritarian control. In *Por la patria*, the family sphere and the nation are superimposed and conflated, parodying and deconstructing the nation/family formulations that were such an integral part of Pinochet's own public discourse.[28] In Roffé's text, censorship is the place where the political and the sexual coalesce, since her concern in *La rompiente* is explicitly to combat repression on both political and genderic levels: the censorship imposed by the Argentine authoritarian state and the more oblique censorship experienced by the woman writer. While Roffé's text locates censorship as the space where political and sexual concerns conjoin, Peri Rossi sees exile as where they come together; indeed, exile in *La nave de los locos* is represented as a simultaneously political, sexual, and textual condition.

In short, a particular relationship between sexuality and politics is suggested by each of these texts. In an excellent study on Argentine literature of this period, Francine Masiello has suggested that the relationship between the sexual liaisons and the political situation in much of this narrative is a metaphorical one: "the relations between the sexes acquire a new metaphorical value in order to represent the dealings between the common citizen and the authoritarian power" ("Cuerpo/presencia" 156). This is certainly one way of characterizing the relation. Yet I would suggest that for women writers the relationship between sexuality and politics is not precisely metaphorical since women live the oppression of the authoritarian regime not as something *like* generic alienation, but as an *intensification* of it. In this way, we can perhaps better understand this relationship as not one between two separate spheres but as one within the other. For example, in another critical study on literature and exile in this period, Elia Kantaris has pointed out that for Argentine writer Marta Traba as well as for Cristina Peri Rossi, "the struggle against a seemingly all-pervasive alienating hegemony must be linked to an exposure of the role played within that hegemony of a patriarchal *sexual* economy in which (male) desire is construed as the desire to possess, and in particular to monopolise the means of (re)production" (248). Indeed, in a similar way, all of the writers included in my study seek to expose the oppressive sexual order that virtually *subtends* authoritarianism. In general terms, then, I suggest that the relationship between the sexual and the political in these works is more metonymical than metaphorical, implying contiguity rather than analogy or similarity.

Yet, while these writers certainly engage in a struggle *against* power (against patriarchal authorities and authoritarian practices), they are also involved in a struggle *for* power, for becoming the subject of narrative by, as Jean Franco would have it, "taking meaning into [their] own hands" ("Beyond" 514). In this sense, the texts I have chosen are not only acts of resistance to or transgression of authority, but active attempts at symbolic transformation. In fact, the power struggle in each text has very much to do with writing, with the re-casting of dominant scripts, plots, and representational modes, with re-writing and transforming discursive models. As we shall see, writing appears as theme (to a greater or lesser degree) in each of these texts. And as theme, writing is cast less as product and more as process, as a form of struggle, as a transformative terrain. In a critical article, Diamela Eltit refers to the radical inequity between the feminine and the masculine in our social order and sums up the importance of *symbolic* transformation:

Producir un cambio cultural en la economía social del género, implica reformular radicalmente el bagage simbólico que ordena enteramente a una comunidad determinada. No se trata, entonces, de un mero accionar de cambios y reivindicaciones en lo *real*—legislación, economía o particularidades de los roles—, sino de movilizar un conjunto mucho más fino y abstracto, como es la subjetividad simbólica que rige la constitución síquica del sujeto y frente al cual lo femenino, adviene desde siempre en su capitulación ante el poder—poder del discurso— ("Cultura" 1).

[Producing a cultural change in the social economy of gender, implies radically reformulating the symbolic baggage that completely orders a determined community. It is not, then, a question of merely enacting changes and vindications on the level of the *real*—legislation, economy or particularities of roles—, but rather of mobilizing a much more delicate and abstract whole, such as the symbolic subjectivity that governs the psychic construction of the subject, and vis-à-vis which the feminine always appears in its capitulation before power—the power of discourse.]

What these comments make clear is that profound change in sociosexual relations can only come about through a radical questioning of the very legitimating structures that constitute power: language and discourse. I dare say that the rest of these writers would probably agree on this point. Where they diverge is in how such discursive structures should be manipulated, what form the questioning of these structures should take, and how subjectivity, to take Eltit's example, can be re-imagined. And this is not to say that such a struggle is only involved with feminist concerns or transformations. As Debra Castillo observes about Latin American letters in general, writing and political commitment to social change often go hand in hand: "Critics and authors of fiction alike have recognized as one of their prime responsibilities the obligation to commit themselves to the 'mad' struggle over the history of meanings, not only to reveal the ways in which rhetorical concerns discursively construct reality but also to intervene in and counter these processes of reality construction" (30). Certainly in the Southern Cone of this time period, meanings and discursive constructions of realities—such as Nation, Security, Democracy—have had particularly deadly results. Yet, for the women writers included in this study, these official constructions *as well as* the discursive formulation of Woman and the Family need to be deconstructed simultaneously, and a new way of structuring our social reality needs to be envisioned. How each of them goes about such a "re-envisioning" is one of the concerns that will guide my readings.

Clearly, such attention to symbolic transformation relates to the "literary/rhetorical" level I mentioned earlier and is bound up with a certain *experimentalism*. Indeed, these writers actively question their relation to language and search for new narrative forms capable of textualizing the almost unspeakable social context. In order to gesture at the internal workings of both patriarchy and authoritarian policies as well as to imagine new sociosexual relations, these narratives all tend toward nonmimetic, nonrealistic forms, involving highly intellectual narratives that suggest an awareness of critical theories of discourse and subjectivity. Each of them entails a marked experimentalism whether principally on the level of linguistic form (*A Casa da Paixão; Por la patria*) or more in terms of narrative structure (*La rompiente; La nave de los locos*).

Such experimental techniques are far from apolitical.[29] Indeed, they can be conceived as an attempt to challenge fixed, authoritarian points of view, as a contestatory practice in the face of authoritarian univocality. Just as the authoritarian regime worked to naturalize certain meanings, so the texts included in this study work to *denaturalize* them and show them up as social, discursive constructions.[30] Furthermore, these experimental texts actively propose modes of reading whereby meaning is not immanent in the narrative but produced, constructed, deconstructed, reconstructed as the reader engages with the text, therefore showing meaning (and, by extension, truth) as difficult to know, far from transparent or "natural," and ultimately constructed through the very process of reading. On the other hand, the experimentalism of these texts also works to break with certain gen(d)eric expectations regarding women's writing. Reina Roffé explicitly refers to these expectations in the testimonial prologue to her novel: "As a woman who writes, I had received the baggage of a series of proscriptions and expectations: that women's writing lacks a symbolic level, that it is subject to the referent, that it contains an excess of unanswered questions, repetitions and details, that it is characterized by a tone of anger and resentment" (*La rompiente* 10). Women's writing, according to this stereotype, is expected to be plodding and referential, not experimental. In a more international context, writing on woman writers and the avant-garde in France, Susan Suleiman observes in *Subversive Intent*: "The avant-garde woman writer is doubly intolerable, seen from the center, because her writing escapes not one but two sets of expectations/categorizations" (15) This is because her writing—and Suleiman is here talking specifically about Marguerite Duras—neither responds to the typically political, adversarial type of avant-garde practice nor does it fulfill the expectations of women's writing as linguistically nonexperimental (15). Further proof of such assumptions about the nonexperimental nature of women's writing is provided in the preface to *Breaking the Sequence*, where the editors of the volume point out that in 1983 an MLA session on "post-realism" included not one women. The editors specifically state that their book of essays on women experimentalists constitutes a response to the mistaken notion that all experimental writers are men. So, given these cultural and literary parameters, the experimental techniques used by the writers I have chosen also challenge notions about gender and writing.[31] In a preliminary way, then, we can say that such experimentalism forms an integral part of the quest to disarticulate both dominant, authoritarian codes and gen(d)eric conventions.

The Crisis of Representation: Allegorical Possibilities and the Will to Meaning

Certainly, the experimental writing techniques of these texts are varied, but, for this study, I am especially interested in one they all share (albeit to varying degrees): a certain use of allegorical procedures. The very etymology of allegory alludes to its *modus operandi*: from *allos* (other) and *agorein* (to speak publicly), allegory tells one story to refer to another.[32] Usually, one concrete story is told to refer to other, less representable or more abstract ideas.[33] One of allegory's more traditional theorists, C. S. Lewis, describes the procedure in straightforward terms, offering the following recipe for mixing up a proper allegory:

> you can start with an immaterial fact, such as the passions which you actually experience, and can then invent *visibilia* to

express them. If you are hesitating between an angry retort and a soft answer, you can express your state of mind by inventing a person called *Ira* with a torch and letting her contend with another invented person called *Patientia*. This is allegory . . . (44–45).

These are, indeed, the typical ingredients and techniques of allegory: abstractions personified to give expression to a symbolic power struggle, often a psychomachy.[34] While I would not characterize the texts I have selected as single, sustained allegories, all of them do use—to differing degrees—such allegorical techniques as abstraction, incorporation of commentary and interpretation, the use of personifications rather than realistic protagonists, all in order to represent a symbolic power struggle. These procedures work to create an allegorical effect or resonance of varying intensity and for distinct purposes.

As will become clear in subsequent chapters, in each text there are indications that one story is being used to tell another, that the narrative bears traces of an/other story that relates to the unspeakable sociopolitical context or to a referent that somehow eludes or defies representation. In many cases, I suggest that a sexual/private story traces a more political narrative. These two stories, of sexuality and of politics, become (in their telling) not singular but so intertwined as to constantly implicate each other. As I pointed out earlier, I see the relationship between sexuality and politics in these texts as more metonymical than metaphorical. While a traditional view of allegory maintains that it functions as an extended metaphor, it can also be seen as having metonymic properties. For example, in her study of the allegorical relationship between romance and nation-building in the romantic novels of nineteenth-century Latin America, Doris Sommer conceives of allegory as two stories that bear the trace of one another, suggesting a metonymic rather than metaphoric connection (41), "an interlocking not parallel, relationship between erotics and politics" (43). Since, as I have pointed out, sexuality and politics are difficult to separate into discrete spheres, a conceptualization like Sommer's is more helpful for my purposes. I do not suggest, however, that the allegorical gestures of the contemporary texts I have chosen offer a sustained or consistent allegory of the political situation. Rather, the power struggles in these texts refer to politics and/or sexuality: sometimes both, sometimes one or the other. For example, on the one hand, these novels can be read as allegories of sexual politics—of how gendering and sexuality are ultimately a confrontation with the power and authority of social structures. On the other hand, as allegories of sexuality *and* politics, these texts show us simultaneously the *political* nature of sexuality as well as the *gender-based* nature of authoritarianism. In both ways, then, these allegorical narratives make a traditionally private sphere into a public and political matter, transgressing and blurring the very boundaries between public and private spaces that authoritarianism attempts to portray as rigid and impenetrable.

Allegorical forms tend especially to appear in times of political contention.[35] It is precisely when something cannot be said directly for metaphysical or political reasons that allegory surfaces (Fineman 28). In the Southern Cone during this period of dirty wars and political terror, many literary texts are indeed marked by allegorical traits.[36] Such use of allegory can be conceived as a function of the virtual crisis of representation engendered by authoritarian discursive practices. Under dictatorship, the sphere of public communication and the media became the property of an elite few (the military and its supporters) who attempt to manipulate them to their own ends, thus making truth more and more difficult to know and turning the production of meaning into the exclusive domain of the authoritarian regime. In trying to "own" signification and direct meanings along a single path, these authorities attempt to take on what Lacanian analysis would call a phallic function as they strive to be the virtual source of meaning and eliminate any plural signification of words.[37] Andrés Avellaneda, who compiled two volumes of the Argentine regime's self-legitimizing discourse, cites a 1980 decree to ban an encyclopedic dictionary because it offers students "a definitely marxist lexicon, through the attribution of meanings to words that, far from faithfully corresponding to the proper significations of the language, tend to substitute these for others that respond to and are typical of that ideology."[38] This is perhaps a perfect example of the will to be the source of the One and Only Meaning. Such discursive practice is a virtual monologue that works to establish and naturalize values without any participation on the part of the people, necessarily alienating a populace whose experiences are not reflected in such representations.[39] In the face of such unidirectionality and the naturalization of discourses that do not correspond to lived reality, literature, as Beatriz Sarlo points out, confronts a "crisis of realist representation," an awareness that "an unlimited confidence in the possibilities of representation is no longer possible" (41–42). Sarlo goes on to explain the response to this crisis:

Al debilitar la idea de una relación necesaria y única entre el orden de lo representado y el orden de la representación, los textos más significativos desde este punto de vista reflexionan no sólo sobre el orden de la representación sino también el orden de lo representado. *Son, en este sentido, ficciones interrogativas de lo real y autoconscientes de los medios y las formas de su interrogación.* La destrucción de las ilusiones organicistas que atribuirían un nexo de necesidad entre el orden de los hechos y el orden de la representación, instala una pluralidad de nexos entre ambos niveles y, en consecuencia, diferentes regímenes de verdad literaria ("Política" 42; emphasis added).

[By weakening the idea of a necessary and exclusive relationship between the order of the represented and the order of representation, the most significant texts from this point of view reflect not only on the order of representation but also on the order of the represented. *They are, in this sense, fictions which question the real and are also self-conscious about the means and forms of their interrogation.* The destruction of the essentialist illusions that attribute a nexus of necessity between the order of facts and the order of representation, installs a plurality of nexus between both levels and, consequently, different systems of literary truth.]

In this way, realist representation as a means to know or perceive reality is thrown into crisis, causing a proliferation of allegorical forms, tropes, and what Sarlo calls "forms of figuration" ("Política" 45).[40] Such a crisis of representation and the resultant antimimeticism could be seen to relate to a postmodern skepticism and espousal of heterogeneity and plurality of meanings, but, as Sarlo's comments show, these techniques respond not only to international literary trends but also to a sociocultural reality that has been obscured and disarticulated.[41] Both the realm of representation *and* the referent continue to be of importance in the fiction of this context.

Sarlo's conceptualization of the use of allegorical technique in literature of this period ultimately revolves around what I would call the ethical function of allegory. Indeed, several of allegory's properties make it useful given the sociopolitical and generic particulars of the texts chosen for analysis. My discussion in the pages that follow focus on three of these obviously interrelated and overlapping features: the ethical dimension of allegory, allegory's capacity for eluding and/or representing the effects of censorship, and its potential for drawing together the personal and the political.

First of all, allegory's relation to ethics is perhaps most obvious in the promotion of good conduct and the moral judgment seen in more sustained and simpler forms of allegory, such as fables. But, especially when we turn to more complex, less overt allegory, the ethics of allegory can go beyond such bald didacticism. Ethics is obviously concerned with values; and any value, as one of the dictionary definitions of the term tells us, ultimately has to do with meaning.[42] It is likewise in the realm of *meaning* that allegory's ethical dimension lies. Most often, allegory demands some degree of ideological compliance from the reader; that is, allegorical modes propose to hold out their own version as somehow true, or at least more true than other versions. In an article devoted to the allegorical procedures at work in postmodern texts, Paul Smith points out that viewing allegory as a plural and decentering trope elides the fact that the allegorical impulse inevitably involves an "authoritative claim to meaning."[43] He goes on to explain that even modern allegories, which cannot depend on epistemological consensus like the allegories of medieval times could, in some way *do* make an appeal to notions of truth and value (Smith "The Will to Allegory" 106–7). Indeed, Smith sees in allegory's will to meaning nothing less than a "reactionary ideological maneuver" ("The Will to Allegory" 120). But, we must ask, is such a will to meaning essentially reactionary? First of all, Smith's position fails to ponder anything but male-authored allegory. His out of hand rejection of any will to meaning as a ruse to maintain dominance and an authoritarian attempt to formulate a new representation, "one over which proprietal rights can be confidently asserted " (114), only considers allegory authored by male writers, that is, the already empowered or author-ized. I contend that a will to mastery can be of quite a different hue when utilized as strategy by unauthorized subjects whose battles are not to maintain dominance or fight off an emasculating "transcience" (as Smith contends is allegory's function) but to move from object to subject positions. What Smith calls allegory's denial of "signifying freedom" can be viewed as either a gesture of domination or a gesture of resistance depending upon the particular configuration of text, author, and context. Indeed, a denial of signifying freedom to previous symbolic orders could be one strategy for women to clear an interpretative space for themselves or a method for citizens living under a state of siege to confound the authoritarian regime's monopoly on meaning. Thus, when addressing the allegorical gestures of the texts included in this study

I ask what kind of signifying power the allegorical mode can lend to a politically oppositional, feminist perspective.

Yet, while allegory certainly involves setting forth its own particular reading of the world, its own interpretation of what is true, this contradictory trope makes no claim to unmediated access to meaning and, indeed, shows its own meaning to be ultimately constructed and *produced*.[44] Allegory is thus ultimately a trope that embodies an ethics but with a duplicitous relationship to authority: it tells one thing to say another, continually deferring its meaning as other and elsewhere. It manages to tell its truth, "but tell it slant." In this vein, Clive Dilnot and Maruja García-Padilla point out that even as allegory takes advantage of certain representational devices it is always self-consciously about *something else*; thus allegory continually "turns and reflects on the conditions of meaning and representation" (44). Bernard Cowan, in reevaluating Walter Benjamin's theory of allegory, also finds allegory's contradictory nature—the simultaneous presence and absence of truth—to be of central importance:

> The affirmation of the existence of truth, then, is the first precondition for allegory: the second is the recognition of its absence. Allegory could not exist if truth were accessible: as a mode of expression it arises in perpetual response to the human condition of being exiled from the truth that it would embrace.[45]

In this way, through its own structure as a re-presentation of something that is never and cannot be present, allegory can virtually set forth the existence of a meaning that is difficult to glimpse, only imperfectly representable, and practically impossible to fix. It is thus perhaps an ideal mode for working in a crisis of representation like the one I discussed earlier. Indeed, by using allegorical gestures, the four texts I examine in this study continually comment on themselves as representations as well as on the problematics of representation itself.

What the previous discussion makes clear is that allegory's formal constitution makes it a prime mode for certain authoritarian political contexts. Telling one story to refer to another, telling an/other, different truth, but telling it slant, allegory is particularly appropriate to the oppressive context of dictatorship. When censorship bans the public telling of some *other* story, allegory can be used to articulate what has been marginalized and silenced. Indeed, many theorists have noted the particular efficacy of allegory in times of tight censorship when authoritarian forces take complete control of public communication.[46]

But silencing and censorship are not only the stuff of dictatorship, although this is perhaps their most explicit and perfected context. One of the tasks of feminism has been to address the schism between the discursive construct Woman (set forth as object in male-authored or patriarchally oriented literature) and the real women who were denied their subjectivity, who were silenced or censored by the (re)production of this image.[47] Censorship, of a decidedly less tangible sort than that wielded by any state apparatus, is very much an issue in feminist analysis. Clearly, for Latin American women writing under the shadow of dictatorship, censorship takes many forms, relating to both the context of gender politics and the context of authoritarianism. Given such constraints, allegory can be an especially powerful tool not only for circumventing censorship but also representing its effects: that is, the crisis of representation engendered by such authoritarian practices.

Another property of allegory that makes it especially useful for the texts included in this study is that it manages to relate the personal to a more collective political struggle. As Fredric Jameson points out, allegory makes its reader rethink the symbolic relationships mapped out between the personal (the libidinal) and the political, so that s/he is forced to see them not as a homology but as a complex "set of loops or circuits which intersect and overdetermine each other" ("Third World Literature" 73).[48] On this modern view of allegory he says:

> The allegorical spirit is profoundly discontinuous, a matter of breaks and heterogeneities, of the multiple polysemia of the dream rather than the homogeneous representation of the symbol. Our traditional conception of allegory—based, for instance, on stereotypes of Bunyan—is that of an elaborate set of figures and personifications to be read against some one-to-one table of equivalences: this is, so to speak, a one-dimensional view of this signifying process, which might only be set in motion and complexified were we willing to entertain the more alarming notion that such equivalences are themselves in constant change and transformation at each perpetual present of the text ("Third World Literature" 73).

This idea of a complex series of changing correspondences is precisely how allegorical technique is being used in the texts I have chosen. In the four works I analyze, the allegorical relationships between public and private spaces make them neither neatly concentric nor absolutely separate spheres. Rather, the borders between the multiple spaces such as "nation," "family," "body," "text," "house," "world" are porous, intermittent relationships and separations—relationships that allegorically "speak the other" not through a one-to-one correspondence, but rather through a complex series of resonances that ultimately transform the borders of these spaces.

What I find most interesting about Jameson's formulations is the suggestion that textual allegories are not systems of one-to-one correspondences but are actually transformative. Yet, even though he makes such a suggestive statement about the transformative properties of allegory, his ideas on the nature of the public and private spheres remain untransformed. For Jameson, the strict separation between public and private is a function of capitalist development and, therefore, the relationship between these two realms is radically different in so-called third world texts (apparently because their social context is precapitalist or noncapitalist). This logic does not offer much in the way of understanding the literature produced during recent military dictatorships of the Southern Cone of Latin America. These governments espoused capitalistic, free market economic policies and kept the population in check through repressive tactics, one of which was the attempted strict division and control of public and private spheres. As Sonia Alvarez observes with respect to the authoritarian regimes of the Southern Cone:

> Political regimes have offensive and defensive policy agendas that reorder social relations of production and reproduction, reorganizing relations between capital and labor, State and family, the public and the private, women and men. This is clearly evident in military authoritarian regimes; *the National Security State delineated a sharpened separation between the public world of ruthless military men and the private world of self-sacrificing, motherly women* (35; emphasis added).

A traditional division between public and private is certainly at the heart of much authoritarian discourse. I would also suggest, however, that the appearance of such a strict separation of public and private was a convenient fiction propagated by the authorities in order to better maintain absolute power over both spheres at once. Certainly, the apparent sharpening of the division between the public and private spheres can be clearly observed in cultural productions such as Luis Puenzo's film *The Official Story*. But what this film ultimately shows, and Alvarez's own study explores, is how those divisions are contradictory and become increasingly difficult to maintain. Specifically, Alvarez points out that even while attempting to maintain a public/private split, the authoritarian regime in dependent capitalist states already depends on the private sectors for the reproduction of class, racial, and gender power relations (33). Indeed, the regime attempted to exercise much of its authority within the private sphere with regard to sexual roles and family values. Nonetheless, by designating such areas as "separate" from the public workings of politics, by casting them as somehow "natural," essential, and beyond question, the authorities could thus disempower them politically. But, as Alvarez's social research also shows, as economic conditions for the poorer classes in these countries worsen, the very sectors the authoritarian regime tries to keep private and in the home are often the *first* to become politicized—hence the wealth of feminist and women's movements opposing the authoritarian regimes, leading to such phenomena as what Alvarez calls the "politicization of [women's] lived experience *as women*" (54–55) The privatized (i.e., depoliticized) sphere often then dramatically reinserts itself into the public realm as emblematized by the Mothers of the disappeared who marched in the public Plaza de Mayo.[49] While the Mothers originally considered their endeavors as privately motivated, they gradually discovered the sociopolitical and collective nature of their personal situations. Writing on the Mothers, Laura Rossi describes their transformation as a process that "did not translate into a decision to 'do politics,' but rather in their comprehension of the social and political nature of their personal tragedy" (150). So, what the Mothers ultimately confront is the way the supposedly personal sphere of a mother's relationship to her son or daughter is crossed and determined by very political interests.

Indeed, in spite of the appearances of a sharp separation of the public and private, the public sphere infiltrates the private realm in an especially insidious way during these regimes. One Chilean cultural critic, for example, sees television as the arm of the authoritarian state, reaching into the private sphere to impose its univocal version of events (Jofré 337). Furthermore, the monologic authoritarian discourse frequently sought to impose particular standards of conduct with regard to such supposedly personal issues as intrafamilial relations, birth control, dress codes, religious beliefs, and sexuality.[50] On the other hand, the political or public realm itself was

marked by a pronounced absence of debate or exchange, with political decisions being made behind closed doors and then handed down
by decree. This produced what some scholars see as a privatization or
even annihilation of the public realm.[51] In sum, then, what these
regimes did was to privatize and demobilize the public sphere of
debate and dissent while simultaneously attempting to dictate private norms of behavior relating to sexuality and family. In this way,
while availing themselves of a radical split between public and private realms, the authoritarian regimes essentially tried to control
both at once.

While the relation between public and private realms is of particular interest to the National Security State, the traditionally perceived split between these spheres is also a prime bone of contention
among feminists.[52] In fact, the virtual slogan of feminism since the
sixties has been that the personal *is* the political. North American
political scientist Catharine MacKinnon has explicated the terms
of this equation for feminism, noting that: "To say that the personal
is political means that gender as a division of power is discoverable
and verifiable through women's intimate experience of sexual objectification. . . ." (21). Given the centrality of the personal and sexual to
women's oppression, much feminist analysis in the United States
and Europe works to show the political workings of the private
sphere, for example, or the ways women have been virtually
marginalized and silenced by being confined to the private sectors.
So, the importance of questioning prevailing notions of private and
public is very much at the heart of feminist theory and practice in
general. Not surprisingly, then, feminist theorists and activists living
under dictatorship have become acutely aware of the fact that
authoritarianism is not an economic or political problem alone and
that seeing the public and private as separate spheres does not
account for the way oppressive power relations operate in society.[53]
An unveiling and transformation of the discursive boundaries
between public and private spheres is thus of prime concern to feminists, especially in the Southern Cone during the authoritarian
period.

In my view, then, rather than the idea that "third-world texts"
simply *are* allegorical because of their a priori "different" public-
private relations (as Jameson suggests), we could say that allegory
provides a medium for conflating the libidinal and political dimensions—a conflation that is crucial for particular cultural productions
for a variety of sociopolitical and generic reasons. In a preliminary
way, I would suggest that the texts I have chosen write sexuality, the

body, and the private sphere using allegorical gestures to stage the private sphere as extremely political, thus enabling a double social critique of gender and authoritarianism. Marginal, dispersive, often sexual spaces are made public political issues in these texts by means of various methods: by encoding sexuality as having to do with control and authority, by allegorically conflating domestic power relations with those of the authoritarian state, and by writing these interior, supposedly subjectivist, feminine spaces in an intellectualized, experimental style. Indeed, the very act of women writing in an ambitiously experimental (and allegorical) way in order to "publicly speak" these other, feminine spaces, is a politically significant one, doubly breaking sociosexual taboos in refusing silence and in not writing in a subjectivist, "typically feminine" mode. Indeed, allegory is considered to be an overly intellectualized, abstract trope; hardly the typical categorizations usually associated with supposedly feminine modes of writing, so often characterized as intimist, particularized, subjective, and immanent (as opposed to transcendent, universalizing, or political). In this way, the allegorical gestures of the texts I have chosen ultimately work to transform conceptualizations of the spheres of public and private, sexual and political. Similar to the way feminist articulations of discursive space have transformed theoretical discourse and threatened traditional systems of representation,[54] so the fictions of the women writers I have chosen write *about* and *through* marginal spaces that confound and deconstruct authoritarian discourses bent on maintaining strict divisions between public and private.

Yet, since all these texts engage in allegorical gestures of different shades or degrees, I am not claiming to put forward a singular theory of feminist allegory. Rather, I merely claim that allegory has certain properties especially appropriate to the sexual/political concerns of these writers, all of whom could be considered feminist and all of whom opposed the dictatorships in their respective countries.[55] These are writers who are concerned, in different ways, with narrating an oppressive political situation as well as with transforming the female imaginary and broadening the repertoires available to women and women writers. Each of these writers necessarily confronts and textualizes the social crises engendered by political and sexual repression. In the following chapters I focus on how specific social and corporal realities are represented in each selected text, how the stupefying context is textualized, how the unrepresentable is represented, how the disembodied is embodied. There is among all of these texts, I suggest, a certain unwillingness to abandon all ethical dreaming and, in several cases, from this reluctance to forego a hope for social change, allegorical gestures emerge. So, allegory forms not the structuring principle of this study but rather a useful writerly and readerly tool, a mediating force between reader, writer, and context, both literary procedure and interpretative attitude.

While my attention to the allegorical gestures of the text surfaces in each chapter, I do not set out to prove that each text "is" an allegory, in order to then monologically tell what that allegory "refers to." Rather, I am primarily concerned with how these texts challenge sociopolitical, genderic, and textual forms of authority. And I believe that the various types of allegorical gestures enacted by these texts help them in resisting those authorities, just as reading allegorically—that is, reading with an eye to the "other stories" traced by each text—can enrich our analyses of these narratives. My goal is thus not to "apply" a theory of allegory to these narratives or to show how they "enact" such a theory. I want, rather, to read the theories (and the practices) these texts themselves suggest, theories of gender and of writing, of how to produce meaning through and against "authoritarian" systems and how to narrate the unspeakable sociopolitical situations that these writers inhabit and that inhabit them.

1

Defiance and Its Discontents: Nélida Piñon's *A Casa da Paixão*

O Estado é a eterna visita em minha casa,
mesmo quando dela se ausenta.

[The State is the eternal visitor in my house,
even when it's not present.]

—Nélida Piñon
"O Jardim das Oliveiras"
O Calor das Coisas

It is no easy task to try to describe Brazilian writer Nélida Piñon's position with regard to politics. For example, questions have been raised regarding her supposed ambivalent position vis-à-vis the military regime (1964–85). On the one hand, she has had to respond to charges of complicity with the regime, making public statements denying any involvement with IPES (Instituto de Pesquisas e Estudos Sociais—Brazilian Institute for Research and Social Studies), a civilian organization that was an arm of the dictatorship.[1] On the other, she has been hailed as "a militant writer" and sees literature and language as ethical and politically charged spheres.[2] With regard to gender politics and women's writing, things seem easier to define. In an interview just before she was to be elected to the prestigious Academia Brasileira de Letras, Piñon observed candidly that the literary establishment along with its artistic models and aesthetic criteria are masculine and that a woman writer must be doubly competent to succeed in such an environment.[3] As one of the most recognized and prolific contemporary women writers of Brazil, author of over ten volumes of narrative, Piñon has succeeded, in spite of the problems faced by women who write, in spite of being termed by some a "difficult" writer.[4] When asked, on another occasion, if she is a feminist she responds that she is "naturally" a feminist, that her feminism is merely a consequence of her being a woman (interview with Clarice Lispector 193).

Certainly, gender plays a significant role in her writing. At least one reader has suggested, for example, that her 1972 experimental novel *A Casa da Paixão* [The House of Passion] is an allegory of the interplay of the masculine and the feminine.[5] But, if this is indeed the case, the ending of the allegory, the virtual "moral" of the story, would seem particularly difficult to take for the feminist reader. Throughout the novel, between *bildungsroman* and psychosexual fable, the protagonist (Marta) struggles for her sexual autonomy, forming a sensual relationship with the sun, rebelling against her incestuously desirous father (pai), and resisting the father's understudy and supplanter (Jerônimo). After a complex series of transformations, however, Marta ends up entering into a mythic sexual union with Jerônimo and finally promises him: "Sou sua mulher, vou para onde você quiser . . ." / "I am your woman, I will go wherever you wish" (122). Both this formulaic final line and the harmonious conclusion in general seem shockingly contradictory and traditional if one has read the novel as promoting woman's radical reappropriation of her own body and sexuality. Yet, interpretations of the text have been surprisingly positive and uncritical in this regard, reading the final outcome as the plausible result of the mystical textual and sexual transformations of the novel.

Naomi Hoki Moniz, for example, explores the cosmic enterprise of *A Casa*, reading the process of writing as well as Marta's psychosexual development from within a Jungian and, to a lesser degree, Lacanian framework. Moniz remains, for the most part, uncritical of the final outcome, seeing it in positive terms in that, first, it does not elide sexual difference or collapse the masculine and feminine in order to attain liberation and that, second, it shows that woman must develop her "masculinity" (her *animus* in Jungian terms) in order to achieve a certain "reconciliation" with her partner.[6] In other words, Moniz reads the ending of the book as a culmination of the utopian impulses in the text, seeing this "reconciliation," this restoration of harmony, as the natural and desired outgrowth of the recuperative strategies of the narrative. In a similar way, Sônia Régis, in her *Posfácio* [Postscript] included in *A Casa*, also takes a positive view of the outcome, pointing out—but not problematizing—how the female body becomes the site of the textual/sexual fecundation that takes place at the end of the novel (143). Régis also sees the ending in terms of the novel's utopian project, finding the mythical union to be a rebirth and, evidently, the groundwork for new beginnings.[7]

Both of these readings seem on target in their appraisal of the utopian function in this text. Piñon's novel certainly does propose a salvation through sexual union. The heterosexual pair becomes a metaphor for the harnessing of the most fertile of human energies; and sexuality is construed as a path for the redemption of the human being, heretofore divided against itself through the binary split between masculine and feminine, mind and body, word and thing. The fusion implied in the sexual union at the end of the novel thus comes to signify a union of two seemingly opposite forces (masculine and feminine)—not only in the carnal joining of Marta and Jerôn-imo but also in Marta's realization of her masculine side (through her contact with the sun) and Jerônimo's affirmation of his femininity (symbolized by his immersion in the river, a feminine element in the novel). Hence, sexual union becomes an allegorical figure for harmony and a sort of dynamic symmetry. Furthermore, as we shall see, this erotic coupling becomes a mystical ritual, a medium for reaching transcendence.

In my view, however, this positive hermeneutic is not sufficient. As we shall see, Piñon's text also launches a vehement denunciation of the patriarchal system and the workings of the "law of the father." In Lacan's psychoanalytic model, the "law of the father" refers to the system of social and psychosexual prohibitions by which the social subject is discursively formed and governed. In Piñon's novel, such a conceptualization of the "law of the father" is implicated, as we shall see, as the unnamed father attempts to control Marta and determine how she becomes a woman. The "pai," seen this way, virtually personifies the father function; indeed he is quite literally "the *name of the father*" in which "we must recognize the support of the symbolic function which, from the dawn of history has identified his person with the figure of the law" (Lacan 67). The utopian goal implicit in denouncing this patriarchal ideology would include the freeing of the feminine subject to take hold of her own desire and sexual pleasure and, therefore, her own subjectivity. Moniz has pointed out this important aspect of the novel: "Piñon affirms and vindicates a woman's right to sexual pleasure and she creates a vocabulary that violates cultural taboos and gives expression to feminine sexuality" ("Ética, Estética" 138). Yet, in this regard, the ending of the novel would seem dystopic in that it is emblematic of the very appropriation of the female body that is endemic to the patriarchal structure. We must ultimately ask ourselves about the relationship between *A Casa*'s critique of the patriarchal structure and its utopian impulse, or, to put it in Fredric Jameson's terms, we need to strive for a "simultaneous recognition of the ideological and Utopian functions of the artistic text."[8]

I agree with Jameson that effective cultural analysis must practice a negative hermeneutic function (uncovering the ideological functionality of a text) while also engaging in a positive hermeneutic (paying close attention to the text's utopian postulations). I disagree, however, with his assertion that marxism is the only critical method that currently assumes this negative hermeneutic.[9] Both deconstruction and feminisms are involved—in different ways—in such a methodology. I do think, however, that the negative hermeneutic function in feminism is often most active in feminist readings of male-authored texts. Indeed, my view of the interpretations of *A Casa da Paixão* is that up to now they have analyzed the utopian projections of the novel without focusing extensively on the ideological critique and the possible ideological contradictions embodied in the text. As Paul Ricoeur has put it, hermeneutics involves a "double motivation: willingness to suspect, willingness to listen: vow of rigor, vow of obedience" (27). When reading texts authored by women, it is especially important for us to be willing to suspect because our *own* utopian projections make us more than willing to listen.

For *A Casa da Paixão*, then, I propose a certain will to suspicion. While acknowledging (listening to) the utopian impulse involved in the realization of the creative possibilities of the feminized body, we must also ask whether the male's realization of his "feminine" side, the celebration of the corporeal on the altar of the female body, is actually any different from patriarchy's traditional use of the woman as sacrificial mediator.[10] Furthermore, the sexual liaison at the end of the novel, touted as a utopian reconciliation of differences, ultimately posits sexuality as "natural" and as somehow outside the social forces against which Marta rebels. Thus, there seem to be conflicting views of the sex/gender system here: one that sees sexuality as social product and thus changeable and another in which masculine and feminine are timeless, essential archetypes beyond sociopolitical context. The possibilities for a female and feminist agency are obviously quite different in these two models. Hence, my goal is twofold: to disentangle the seemingly conflicting strains of the narrative—simultaneously a critique and a utopian foundation for a "new order"—and ultimately to explore the political implications of the resolution posited by Piñon's text. To accomplish this I focus on both *A Casa*'s ideological critique as well as the contradiction between this critique and the novel's harmonious conclusion.

To my mind, *A Casa da Paixão* involves a blatant critique of
the status quo regarding the process of gendering. The story of Marta
and her sexual development radically transgresses various patriarchal
patterns of narrative, undermining many of the "scripts" that ideologically govern how one "becomes a woman".[11] Piñon's particular
allegory of sexual politics defies and delegitimates several narratives
that place women in passive roles: the traditional gendering sequence
where the female is successfully socialized in the image of male
desire, the exchange plot where women are traded amongst men,
and the transformation myth plot where the hero rescues his woman
from the clutches of an evil, powerful female figure.[12] Even though,
as we shall see, this text ends up reinscribing the status quo in its
contradictory and conservative finale, it *does* manage to enact, along
the way, a surprisingly radical series of transgressions that serve as
emblems of resistance to patriarchal authority and that promote
woman's reappropriation of her own body and sexuality. Such defiance of the father's law indeed becomes a way to open a new narrative space, to attempt to write what has rarely been written: a feminine erotics where the female body is not merely an instrument of
male pleasure.

But there is also another area where I suggest a certain will to
suspicion. As my discussion so far attests, *A Casa da Paixão* seems
to be a "political" text principally with regard to gender. There is
hardly any explicit reference at all as to a specific sociopolitical
context. This undoubtedly has to do with Piñon's literary concerns
at the time, that is, her preoccupation with language, with myth,
and with creating new forms of expression. It may even have to do
with the level of state censorship in effect in the early 70s when the
military regime was clamping down on any form of resistance to its
authoritarian policies.[13] Whatever the cause, politics is often only
obliquely present in much of Piñon's earlier narrative. As critic
Lúcia Helena Costigan points out, Piñon had usually been noted
for linguistically transgressive, "intimist" and "poetic," but not
necessarily politically engaged, prose (148). Even so, Piñon insists on
the political and ethical implications of literary language in interviews. She explicitly associates the literary avant-garde with "a permanent critique of the social and linguistic system" and an "intransigent ethical attitude in the exercise of the means of expression"
(interview with Lispector 189). Her experimentation with language
is thus far from apolitical.[14] For her, language and power are very
closely aligned (interview with Lispector 192). Nonetheless,
sociopolitical themes and specifically the Brazilian dictatorship are

even more explicitly explored in her later narrative when, it must be pointed out, state repression had been considerably relaxed. For instance, her collection of stories *O Calor das Coisas* [The Heat of Things] (1980), which contains representations of political repression and torture; the historical saga *A República dos Sonhos* [*The Republic of Dreams*] (1984), which narrates four generations of a Brazilian family; and *A Doce Canção de Caetana* [*Caetana's Sweet Song*] (1987), which takes place in a small town in Brazil during the military dictatorship's supposed "Economic Miracle" of the 1970s, are all directly engaged with the sociopolitical context of authoritarianism.[15] Compared to these somewhat more "realist" texts, *A Casa da Paixão* seems far less historically referential and far more aesthetically preoccupied. Yet, without trying to reduce or bracket the aesthetic complexities of the text, we must also consider what happens when we read *A Casa* in its political context, when we read its indictment of the gendering process as well as its linguistic experimentalism *within* the context of Brazil's oppressive military regime. What happens, in other words, when we read the private, even intimate "house" of the "House of Passion" as an allegorical figure for the public "house" of the nation under authoritarian rule?

In this chapter, then, we will see how transgression—manifested in this novel as daughterly defiance or rebellion against paternal law—provides a means of imagining both a female sexuality not predicated on the phallus as ultimate signifier of desire and a women's writing not subject to the same old narrative patterns. Such a challenge to patriarchal law not only deauthorizes dominant sexual and textual codes but also, as I will suggest, obliquely questions the authority of the dictatorial, paternalistic political regime in Brazil at the time. Finally, we will turn to the troubling ending of Piñon's work, to that place where her radical disarticulation of oppressive patterns bumps up against ideological constraints that necessarily provide the context for her text.

Defying the Patriarch's Plots:
Transgression as Narrative Strategy

The narrative of *A Casa da Paixão* seems at once strikingly original and eerily familiar. It is, on the most basic level, the story of how Marta strives to "become a woman," how she struggles to assume a subjectivity and sexuality of her own, through and against the various "scripts" laid out by masculine dominated systems of representation. In this way, Marta's story retells a very old and well-known tale: the drama by which we become gendered subjects. Told without the euphemism and adornment of mimetic description, Piñon's often abstract rendition of this sequence lays bare the very political nature of the gendering process itself. As the father plots out the path for Marta to follow, she, in turn, repeatedly rebels against this preordained order, frustrating the father in his attempts to take control of her body and sexuality. As we shall see, Marta defies her father's will to control her destiny by enacting a transgressive, antipatriarchal sexuality, thus attempting to seek out her own sexual autonomy and, ultimately, to write her own story.

Certainly, *A Casa* details Marta's struggle to assume a sexuality and a subjectivity of her own. But the narrative path of the first five sections of the novel is plotted not by Marta but by the father. During the first part of the novel, Marta hardly speaks and we are informed of her attitudes and behaviors through a third-person narrative. Indeed, Marta is seen and observed but rarely heard until she reacts to Jerônimo in the sixth (and central) section of the book. At that point, as we shall see, Marta takes control of events, stops reacting and starts acting, forcing the father and Jerônimo to follow in her footsteps. In other words, Marta takes up the plotting prerogative, becoming the one who determines the direction of the narrative.

But, in the beginning, while Marta is hardly passive, her modus operandi is mainly to escape, to defy, and to negate the father's plot. The goal of Marta's defiance is, in a sense, to attain signifying power, to assume the subject (rather than object) position in her narrative. Indeed, as Moniz points out, "Marta's appropriation of sexuality in the initiation rite and her becoming 'a person,' is an act similar to the one that Lacan denominates the 'initiation into the symbolic'" ("Ética, Estética" 138–39). Yet, her entry into the symbolic is especially treacherous. The relationship between the father and daughter is, as Moniz observes, tense and dependent, due to the tradition that governs their interaction: "the tradition established between them, for one to be the shadow of the other."[16] Marta attempts from the beginning to take an active part in this specular, mimetic relationship:

> Marta reconhecia-o sua sombra e construiu aquela silhueta como quem levanta uma casa, projeção de sua vontade, iam crescendo portas, paredes, telhados mil, disfarçados em outros telhados, enigmas soltos, todos abrigando intimidades (15).

[Marta recognized him as her shadow and constructed that sil-
houette as one builds a house, projection of her will, doors,
walls, roofs were emerging by the thousands, disguised in other
roofs, unfettered enigmas, all sheltering intimacies.]

The "house" here refers to Marta's symbolic house that she herself
constructs, using the father's shadow in order to project and encode
her desires and create her own imaginary.

Yet, try as she may to project her own desires and to plot out
her own sexual and textual meanings, the father, authority figure
that he is, strives to design surreptitiously the very paths she would
construct as her own. Indeed, the father's attempts at dominating
Marta are enacted as endless chase scenes where he tries never to
lose sight of her and to keep her always on paths constructed by
him:

O pai aprendera a deslizar como índio, embora algumas vezes
perdesse Marta e aquela perda, ainda por horas, doía-lhe pelo
corpo. . . . Marta surgia horas mais tarde, até o pai compreender
com os anos que antes da filha criar novos caminhos, devia ele
inventar outros que fatalmente ela percorreria, sendo ela filha
da sua carne (15).

[The father learned how to slink like an indian, although sometimes losing Marta and that loss, even just for hours, caused
him pain thoughout his body. . . . Marta would appear hours
later, until the father understood with time that before the
daughter created new paths, he should invent others upon
which she would inevitably, fatally travel, her being the daughter of his flesh.]

Space here is entirely abstracted and nonreferential, thus making
the father's and Marta's actions all the more symbolically resonant.
The paths inscribed here by Marta or the father can thus be read as
narrative paths, as ways to make meaning, as plots "written" to be
followed. In this passage, it becomes particularly clear that the struggle is one for path-making or plot-tracing control, for signifying
authority. By keeping her on *his* tracks, the father assures himself of
Marta's being "daughter of his flesh"; that is, he maintains control
over her ability to signify and can consequently, as we shall see, use
her as a mirror in which to see himself.

This key scenario, of prime importance in understanding the
father/daughter dynamic in the novel, is also an eloquent expres-

sion of the most basic challenge facing women's writing: how to make new meanings, how to trace new paths ("novos caminhos"), when, as Irigaray would put it, all the subject positions are being appropriated by the masculine.[17] Indeed, Marta's struggle and *A Casa da Paixão* itself are emblems of this dilemma: in short, how to write *against* and *through* current systems of representation.

So, Marta's struggle is against what I have called the patriarch's plot, both the father's particular plans for her *and* the dominant mode of scripting women as Woman. Summarizing recent feminist theorists, Sally Robinson provides an excellent and succinct account of what is at stake in the distinction between Woman ("a discursive figure most often constructed and mobilized according to the logic of male desire") and women ("actual female persons engendered by and engendering social and discursive practices") (4–9).[18] Of course, women's literature often puts into discourse the contradictions faced by "actual" girls or women as they grapple with the construct Woman. Meanwhile, what I have called the patriarch's plot makes it appear that the only way for girls to become women is through adopting the primarily passive role of Woman. In this way, the patriarch's plot marked out in *A Casa*, the "master narrative" that the father attempts to enforce, is not of his own invention but rather forms part of an already established cultural norm. Referred to only as "pai" [father] throughout the novel, the father in the text virtually personifies the abstract "law of the father," the idea or function of paternal authority according to governing psychosocial codes. Indeed, the father/daughter positions are inscribed here as predetermined—"desde sempre lutaram" / "they had fought since forever" (12)—and their respective roles as pre-established—"ela em oferta, sobre altares *que o pai não construía mas respeitava*" / "she in offering, on altars *that the father had not constructed but respected*" (15; emphasis added). That is to say, in many ways, the relationship between Marta and the father is the concretization of abstract cultural laws perceived as always already in place.

But, even though the father's plot is as old as the hills, it nonetheless serves his own immediate psychosexual purposes. Indeed, the father's efforts at marshaling Marta along the road to an appropriate marriage are revealed by Piñon to have little to do with Marta and everything to do with *his* own self-affirmation. The father's incestuous desire is ultimately a desire for a means to knowledge, for a medium between himself and the world, for a conduit to the most inaccessible parts of himself. For the father, Marta embodies at once a treasure and a mystery. When he comes upon her sunbathing, the narrator tells us "O pai fingia não ver a rapidez com que fechava as pernas, escondendo tesouros, sabedorias raras. . . . Ela escondia daquele homem seu precioso segredo" / "The father pretended not to see how quickly she closed her legs, hiding treasures, rare wisdoms. . . . She hid from that man the precious secret" (10). The "seu" here is ambiguous; the secret is both "hers" and "his." In fact, the treasure, the knowledge, and the secret are all at once hers in that her body encloses them and yet also the father's in that he views her as embodying the answers to his own enigma. He speculates that Marta, as his offspring, is the very embodiment of the mystery of life, she is "to whom he owed the certainty of all mystery" (20). She is, for the father, mystery incarnate, doubly mysterious in that the mother has died. As such, Marta is both his potential savior (as a connection to his own seeds of life, his own fertility) and his perdition (as an embodiment of that very schism between himself and the immortal origins of life itself). While he refers to her explicitly as "the daughter of his perdition" (29), the father also sees her as his salvation, crying out, after contemplating his desire for his daughter: "it is not for desire, I well know, it is for fear, people like her save our soul. Or one never comes to know God" (18). From the father's point of view, then, Marta becomes the means to know God, his path to reach the divine. She is, in Simone de Beauvoir's terms, his Other.

Indeed, the patriarch's plot here is the very one Simone de Beauvoir has described and critiqued in *The Second Sex*. Beauvoir shows how the function of woman as man's Other is similarly one of mediation: between man and nature, man and divine inspiration, man and the gods. It is through the Other, materialized in Woman, that Man seeks to know himself (Beauvoir 139). She is established as everything he is not, timelessly ambiguous, chaotic, and yet mediator between man and nature. Essential to this process then is projection: "he projects upon her what he desires and what he fears, what he loves and what he hates" (Beauvoir 197). This mechanism alienates woman from herself for, as Beauvoir puts it:

> She is All, that is, on the plane of the inessential; she is all the Other. And, as the other, she is other than herself, other than what is expected of her. Being all, she is never quite *this* which she should be . . . (197–98).

One could also say that as his Other, the woman's body and sexuality are never her own, but rather are appropriated as a foundation for patriarchy's symbolic house. As Catharine MacKinnon says specifically of women's sexuality: it is that which is most her own yet most taken away.[19] The father's struggle to maintain control over Marta effectively lays bare the very tactics of appropriation of the female body that feminist theorists have also denounced. Seen in this light, the relationship the father strives to have with Marta is revealed to be a very old (and oft-repeated) story: he is trying desperately to make her Woman, his most complete Other, which involves laying claim to her body and sexuality. So, the struggle in *A Casa da Paixão* is a territorial battle with the terrain in dispute being Marta's body: the very "house of passion" itself.

The conflict arises since Marta's body becomes, as we have seen, the site for the father's self-realization and yet also the source of Marta's own salvation, as she herself had realized even as a young child: "the salvation of the soul is between my legs, I sensed it even as a child" (60). Thus, Marta's quest is in direct conflict with the father's since both involve power and control over Marta's body.[20] The father, prisoner of his own passion, pursues Marta incessantly in a mythical and repetitious chase, driven by his desire for the Other, for that which embodies all that he is not. His pursuit of Marta is propelled by an essentially insatiable desire to possess his own truth, not hers. It is not that he desires her or wants to possess her as much as he desires her recognition, which is ultimately the ground upon which he constructs his own subjectivity. As Lacan puts it: "Man's desire finds its meaning in the desire of the other, not so much because the other holds the key to the object desired, as because the first object of desire is to be recognized by the other" (58). This seems to be precisely the nature of the father's desire in *A Casa*. After the father chooses her horse for her, imposing his will in this seemingly insignificant way, Marta realizes:

Mais lhe parecia que o pai selecionando os animais se reservava o direito de também um dia colocar em sua cama de espinhos um homem vizinho ao seu corpo e a haveria de abrasar, *para que invocasse entre gritos de amor o nome do pai, e não por desejar sua carne, mas somente aquela figura era viva e palpitante em cada hora de sua vida, e a que deveria reverenciar mesmo no amor.* Olhava-o com raiva (40; emphasis added).

[More so, it seemed to her that by selecting the animals the father reserved for himself the right to also someday place a man in her bed of thorns neighboring her/his body and he

> would have to consume her by fire, *so that she would invoke*
> *between cries of love the name of the father, and not for carnal*
> *desire, but only that figure was alive and palpitating in every*
> *hour of her life, and she should revere it even in the act of*
> *love.* She eyed him with rage.]

Again the "seu" of "seu corpo" is ambiguous; the man elected by the father would not only lie next to "her" (Marta's) body but would also somehow be an extention of "his" (the father's) body. Furthermore, as Marta sees it, it is not that he wants her in the flesh; he wants to be the name on her lips at every moment of her own desire, he wants to be ever-important, ever-present to her because he can, in this way, affirm his own transcendence. She is his mirror—"the daughter was the only mirror, [the father] admitted, offering her animals, epic dogs, and jewels" (41)—and he ultimately desires her, pursues her, and strives to control *her*, to affirm *himself*.

   In effect, the patriarchal script of gendering, the father's designs on Marta's body, would remake and socialize Marta according to male desire. In this way, Piñon's narrative shows gender identity to be not static and essential but to be constructed with great difficulty through an eminently political process. But the patriarchal plot is ultimately threatened by Marta's relationship to the sun, by her insertion into the masculine lineage (the symbolic), by her insistence on owning her own body, by her appropriation of her sexual pleasure for herself, and, ultimately, by her tutelage of Jerônimo, through which she encourages him to delve into his own body.

   The first challenge to the father's dominance is her insertion into the masculine lineage through her very imitation of the father. The father is puzzled and troubled by Marta's willful behavior. He views her, ultimately, as the product of his creative energies ("daughter of his flesh" 15) and is thus alarmed by her own will to creative power. In his despair he consults a physician, demanding an explanation for Marta's inclinations (16). The doctor discovers, in fact, that Marta is copying the father, that she is following in his footsteps even more closely than the father had bargained for: "he discovered that daughter copying what the father concealed, like a slave chained to the slaver's ship" (17). He explains this to the father, "wanting to insinuate that Marta was of the same domain as the father" (17). By her very mimicry, by imitating the father too closely and by aspiring to his signifying powers, Marta challenges the father's dominance and transgresses the father's authority. According to traditional scripts, such a position of signifying power is closed to her because of her femaleness.[21] Yet to become a subject of her own story, she must usurp that position. The problem for Marta, ultimately, is how to develop a representational economy of her own while still so limited, "like a slave chained to the slaver's ship."

In spite of the antagonism between them, Marta is obedient to her father in attending mass. The church, in turn, becomes the site of the initiation of the exchange rituals involved in marriage rites yet also the first site of active resistance on Marta's part. The ceremony as enacted in Piñon's narrative tellingly reveals the power relations and "policies" of our sexuality as constructed by social contract.[22] This system is portrayed as already in place with the father merely carrying out the role assigned to him: "O homem que era seu pai sabia-se parte da cerimônia e concedia" / "The man that was her father knew himself to be part of the ceremony and conceded" (22). The construction of the sentence emphasizes that the man (the biological male) occupies the social and symbolic position of her father; he is merely acting out his part in the psychosocial script. Marta, however, rejects the men who look upon her as an animal at market. Indeed, it becomes clear that she has come only to express her sexual preference for what Annis Pratt has termed a "green world lover": "The men understood that she came there only to proclaim her disdain, exchanging their flesh for the flesh of the tree" (23). Marta thus prefers the sensuality of the earth and the elements to that of the men offered to her, and insists repeatedly on her sexual autonomy: "I look after the honor of my house" (25), "I look after my own body" (20). So, while the father is concerned about her body as the depository of his family honor ("The father feared for the familiar destiny" 24), Marta claims her house, her body, as her own and takes charge of its well-being. Her will to autonomy, her identification with the sun and the natural world, and her refusal to be initiated into the patriarchal structure as an object of exchange all threaten the very specular dialectic relied upon by the father for his own self-affirmation.

This patriarchal structure is further threatened by the relationship between Antônia, the old maidservant, and Marta. Moniz describes the protean nature of Antônia, how she assumes the many different manifestations of the Magna Mater: she is the destructive Lilith, the protective maternal figure, a cross between human and animal, the primitive mother with ties to the earth, the midwife with overtones of witch or sorceress (Moniz 133). Nonetheless, for all her feminine traits, Antônia is described as androgynous (33), and the relationship between her and Marta is predicated on forces of both sex and power. What Marta most desires in the old woman are her powers: her knowledge of the earth's secrets, her "virility" (32), her contact with sexuality and powers of reproduction. When Marta goes to the barn to see Antônia, she recalls the time she observed Antônia in the henhouse, picking up eggs and enacting a sort of fertility ritual (32–36). After the highly erotic scene with Antônia and a recently laid egg, the old woman fries the egg for Marta and insists that she eat it. In this way, Antônia's role is like that of a high priestess in Marta's sexual indoctrination.[23] Later, in the barn, Antônia touches Marta sexually and promises her that her salvation lies in her own sexual pleasure: "Antônia slid her hand over and touched Marta's sex and told her with a voice like barbed wire: I am old, ugly, but from here will come your happiness: Marta raised herself up, anointed with Antônia's consecration . . ." (37). Antônia thus initiates Marta to her bodily sexuality and Marta wants this contact to continue, feeling the fertility and sensuality of the egg still in her body, desiring the same type of fiery, transformative sexual experience with Antônia that she has with the sun (37). But Antônia feigns sleep and admonishes her at the end of the chapter in a threatening tone: "Do ovo, nós sabemos. E de teu sexo de sol?" / "About the egg, we know. And what about the sun of your sex?" (38). This line is quite ambiguous and could be read many ways. Yet, by all accounts, this comment indicates Antônia's function of indoctrinating Marta into her carnality, of drawing attention to Marta's sexual relationship with the sun, and, ultimately, of insisting that she look for sexual fulfillment in a more conventional or earthly sexuality. Antônia is, then, priestess in Marta's initiation into a more mundane and specifically feminine sexuality, beyond or in addition to her relationship to the sun.

Just as the father looks to Marta for the key to his secrets, Marta, in turn, looks to Antônia for the answers to her own mysteries: "She tracked Antônia to discover in her the secret, her unsubmissiveness in the face of any virtue" (27). Furthermore, Marta's desire for Antônia is for her powers and for the power Marta herself could have over such a body: "A desire to mount the woman, not to touch her body, . . . but to dominate her . . ." (30). Indeed, the relationship between the two women mirrors the relationship between the father and Marta, as the father's initial thoughts on the matter reveal:

O pai via a aproximação das duas mulheres, uma quase excremento de animal, a outra a filha da sua perdição, compreendendo que a união dos seres raros era uma destinação natural, também ele seguia a filha, fiel e desonrado, . . . Marta perdia-se em Antônia e em quem também ele se perdia? (29).

[The father saw the closeness of the two women, one almost animal excrement, the other the daughter of his perdition, understanding that the union of rare beings was a natural destination, he also followed the daughter, faithful and dishonored, . . . Marta lost herself in Antônia and in whom did he lose himself?]

Yet the father's view on their relationship becomes more negative as he gradually loses control of the situation. He feels threatened by the feminine solidarity between them and views their relationship as a conspiracy: "'For years you and Antônia have been conspiring, I will never forgive you.' The father denounced the lack of order in the house, of which he had never spoken before" (80). Thus the joining of forces of Antônia and Marta precipitates the "disorder" in the father's house, the patriarchal structure is upset by the "goods" getting together, by the women speaking among themselves.[24]

The threat to the father's authority reaches its climax in the fourth section of the novel, where the father observes Marta communing with the sun. He becomes enraged and at that point decides to bring Jerônimo into the picture. Indeed, Marta's sensuous and mystical relationship to the sun is what most threatens the patriarch's plot.[25] The narrator minces no words, clearly telling us that although Marta is her father's daughter, her "longing for the sun reduced him to ashes" (44). Obsessed, the father follows her into the woods where she, the primeval woman, "the first creature after the creation" (44), goes to the river to bathe in a feminine ritual. For him, this ceremony is going to reveal her truth to him once and for all and he will no longer be possessed by his desire for her or for knowledge of the feminine (44). After coming out of the river, Marta lies out in the sun, exposing her nude body to its rays while the father looks on. Her act of sexual autonomy becomes an act of aggression against the father: she removes her clothes "until she exposed the sex, covered with dark grass, and laid down on the ground, nude and white, condemning the father" (45). In seeing her offer herself this way, the father becomes alarmed, taking her challenge as an affront to his authority, vowing to take his revenge and be the one to determine her sexual partner: "He remembered the man in the church, the hand of a tree, he had then judged him

severely. 'If it is a male she needs, I will give her one'" (47). This man
(Jerônimo), who has "the hand of a tree," had approached Marta in
the church and she had let him touch her because he was neither her
father nor one of the other participants in the market/ceremony.[26]
The father had looked upon Jerônimo severely then, as outside the
patriarchal economy. But now the father thinks of bringing him to
the house so that he (the father) will be the one to give Marta a man.
The father thus decides, in light of Marta's threatening sexual autonomy, to call for Jerônimo as a desperate attempt to maintain his
authority over Marta. This, of course, is the same strategy employed
before by the father: plotting out even the trails Marta herself would
blaze in an effort to control meaning, to be the author of Marta's destiny, and, ultimately, to retain all (signifying) power for himself.

The series of transgressions and affronts to authority we have
just examined, in addition to constituting an effective narrative
strategy, also bear, I suggest, an oblique critique of the Brazilian
political context. Between 1968 and 1974, in response to worker
and student protests, the Brazilian military tightened its grip, using
increasingly repressive tactics to terrorize and control the country
(Alvarez 8). So in 1972 (the year *A Casa da Paixão* was published),
the authoritarian regime was at its most restrictive. An authoritarian
figure such as the nameless "pai" takes on a sociopolitical significance given the patriarchal dictatorship in place, and indeed at its
oppressive worst, when the novel was published. Asked in an interview whether literature's task is to undertake political critique,
Piñon affirms her commitment to provoking a change of consciousness but in an indirect way: "The writer denounces, but not in a
direct way. If not, he or she will produce a text which is everything
but a literary or artistic text. The writer has a committment to
arouse the rage born of conciousness" (interview with Moraes Neto
8). Likewise, in *A Casa da Paixão*, Piñon's explicit attack on sexual
and textual authorities, enacted by writing the body in such transgressive ways, can also be read as an indirect critique of an authoritarianism that tried to silence dissent in Brazil in the late 60s and
early 70s. In any case, an overt attack at this point would have been
out of the question and, as it was, the novel encountered difficulties
with state censors because of its unconventional, sexually explicit
episodes.[27] Piñon herself has the following to say about writing in
times of censorship:

> Aunque se haya establecido la censura sobre nuestras cabezas,
> es difícil admitir su existencia. . . . De algún modo u otro

venceremos. Si nos prohíben hablar del cuerpo, . . . significa entonces que pasaremos a discutir lagartos y sus equivalentes históricos. Sabiendo, sin embargo, que los lagartos sólo expresan lo que no podemos asumir públicamente. Las fábulas son un ejemplo de la falta de libertad del hombre. Se esconde detrás de algún subterfugio para engendrar una verdad mejor aunque difícil (interview with Farida Issa 137).

[Even though censorship has been installed over our heads, it is difficult to admit its existence. . . . In some way or other we will triumph. If they prohibit us from speaking about the body, . . . then this means that we will turn to discussing lizards and their historical equivalents. Knowing, nevertheless, that the lizards only express what we cannot assume publicly. Fables are an example of the lack of freedom of man. One hides behind some subterfuge to engender a better, if more difficult, truth.]

Clearly, Piñon views allegorical technique as a viable form of resistance to censorship and lack of textual freedom. Without belaboring the point, I suggest that the power struggle in *A Casa* against a suffocating, authoritarian patriarch as well as against limiting social discourses can be read as an allegory of political resistance. Such a correspondence between the questioning of the father's authority and resistance on a wider, more public level seem to be what Marta herself intimates when she says: "o que se fizer em minha carne se estará fazendo no mundo" / "what is done to my flesh will be done in the world" (68). Seen this way, Marta's defiance of the patriarch's plot takes on not only sexual but social resonance; her resistance to the paternal signifying authority becomes—by reading in context—an indictment of an authoritarian system that sought to remake Brazilian society in its own image.

The Patriarch's Puppet: Jerônimo and Marta's Critique of Masculinity

The transgressions examined earlier are strategies Marta uses in her quest for a sexuality outside the patriarchal economy. Gaining sexual pleasure from the sun, rejecting her role as object of exchange, engaging in a same-sex sensual relationship with Antônia are all transgressions of the traditional gendering sequence and ultimately open possibilities for rewriting the script. Jerônimo's entrance on

the scene considerably complicates Marta's search for sexual autonomy and, in many ways, constitutes the ambiguity and complexity
of Piñon's novel. Jerônimo is an ambivalent figure in *A Casa da
Paixão* precisely in that he occupies a key role in the patriarch's
plot and yet also in Marta's attempted rewriting of the script. While
she desires Jerônimo's body, she patently rejects his position within
the father's plan. Indeed, her complex ambivalence regarding Jerônimo textually figures a critique of traditional masculinity and
becomes a way of calling for a different, more bodily male sexuality.

Jerônimo's role at first seems to have much more to do with his
relationship to the father than to Marta, who immediately pegs
Jerônimo as a slave to her father, as a mere puppet of the patriarch's
plot; "servo do pai" / "servant of the father", "escravo do meu pai" /
"slave of my father" Marta repeats over and over. Indeed, Jerônimo
follows the movements of the father, obedient to his signals, and
the initial scene in the father's house appears to be one of male
bonding: "Jerônimo accepted the cigar, he was imitating the father's
movements" (51). The meal the father invites Jerônimo to share is
akin to a medieval challenge and exchange. Jerônimo rejects the
invitation at first on the grounds that eating from a stranger's table
would be poison. Yet the father challenges him again, and the
younger man, after declining the overtures of the elder, finally agrees
to accept the deal. The "contract" involves, however, not only the
ritual exchange of a woman between men traditionally used to bind
the men to each other (i.e., kinship structures), but also the genera-
tional confrontation where boys come up against paternal authority
(i.e., the oedipal crisis). Jerônimo agrees to obey the father's desire
not only because he will get the daughter or because he can thus
associate himself with the powerful father, but because the father
promises him his own freedom as well: "Jerônimo obeyed in view of
the promise: more than the daughter, you will have freedom afterwards" (54). Here the younger man agrees to his role in order to
become subject of his own quest for autonomy, to attain his own
degree of signifying power; in short, to "become a man."

Thus the relationship of Jerônimo to the "law of the father" is
ambiguous; he feigns obedience to phallic law but simultaneously
strives for his own independence and scripts himself into the position of saving the daughter from that law.[28] At dinner Marta enter-
tains thoughts of saving herself, of not having to accept this stranger,
this representative of her father's will: "The slave of the father would
not be her master, thought Marta . . . she could save herself however
without depending on the stranger" (52). Later in the same dinner

scene, Jerônimo's textual function becomes even more ambiguous. Antônia brings a towel and water and Jerônimo proceeds to wash Marta's face, removing the wild scent from her skin. All the while he is whispering to Marta, ordering her to open her eyes, asking her to comprehend the ritual to which he is submitting himself in order to save her. Throughout this scene he appears to be engaged both in domesticating Marta (removing her wild scent) and in helping her to revolt against the father. Jerônimo feigns compliance with the father's agenda ("Jerônimo, smiling, pretended to be submissive" 55) and at the same time establishes his own program for convincing Marta of his independence from the father. He is effectively playing both ends against the middle. Marta, in part seduced by the gentleness of his touch, listens to him sympathetically, although she continues to resist him as the "slave of my father" (53). She remains convinced that he forms part of her father's designs on her body and hates him for being an instrument of the father's will. Jerônimo, in turn, is ambivalent; he finds himself taken by Marta such that he is tempted to abandon his preconceived plan in order to please her.

So while Jerônimo's position is complex and ambiguous, it is further complicated by Marta's attempts at re-writing the sexual script. Marta's autonomous sexuality is an affront to phallic law from the beginning of the novel. While Marta is seen in a passionate rapture with the sun in the very opening scene of the text, it is in the middle chapter of the book (59–68) that Marta's unsettling *jouissance* is given full expression as both sexual and textual pleasure. In this section of the narrative, Marta articulates her view of the events up to this point, her relationship to the father, her sexuality, and her dilemma vis-à-vis the arrival of Jerônimo. Beginning and ending with "eu," the chapter breaks even further with traditional syntax; there are no sentences, no paragraphs, only phrases that continually open out onto the next. In this way, the discourse presses onward, yet is circular and never unified under one thesis, thus bearing resemblance to what Cixous and other feminists have denominated *écriture féminine*. Remaining multiple and elusive, this writing explores the complexities and disruptions of feminine *jouissance* and its problems with the "men of this world."[29]

While it would be both time-consuming and of dubious value to attempt to synthesize the entire chapter, certain themes do emerge that merit close attention in order to understand Marta's critique of traditional masculinity. For example, throughout the chapter, Marta reiterates her view of her sexual relationship to the sun. Marta begins the chapter by celebrating her sexual relationship to the sun and vowing her fidelity to a sexuality that is otherworldly: "I will sacrifice myself to the sun" (59). Specifically, she articulates her body as sacrificial altar through which and upon which the sun becomes man: "ventre meu, falo teimosa para não esquecer, é de altar, para sol virar homem e me penetrar" / "womb of mine, I speak stubbornly so as not to forget, is like an altar for the sun to become man and penetrate me" (63). While, through the mediation of her body, the sun is embodied in man in order to make love to her, Marta also views herself as an incarnation of the sun's sensual energy: "I am the body of the sun" (65) Thus, both man and woman are articulated as carnal manifestations of the sun. So, even though the sun is often construed as a masculine element, in *A Casa* it signifies primarily a sexuality beyond sexual difference but not obliterating the differences within it: "sol é o meu ventre, sol é o pênis precioso da minha terra encantada . . ." / "the sun is my womb, the sun is the precious penis of my enchanted earth . . ." (62). In this way, the revolutionary sexuality Marta embraces is based on the sun as an erotic energy common to both a masculine and a feminine libido.

It becomes increasingly clear that the light of the sun is absolutely necessary for Marta to formulate a new feminine sexuality, for any revolutionary sexual union to take place. Indeed, I would argue that the insistence on the realm of the elements, on the power of the sun to give sexual pleasure, becomes a strategy for deauthorizing the law of the father, for calling into question the patriarchal structure and its usurpation of all rights in the deployment of sexuality. Marta declares:

> Odeio os homens desta terra, amo os corpos dos homens desta terra, cada membro que eles possuem e me mostram, para que eu me abra em esplendor, mas só me terão quando eu ordenar, homem que for herdeiro do meu corpo eu acusarei em via pública . . . (63).

> [I hate the men of this earth, I love the bodies of the men of this earth, each member that they possess and show me, in order for me to open myself in splendor, but they will only have me when I ordain it, a man who will be heir to my body I will denounce in public.]

In this way, she rejects the law of the father, the patriarchal system whereby a man "inherits" his right to a woman by virtue of his forming part of the masculinist lineage. Marta summarily rejects the father's imposition on her sexual rights, attempting to make a distinction between the man he has chosen for her and the man she chooses herself. Marta sees the male body as erotic, asking whether man is not there precisely to give her pleasure, to give her body what it desires: "and so does not man come forth to satisfy what the body at last should know" (65). But the man who could participate in this solar sexuality is *not* the man brought by the father, thus placing these two figures in opposition: "The man, father, that you brought, ah, Jerônimo he is called, and I would kill him a thousand times on my altar, he is the slave of your vestibule, of your will" (65) and "I hated the man that my father brought me and in whose eyes I saw the nocturnal assault" (68). Indeed, the darkness is used to cover "seus sexos oficiais," "their official sexes," the official phallus of patriarchal sexuality, while the new sexuality formulated by Marta herself would be bathed in light and would not be hidden.

Throughout this key chapter, Marta lays bare her ambivalence regarding Jerônimo. She says of him: "vinha para minha cama, privava-me dos agasalhos, ordenava, mulher é minha sempre que eu entro nela, e me entrava eu não queria, ou queria, que não podia aceitar . . ." / "he came to my bed, he deprived me of warmth, he ordered, woman is mine every time I enter her, and he entered me and I did not want it, or I did, but could not accept . . ." (67). The final phrase here is particularly ambiguous in the Portuguese: either she could not accept him (as I translated it above) or, alternately, the fact that she indeed wants him is what proves unacceptable (whereby it would read in English "or I did, but that could not be accepted"). What this all points to is that it becomes more and more difficult in the oppressive atmosphere of her father's house for Marta to even be sure of her own desire. Further along she says, "eu invento assaltos para enfeitar a morbidez do meu desejo, ou a morbidez dos outros" / "I invent assaults to embellish the morbidity of my desire, or the morbidity of others" (68). Marta's desire becomes elusive, and yet she remains opposed to the type of coupling offered to her by this representative of the father's law and his paternal desire. After imagining the "nocturnal assault," how Jerônimo would take her according to a traditional sexuality, she describes how this earthly man *could* please her, how he *could* participate in her other sexuality: he would "transport me to the river, there, and only there, fecundate me *bathed by the sun* . . ." (68; emphasis added). Marta's ambivalence thus arises because the distinction between a potential Jerônimo of the sun and the slave of the father's law becomes ever more difficult to imagine as these two men are one and the same. Marta only desires Jerônimo outside of the economy designated by the father, and, consequently, the act of calling him "Jerônimo" instead of "slave of the father" becomes an emblem of this desire. And yet, it seems that a desire outside of this economy is doomed to failure, doomed to being reinscribed in that very same economy all over again. As Naomi Hoki Moniz points out, the very name "Jerônimo"—from *ieros* (sacred) and *onymos* (name)—is a manifestation of the sacred, Adamic activity of naming (134). He is then, from his very name, the enactment or incarnation of the father's law. This seems to be the realization Marta comes to when she says:

> eu o chamei Jerônimo uma única vez, ele enrubesceu e seus olhos como que ordenavam, chame uma outra vez, eu fiz que sua carne amargasse ter vindo com o pai, ser escravo do pai e não disse Jerônimo, embora dentro tudo gritasse, sim, eu tinha desejo de dizer Jerônimo, o homem Jerônimo, a carne Jerônimo, o sangue Jerônimo, ele mais parecia o título da terra, a terra se batizara segundo Jerônimo, e Jerônimo batizando a terra com seu nome batizava meu ventre de Jerônimo, como flores, como animais, eu expulsava o batismo, Jerônimo dizia, meu, eu te chamo agora Jerônimo, em vez de Marta eu sou Jerônimo, como Jerônimo também eu possuo seu imenso sexo, sexo que me desonrou só pelo olhar e meu ventre carregando aquele sexo mais parece um hermafrodita sofrido, séculos o separavam de vida, e eu era a vida, Jerônimo escravo do meu pai dizia, vamos copular, não, ele não dizia, seus olhos cumpriam a ordem, então eu fui dormir . . . (66–67).

[I called him Jerônimo only once, he blushed and it was as if his eyes ordered me to call him again, I made his flesh become bitter for having come with the father, for being the slave of the father and I did not say Jerônimo, although inside all of me shouted, yes, I had the desire to say Jerônimo, the man Jerônimo, the flesh Jerônimo, the blood Jerônimo, he seemed more like the inscription of the earth, the earth was baptized according to Jerônimo, and Jerônimo baptized the earth with his name, and Jerônimo baptizing the earth with his name baptized my womb as Jerônimo's, like the flowers, like the animals, I drove away the baptism, Jerônimo said, mine, I now call you Jerônimo, instead of Marta I am Jerônimo, like Jerônimo I also possess his immense sex, the sex that dishonored me only by looking at me and my womb bearing the burden of that sex seemed more like a suffering hermaphrodite, centuries separated it from life, and I was life, Jerônimo slave of my father said, let us copulate, no, he did not say it, his eyes carried out the order, so I went to bed . . .]

I have cited this lengthy and complex passage not only to give a sense of the rhythm of this chapter, but also because it effectively sums up the ambivalence Marta feels toward Jerônimo and lays bare his ambiguous and confusing position vis-à-vis the dominant power structure. While Marta desires Jerônimo's body, his flesh and his blood, the idealizing and universalizing functions he takes up threaten to overwhelm her autonomy; in other words, his naming of the world, his brandishing of the phallic function, threatens to overtake her own subjectivity and completely subsume her to him. The baptismal ritual where Jerônimo ultimately names her womb as his own is a figure for the danger Marta sees in a phallic masculinity that would usurp her identity completely. In the sexual order of a traditional phallic masculinity, Marta would literally become Jerônimo ("instead of Marta I am Jerônimo") as he, in effect, carried out the patriarchal plan. As Moniz accurately observes: "Jerônimo, brought by the Father . . . represents all oppression and repression, patriarchal and Christian, of the feminine" ("Ética, Estética" 135). Indeed, Marta realizes this and thus rejects and tries to ignore this representative of patriarchal power ("I went to sleep"). Yet, the fact remains that she sees erotic possibilities in a coupling with the flesh of the man ("the man Jerônimo, the flesh Jerônimo"), with his body and his penis, if not with his phallic powers and privileges.

The distinction penis/phallus has been articulately summarized by Jane Gallop in *Thinking Through the Body*. Referring to Freud, Gallop explains that the phallic phase refers to a sexuality organized around the opposition between having a phallus or having nothing, while adult sexuality finds its logic in the distinction between the masculine and the feminine (125). Thus, Gallop points out that "the phallus thus belongs to a monosexual logic, one that admits to no difference, of no other sex; whereas the penis can be inserted into the realm of adult sexuality where it can encounter the feminine" (125). Regarding the passage from *A Casa* that I cited earlier, the phallic phase certainly seems to be operating here: there is no space for femininity, or even a penile masculinity that would recognize femininity. Both sexual organs are collapsed into one immense phallus ("like Jerônimo I also possess his immense sex, the sex that dishonored me only by looking at me"); all sexuality is usurped by the powerful, transcendent (male) sex.

Gallop goes on to point out that for Lacan the phallus is not only emblematic of infantile sexuality but is a linguistic concept: "It is a signifier, which is to say it belongs to what Lacan calls the symbolic order, which is the order of language. It is neither a real nor a fantasized organ but an attribute: a power to generate meaning" (126). Yet no one can be at the center of language, no speaking subject controls language in that way; language, as Lacan might put it, "speaks" the subject. Furthermore, the constant slippage between phallus (the power to mean what he says and to say what he means) and penis (male sexual organ) enables the dominant phallocentric culture to continue, as Gallop lucidly observes: "as long as the attribute of power is a phallus which can only have meaning by referring to and being confused with a penis, this confusion will support a structure in which it seems reasonable that men have power and women do not" (127).

The sexuality Marta advocates, predicated on the power of the sun, works to divest the phallus of its power. Indeed, the sun comes to function as a new transcendent signifier, an ambiguously gendered power that could delegitimate the phallus as the symbolic reference point for all sexuality. In practice, the sun can operate as a generative principle in a similar way to the phallus; it "names" all things in that nothing can be seen without its light. The sun is portrayed as just such a generative function at the beginning of *A Casa da Paixão*: "a certain powerful light making it necessary to close the eyes, under the threat of blindness, so that it could ever discern the objects which it named, leaves, fruits . . ." (10). Ultimately, Marta wants the sexual relationship between herself and Jerônimo to be mediated by the sun, envisioning them both as carnal instruments of an erotics of the sun rather than an erotics of the phallus where they can obviously never be on equal footing. Thus, what Marta wants from Jerônimo is a carnal, *penile* sexual relationship, not a relation to the phallic function. She is looking for a bodily Jerônimo with his flesh and blood, not a Jerônimo with a privileged link to phallic power. We could say that Jane Gallop, in the end, advocates the same thing: a penile, masculine sexuality as opposed to the phallacy currently in place. She hypothesizes about the possibilities of a bodily masculinity:

> I cannot disintricate the penis from phallic rule but neither is it totally synonymous with the transcendent phallus. At this

point in history I don't think they can be separated, but to insist on bodily masculinity is to work to undo the heterosexist ideology which decrees the body female, to be dominated not by a male body (too disorderly to rule) but by an idealized, transcendent phallus. I want to render that idealization impossible (131–32).

It would certainly seem that this is what Marta wants to do as well. She searches primarily for the masculine *body* and her view of Jerônimo is so ambivalent because she, too, has difficulty in trying to "disintricate" the bodily masculinity she desires from the phallic role Jerônimo has been scripted into.

What this all adds up to is that both Piñon's fiction and Gallop's theoretical intervention reflect on the pressing need to rearticulate masculinity as bodily rather than universal and transcendent. Clearly, this is not women's work alone. In *The Body Hispanic*, Paul Julian Smith has observed that this is precisely the goal of an emerging men's studies: to examine man as particular and as a male gendered *body* rather than as a "universal representative of humanity" (4). Indeed, in order for man to maintain his transcendent position, to *be* the universal, the male body must be rendered invisible.[30] Regarding the invisibility of the male body, Smith points out: "The erasure of the male body thus has a contradictory effect. It both ensures the persistence of male dominance and prevents men from knowing themselves" (5). This is certainly true and is born out in *A Casa da Paixão*. Smith goes on to add that even though his focus is on male identity, "so naturalized as to be invisible," he notes that he cannot ignore woman, for "any attempt to move man to the centre of the stage must also examine that stage itself. And the ground on which man takes up his position is, inevitably, woman" (5). Inevitably? Smith's formulation draws attention to the way the construct man has consistently used woman as his eternal Other. But surely we might question this state of affairs. Indeed, it is this very "inevitable" use of woman as man's "stage" that translates into real limits on women's subjectivity. It is, in many ways, against such "inevitability" that Marta struggles. Yet, curiously enough, we shall see that, although *A Casa da Paixão* attempts to articulate a sexuality that would move beyond the phallic through its emphasis on the sun, which would resist the appropriation of the woman's body, Piñon's novel also moves man to "center stage" where he promptly takes up his position (inevitably?) on the body of Marta. But why does this happen, why does the same old story repeat itself, as dissonant as it is with Marta's and the narrator's resistance to that story? What does this outcome say about the possiblities for women designing/writing their own quest, about their ability to become women (active social subjects) while grappling with the social constructs of Woman? And, perhaps even more intriguing, if more difficult to make explicit: what does the outcome of the sexual narrative in the novel imply about the possibilities and limitations of resistance in the sociopolitical sphere?

As we shall see in the last part of this chapter, *A Casa da Paixão* does not answer these questions but rather asks them in a particularly poignant way at the end of the novel. Nonetheless, what Marta desires, in the meantime at least, is an erotics outside the phallic economy. Her quest for this bodily maleness that would exclude the function of the phallus by replacing it with the sun, provides a powerful critique of traditional constructions of masculinity, of the dominant gender script. She says she hates the men of this earth but loves the bodies of the men of this earth (63); the problem of course is whether at this point such a separation can be made between the official, phallic, universalizing male and the bodily, penile, particular male. In any case, the attempt to disarticulate these, like the attempt to disarticulate phallus/penis, could be seen as a step toward deconstructing the "heterosexist ideology" Gallop talks about.

Marta's Script: Re-Plotting Gender and the Struggle for Authorship

While Marta's rejection of a sexuality predicated on phallic principles certainly enacts a critique of traditional constructions of masculinity, her quest does not stop there. Attempting to move beyond defiance, Marta embarks on her own narrative path, setting the pace for the father and Jerônimo to follow. Determined to resist the father's plans for her, she struggles to maintain her autonomy, to refuse the man the father wants to impose on her. Jerônimo is at once the father's representative and object of Marta's desire, occupying, as we have seen, a contradictory position. For this reason, Marta designs a ritual whereby she will drop three vases, on the third deciding who will be her earthly sexual partner. This rite symbolically reiterates that she will only have the man of *her* choosing, that she is writing her own passage into womanhood. Indeed, Antônia explicitly refers to Marta's ritual as *writing*: "*A filha escreve*: os dois vasos quebrados e eu parto" / "the *daughter writes*:

two glasses broken and I depart" (99; emphasis added). In this way, Marta tries to write her own law, a law based on her feminine desire and on a solar, as opposed to a phallic, sexuality. Marta will not accept a patriarchal sexuality carried out in darkness, in the father's house, in closed spaces or in the spaces defined and delineated by man's time. Earthly sexuality will only be actualized if her conditions are met, hence the demands and the ordering of events (the narrative pattern) that Marta imposes in the second part of the book. My vocabulary of writing in this chapter thus not only refers to the fact that Marta's activities at times quite literally involve writing, but it also reflects the resonance between agency and authorship when it comes to social scripts of gendering. In this way, the struggle for a more active subjectivity and the role of agent in the story of gendering can be read as a struggle for authorship.[31]

Perhaps the first indication that Marta is transforming the script is the change in the relationship between the father and Jerônimo. Marta's refusal to accept the father's will passively, indeed her defiance of the father and her consequent rejection of Jerônimo as slave of the father, is what causes Jerônimo to seek his own independence from the patriarch's plot. The phallic alliance has become problematic for Jerônimo and, at this point, he rejects patriarchal law and decides to act on his own behalf against the father. Jerônimo begins his own narrative—his rendition of the events dominates the seventh section of the novel—by telling the father that he is now his own man:

> Obedeci no início, mulher eu sempre quis, destino de homem é resolver-se sobre coisas valentes e abusadas, obedeci então, a filha acusou-me de ser teu servo, fui até agora, mas meu tempo de servidão terminou . . . (70).

> [I obeyed at the beginning, I always wanted a woman, the destiny of man is to realize himself upon things brave and abused, I obeyed then, the daughter accused me of being your servant, I was until now, but my time of servitude has ended . . .]

Jerônimo now proposes to act according to his own "nature" as opposed to complying with the father's desire (70) and the father becomes the third term that separates the lovers. As Jerônimo sees it: "the father between us, to control any breath to which we dedicate ourselves" (73). And indeed the father has become wary and jealous of his over-eager ally.

In this way, Jerônimo begins to script himself as Marta's savior, as the hero of his own quest plot where Marta becomes the treasure he seeks. An oedipal-like situation thus comes into full force; the father becomes jealous of his own stand-in and legal successor just as Jerônimo rebels against the father's will by becoming Marta's ally and rescuer and, ultimately, author of his own story with her. As Jerônimo attempts to become the subject of his own quest, fighting subjection to the father's will, he challenges the father's authority and consequently loses his authorization. Thus, Jerônimo moves from legal, official representative of the father's law to illegal rebel and potential usurper at the precise moment that he proposes to assume narrative control, indeed just as he moves from actor authorized by the father to author in his own right. The struggle in the constantly shifting triangle of pai-Marta-Jerônimo is thus primarily for subjectivity, for narrative power or what I have called the plotting prerogative, for the position of author or agent in the (patriarchal) social script.

The shifting power relations and the oscillation of the plotting prerogative become increasingly clear in the way chase scenes are enacted in the second half of *A Casa*. A common element of the rituals of sexual relationship is the chase, the pursuer typically being the male and the driving force male desire. Until that point in the novel, this has certainly been the case: we have seen mostly how the father and Jerônimo pursue Marta and how she eludes them. In the second half of the novel, however, Marta re-plots this protocol of the sexual quest, imposing her own desires and designs in a more active way, making the man pursue her because *she* desires *him*. Jerônimo recounts his pursuit of Marta, viewing her as a keeper of secrets and repository of primordial creative energies: ("it was as if she deciphered codes from Mesopotamia" 71), as a "fruit of creation" (71). Perhaps most importantly, he explains how he becomes her "tesouro," how he becomes an object of her desire: "admiti que a mulher aceitara minha mão como aquela que sempre buscou escondida dentro da terra, eu era o seu tesouro" / "I allowed that the woman had accepted my hand as that one she always searched for hidden in the earth, I was her treasure" (72). The syntax of the sentence in Portuguese almost feminizes Jerônimo: he is the hand (the feminine "mão") that she has been looking for. He is following her tracks, tracing her movements; as he himself says "I thus began habituating myself to the life exercises of Marta" (73).

In effect, by pursuing her this way Jerônimo becomes her apprentice, unknowingly learning the ropes of the revolutionary sexuality Marta so desires. At this point, however, what he most desires in the chase is Marta's body, claiming that what he really needs is her flesh to experience pleasure: "I only needed her body, to nourish myself as one who bathes in cleanliness, and is assured pleasure forever, ah, the foolishness of going after Marta" (74). Throughout what amounts to an allegorization of courtship rituals, Jerônimo's potential sexual experience is all banked on Marta's body while his own body remains surprisingly—or, considering our discussion above, not so surprisingly—textually absent. Yet as Marta leads him through her "exercises," as she makes Jerônimo pursue her, she becomes his teacher, obliging him to follow in her steps toward new sexual and textual possibilities. That is not to say, however, that Jerônimo is always a willing and compliant student of Marta's lessons. When it comes to Marta's writing, for example, he takes issue with her autonomy and authority, in short, with her authorship of a sexual desire all her own.

Marta's attempt to re-plot her own erotic rituals, at one point, becomes even more explicitly an act of writing the body, an act of assuming authorship of her own sexual desire. Jerônimo observes as Marta effectively writes her own desire on the wall, using her menstrual blood: "Now she probed her sex, scrawling on the wall with the blood that trickled down between her legs" (75). He later reads what she has written: "later I read the woman's words, nearly vanishing: *when he comes, I will know how to choose*" (75; emphasis added). Thus, what she writes on the wall has to do with her sexual autonomy, her lover defined by *her* desire in the revolutionary, solar sexuality she advocates. With this act Marta summarily rejects her father's attempts to choose her mate for her by inscribing her determination to choose her own lover. This reappropriation of her own sexual and textual *jouissance* enacts a "writing the body" as an act of resistance to patriarchal law. Furthermore, the fact that she inscribes her desire using menstrual blood makes this act doubly transgressive: it breaks the code that would exclude women from writing and also uses a substance to do so which is outside (and indeed confounds) the masculine signifying economy. As Jane Gallop has observed: "Menstrual blood cannot immediately be absorbed into the category of female sexuality as phallic turn on, phallic receptacle, or the category of maternity as carrier of phallic products, reproductions of the phallus. Thus it remains an embarrassment for either classic feminine representation: the mother or the whore" (*Thinking Through the Body* 54). What Gallop's comments point to is that menstrual blood bears no meaningful relationship to a phallic desire and indeed exceeds the boundaries of such an economy. Marta's writing on the wall turns menstrual blood into language, making it signify her desire in a revolutionary act of sexual autonomy. This activity is one more lesson in the feminine sexuality not determined by the phallus and its methods of meaning.[32]

Significantly enough, Jerônimo reads her writing, yet resists this lesson, preferring to imagine a flowing of blood as a result of her defloration, as a result of his penetration. The chapter ends:

> porém ela preferira o sangue, a mensagem transitória, vi de repente, a raiva me fazendo correr, eu esbarrava em coisas da terra, eu queria Marta, e na sua frase estava o enigma, situava-se sim, ele, numa imensa parede branca marcada de sangue, regalo de sua abundância mensal, mas jamais o sangue que lhe teria o meu corpo provocado, hemorragia do prazer, se me tivesse ela chamado para participar do festim, eu ingresso em seu corpo, ela gritando, pela dor e a alegria, ambos rabiscando a parede, ela era a fonte sangüínea, eu o gerador do seu suplício, ela (76)

> [but she had preferred the blood, the transitory message, I saw suddenly, the rage making me run, I collided with things of the earth, I wanted Marta, and in her phrase was the enigma, it was situated, yes, on an immense, white wall marked with blood, boon of her monthly abundance, but never the blood that my body had provoked in her, hemorrhage of pleasure, if she had called me to participate in the feast, I enter into her body, she crying out, in pain and in happiness, both scrawling on the wall, she was the bleeding fountain, I the generator of her torment, she]

Her sexual autonomy threatens him, makes him feel excluded and angry, and he figuratively re-writes the blood on the wall as a coproduction produced by his penetration of her body. The production of meaning he envisions is not, however, only predicated on some univocal phallic pleasure or "phallic turn-on." It is a dual, mutual pleasure: he is the "gerador" ("generator") but she is the "fonte" ("fountain"). Nonetheless, it is the phallic penetration that would be the provocation of her pleasure; the pedagogical flow here would be primarily from male to female, and less so the reverse.[33] Furthermore, Jerônimo's re-writing of her desire effectively undoes her claim to the exclusive authorship of her desire, as he cleverly writes himself into the prime subject position as the more active agent (the "generator"). Again, the struggle here is for narrative power and Marta's quest for the right to generate meanings comes into direct conflict with the father's and Jerônimo's desire to do the same. Perhaps these desires would not be on such a collision course if the "inevitable" place of the inscription of meanings were not the female body.

Yet, Marta's plan, with its pedagogical element, seems actually to foment the use of her body as mediator. While she has taken up the plotting prerogative, her pedagogical path involves mimicking the woman's traditional roles as object of desire, as mystical mediator between man and himself, between man and the world, man and sensuality. Marta envisions her function as leading Jerônimo to the depths like Euridyce, to where he can experience his own sensuality: "It would be up to her to conduct him to the center of the earth. She had acted like this with the father. All of them pursued and the eternal hunt" (80).[34] When Antônia indicates that they should continue to look for Marta in the North, the father concludes: "In the north the salvation of Jerônimo's body" (98). His comment prefigures Marta's sacrificial function as a medium to bring the masculine back into contact with its corporality, to lead Jerônimo to assume his own sexual body.

More evidence of Marta as mystic medium is the use of music in the text. There are several instances when Marta plays the piano for the men, first for her father, then for Jerônimo and the father together. She is their contact with the feminine, which in this case corresponds to the Dionysian, characterized by Nietzsche as a disruptive, conflictive but necessary force for creation.[35] The effect of her music on the men—on the masculine—is dramatic. When she plays, Jerônimo describes the effect it has on him:

Não sabia explicar mas a arma assassina era o piano, porque quando Marta tocava, partes inteiras do seu corpo silenciavam, sem explicar a anestesia, seria acaso feitiço, ou a simples aproximação do corpo em vapor de Marta . . . (83).

[He did not know how to explain it but the murderous weapon was the piano, because when Marta played, entire parts of his body became silent, without explaining the anesthesia, perhaps it was a spell, or simply the closeness of the vaporous body of Marta . . .]

His response to the music is eminently corporal: it becomes a profound experience of his own body as well as of Marta's. Yet his body is only "silenced" and the rest of the passage focuses on Marta's body, which Jerônimo finally proclaims: "the most perfect jewel" (83). This is ultimately a learning process, evident in that Marta explicitly looks upon the men as her pupils: "Marta esquecia Jerônimo, sua *aprendizagem* destinava-se agora ao pai" / "Marta forgot about Jerônimo, her *learning* was now directed toward the father" (85; emphasis added). While the men continue to believe they are the masters, it is Marta who takes control of the pedagogical structure. She is leading them through her steps, training them according to her own design.

But the fact that she has assumed an active subject position, indeed seeming to be the prime socializing agent in the latter half of the novel, makes it all the more unsettling that the role she scripts for herself is so close to the traditional role of woman. The question is: is her attempted defiance of phallic law really a re-writing of the script or does it merely chronicle the same old story? As Althusser has shown, the way ideology works is to interpellate "free" subjects who seem to assume their place in the social structure voluntarily (182). Likewise, Marta seems to be freely re-plotting the story, but as the story progresses, it begins to look alarmingly like the traditional structure. The difference lies in that she is the agent, seemingly author of her own role, in narrative control. Mimicry of a traditional role as a way of attaining agency is a notoriously treacherous path but one common to women's writing, as Irigaray's work attests. Clearly, there is a fine line between repeating a role and parodying it, but, as Judith Butler suggests, "agency can only be located within the possibility of a variation on that repetition" (145). Indeed, as far as it goes, Piñon's text *is* a variation, in granting Marta the role of agent and would-be author of her story. Contradictions necessarily arise, however, given that the story was never—nor could it be—Marta's alone. As she battles to be subject of her experience, so too do Jerônimo and the father struggle toward their own goals, enacting their own quests that have an already established tradition. Indeed, as Marta strives to appropriate her sexual experience for herself, thus assuming an active subjectivity, it becomes increasingly clear just how experience is, as Diana Fuss puts it, "ideologically cast," how it is inevitably bound up with social relations and systems of signification already in place.[36]

Jerônimo's role in the text illustrates just how experience is never unmediated. Is he the father's "slave" or Marta's savior? Is he outside the patriarchal economy with his "hand of a tree" or privileged understudy of the father himself? In many ways, the struggle portrayed in the text is over what Jerônimo signifies; and his significance, his meaning within an entire social system, will necessarily color Marta's experience of him. It is interesting to note, in this regard, that the father's ingenious strategy of giving Marta the very man she desires is often how patriarchal law gets what it wants. The father does not impose his choice on Marta but rather divines her desire and then, by bringing Jerônimo on the scene through his paternal authority, effectively converts the consummation of her own desire into an act of obedience to his law. This is not unlike the patriarch's plot we examined earlier where the father struggles to keep the daughter on symbolic paths constructed by him, essentially foreclosing her signifying capabilities, by surreptitiously designing and appropriating any trails she would attempt to blaze. So, as Marta resists the patriarch's plot, she struggles against this type of appropriation and the chronicle of her struggle forms the text of *A Casa da Paixão*.

Indeed, while Marta tries systematically to refigure the traditional gender script, she encounters increasingly violent resistance from the father just as her patterns begin to take hold. Marta reminds the male figures that the rituals of courtship, in fact the entire gendering process by which she will become a woman, is being re-written by her: "There are two days left for me to decide. At the end of each day I will break a vase. And when there are none left, *I become a woman*" (84; emphasis added). For Marta, thus, her "becoming" is completely tied up with her entering into a sexual relationship with a man of this world.

What this amounts to, then, is that Marta's *bildung* conflates becoming a woman with becoming Woman. This is, perhaps, the fatal error of her plot. She makes the goal of her quest resonate with the traditional goal of the romance plot: finding a man and "settling down." The possibilities of "becoming a woman" via a lesbian eroticism are explored through the liaison between Marta and Antônia. While this relationship seems to challenge the "inevitability" of heterosexuality, it is ultimately not sustained and Marta's plot falls back in line with the heterosexual script.

In spite of the fact that her own plot ends up being what the father wants for her, he is outraged at what he views as Jerônimo's and her insurgency. The father attempts to impose his law and to usurp her narrative of "becoming a woman" by revealing to Marta that Jerônimo does not constitute her own choice but is there only in obedience to the father's law. The father proclaims: "'It was not you who chose Jerônimo, I hired him just for this, never forget,' the father spewed out live words, like frogs jumping from his mouth" (84). Thus the father becomes a monstrous fury, spitting words and food, as he tries to take control of Marta's desire and her re-writing of the gendering process. While the father wants Jerônimo to triumph, he refuses to "liberar a carne," he refuses the possibility of a sexuality not predicated by his law; in other words, he only wants Jerônimo's bid for Marta to be successful as an agent of *his* law.

So, the father resists this process initiated by Marta precisely because the "incarnation," the transcendent made flesh, threatens his phallic law, which operates according to an idealizing, disembodied, masculine control. The new chase scenes, the courtship rituals under Marta's instruction, all the activities the four characters undertake become a virtual "intense laboratory of the flesh" (91). Jerônimo begins a protocol of perfecting his body, following prescribed steps that lead him through a gradual conversion or transformation process. His corporeal preparation and transformation is required by Marta as a prerequisite for becoming her earthly lover. This entire process has many of the typical rites usually enacted in conversion processes such as baptism, ritual cleansing, and pilgrimage. Jerônimo's conversion, rather than from one religion to another, is from one type of sexuality to another, from a state of idealization of the body to a more carnal experience of the body. Similar to the mystic saints, Jerônimo takes it upon himself to perform purification rituals, attempting to cleanse his body in the river. Yet, this bathing in the river functions as a sign of Jerônimo finally locating his sexuality in his own body as opposed to projecting it only onto the body of Marta. Saying he is in need of atonement (88), he goes off and eventually bathes in the river where he experiences and locates his desire in his own body. "He fled toward the river, submerged himself in its waters. The animal was waiting quietly. Jerônimo's body now reflected no anger. The muscles yes, they worked. As long as I swim in a perfect way, in a perfect way I will possess Marta" (89). As he swims in the river, a traditionally feminine symbol, he begins to experience his own body, his own carnal desire, and aspires to a oneness with his body. In this way, Jerônimo's masculinity is in a process of transformation, now more capable of meeting the feminine. As he swims, his sex overtakes the rest of his body at the sound of Marta's name:

> Marta, ele gritou e sentiu dentro da água nadando o sexo crescer como se antes dos seus braços prosseguirem para arrastar o corpo, seu sexo o ultrapassava, grande e erguido, ele orientava e o trazia para o futuro. Nome de Marta é o sexo orgulhoso (89).

[Marta, he shouted and in the water felt his sex growing as if before his arms proceeded to drag his body, his sex overtook it, large and erect, guiding him and bringing him toward the future. Marta's name is the proud sex.]

So her name provokes his desire, her name becomes the sacred one, her name becomes sex in a reversal of the previous situation where his name was sex, his name named all. As he names the object of his desire, his desire grows, becomes alienated from himself. His penis becomes alienated from the rest of his body, becoming the "pariah of my body" (89) as he swims violently, as he proclaims his hate for Marta in order to keep his desire under control. He cleanses his mouth, washing it out with water, searching for a form of atonement as he prepares himself for the sexual encounter with Marta, which has taken on mythic, religious dimensions.

The sexual act, which finally takes place in the last chapter, becomes another means for attaining that which is beyond the body, beyond the word. At the beginning of their sexual encounter, Marta and Jerônimo explore his body together. Marta confesses that she has never seen the naked body of a man, while Jerônimo admits that this is because "in my most distant memory, I forbade you" (112). In other words, they are focusing on his body in a way that man has heretofore prohibited through social mores and tradition. They look at his flesh and he speaks about his own masculinity, his very real experience of his sexuality, in frank terms.

Maior dor eu conheço aqui, neste arbusto grosso, cresce e diminui e de que não sou senhor, dói tanto, Marta, às vezes encosto-o contra uma árvore, meço quem é mais forte, ele ou a casca da árvore, uma luta de senhores, ficamos esticados, eu feroz de sexo em pé, até a perdição, e não aceito mulher nestas horas, só depois vou em busca delas e pronuncio, vocês abrigam espinho de homem, e me liberto por algumas horas, vou rasgando tudo, sou um instrumento de guerra, Marta (113).

[I feel more pain here, in this thick shrub, that grows and diminishes and of which I am not master, it hurts so much, Marta, sometimes I lean it against a tree, I measure who is stronger, him or the bark of the tree, a struggle of masters, we remain taut, I ferocious with my sex upright, until disgrace, and I do not accept a woman during these hours, only afterwards do I go looking for them, and I pronounce, you harbor the thorn of man, and I free myself for a few hours, I go tearing everything apart, I am an instrument of war, Marta]

Thus, Jerônimo discusses his body, his penis, his experience of his sexual desire in nonidealizing, and yet compelling, terms. He explains how he feels a slave to his desire, often experiencing his sexuality as uncontrollable and conflictive. This seems to be the very thing Gallop and Smith imply is necessary at this point in time: a male articulation of how they experience their own bodies, disentangled from the idealization and universalization to which they so often resort.

Marta insists that the man that is to enter her body participate in the feminine and not flee the bodily realm. At one point, she envisions Jerônimo attending to her as Antônia would: "Jerônimo should wash my sex with water from the river, my sex adorned with blood, he must help me *like a woman*, collaborating in the discreet delivery, just like Antônia . . ." (102; emphasis added). She demands that Jerônimo partake of the feminine, that he act as her midwife and take her body's needs into account. At another moment, she imagines the future scene of fertilization in the river: "its waters should witness the fecundation, the man submerging in my flesh, will also immerse himself in the hands of the river, the vow being his secret" (105). The man who takes her must delve into the river as he plunges into the feminine in an act that seems to have to do with sexual copulation as a figure for the joining of differences (here masculine and feminine) as a means of creation. As Marta prepares herself for the final scene of sexual and poetic fecundation, she leaves tracks for the father and Jerônimo to follow her. Yet, even as she desires the latter, she continues to remain ambivalent. The protocol of the chase is inverted: "The woman after the man. Servant of Jerônimo, she recognized herself. Her new condition brought pride. But, no. Servant of anyone but him." (106). It becomes increasingly difficult to distinguish who is obeying whom as the mythical chase scene reinscribes the dialectic of desire and the other. As they circle each other, approaching each other and then distancing themselves again, Jerônimo loses Marta repeatedly because he tries to follow her. It is only when he stops pursuing her that they are able to come together. He tries to explain that his desire for her originated with him, that it was not set by the father's law. He reveals that he was the man that had touched her in the church, that he was not among the men originally set out for her by the father: "before the father called me, I wanted you in the church . . .

'Servant of Marta,' he spoke, explaining" (109). She accepts him then as the man who will be her first earthly lover, but she sets the condition that they wait till sunrise to consummate their love, for "'Without the sun, my body will not open'" (109). They lie together, their bodies sensually entwined, but they do not make love till morning since the new sexuality Marta seeks must be unhidden, unlike the "nocturnal assault" (68), and bathed in the radiance of sunlight.

The plot of the narrative, in many ways, seems to be a re-writing of what Erich Neumann has called the traditional transformation myth. In the traditional scenario, a male hero liberates a captive woman, extricating her from the clutches of a "terrible mother" or a monster. Here, however, Marta has embarked on her own transformation quest, striving to transform herself into a woman as well as re-forming Jerônimo in the sun's image and reconnecting him to his most bodily, sensual and even feminine attributes. While the traditional myth plot, as Rachel Blau DuPlessis explains, allows the male hero to rescue the "good" aspects of the feminine from the "bad," destructive aspects, this new mythic plot attempts to allow the heroine to discern the oppressive, phallic, authoritarian masculinity from a more productive, bodily, benevolent masculinity. Yet, even as Marta re-writes the transformation plot, Jerônimo engages in his own heroic quest, scripting himself as the rescuer of the female, Marta, from the clutches of the authoritarian, incestuous father. But, here we have to ask, which plot takes precedence? Which figure—Jerônimo or Marta—takes the plotting prerogative? One could argue that the either/or question is inappropriate to the both/and story line. But the unsatisfactory ending suggests otherwise. Both Marta and Jerônimo are authors of a quest; and the ambivalence and confusion at the end of the tale are evidence of the resulting struggle for narrative power. While Marta tries to impose her law, Jerônimo also scripts himself as hero and rescuer. As Marta tries to lead Jerônimo to an experience with his body and sensuality, her actions ultimately fit into a traditional pattern of female serving as the male's link to the sensual realm.

In the end, the outcome of this struggle for authorship is a disappointment to Marta, to her narrator, and ultimately to her reader (to this reader anyway). Perhaps we can view this confused and confusing quest as evidence of the difficulty of women's struggle for authorship, as an expression of the struggle with a textual, sexual, and, ultimately, political authority by which Woman is written but does not write. Indeed, Sally Robinson points to the continual derailments of Martha's quest in Doris Lessing's *Children of Violence* (a quest narrative not unrelated to Piñon's text), as evidence of "the problems encountered when a woman desires to be the subject of her own narrative and history" (20). Similarly, the problems encountered by Piñon's Marta, who attempts to resist the objectification and passivity traditional gender scripts offer her, are evidence of just how difficult it is to rewrite the script through and against existing signifying practices. As Robinson makes clear in her analysis of Lessing's narrative, and indeed, as the work of many feminist critics ultimately shows, a woman's desire to become a subject *of* her own narrative always involves negotiation with the socially scripted representations she is subject *to*. So, making meaning always involves some degree of repetition of existing cultural forms and the ambivalence at the end of *A Casa da Paixão* can be read as the difficult uneasiness of finding and writing a female agency within that meaning-making process.

"She saw her misfortune": An Allegory of Women's Writing

Surely, Marta strives to defy the patriarchal plot and struggles to become author of her own narrative. This enterprise, as we have seen, is not without its contradictions and ambiguities. Yet Marta's more radical propositions are even further unraveled and contradicted in the final chapter of the novel where Marta finally accepts Jerônimo as the man she will take as her earthly lover in her quest to become a woman. That is not meant to erase, however, the real accomplishments of Marta's quest (and Piñon's text). Even though Marta seemingly acquiesces in accepting Jerônimo in the end, their sexual union is governed, in many ways, by the logic Marta has tried to inscribe. For example, through Marta's decree, this union cannot be achieved without the presence and participation of the sun (111). Marta has set certain conditions (which Jerônimo ultimately accepts), and she rejects a passive role even in entering into this bodily liaison. She insists that he is not the source of her sexual awakening, but that she has loved a thousand men in loving the sun (113). Jerônimo, alarmed by her erotic autonomy, orders her to assure him that she is his exclusive property, that she was alone before him, to which Marta responds: "I am free to accept your body, but do not command me, man" (114). So, even as Marta accepts Jerônimo, she is still determined to be the author of her own experience and not to have her hard-won subjectivity impinged upon.

Marta's insistence on her erotic autonomy draws attention to the male/female power relations at work in sexuality. But, beyond sexual politics, their erotic encounter is also seen by both Jerônimo and Marta as a means of attaining knowledge and achieving transcendence. Such a resurrection is not of the spirit or psyche alone but ultimately of the body as well. At the beginning of the encounter, both proclaim not their immortality but their mortality:

—Sou mortal, Marta, [Jerônimo] exclamou com júbilo. Esfregava discreto sua pele na dela, porções reduzidas no início, ainda não o incêndio total, mas algumas purificações. Ela sentiu que vivera até então no obscuro, protegida pela imortalidade. —Conhecer a carne é isto, então, Jerônimo? (111).

['I am mortal, Marta,' [Jerônimo] exclaimed jubilously. He discreetly rubbed his skin on hers, small parts at first, still not the total fire, but some purifications. She felt as if, until then, she had been living in darkness, protected by immortality. 'So is this what it is to know the flesh, Jerônimo?'"]

A purificatory fire and a religiouslike awakening, sex becomes a brush with death, with mortality, with our most bodily origins as well as with our own most human desires. As a moment of utter carnality, the sexual encounter between Marta and Jerônimo will literally embody the disembodied ideals both of the phallus and the sun.

Eroticism in *A Casa da Paixão* is cast as a utopian, mystical experience, as a means to achieve a boundary-breaking unity and transcendence. This hoped for experience of continuity, which Georges Bataille has shown to be what aligns eroticism, religion, and death, finally culminates in the sexual union of the final section.[37] Indeed, through their sexual experience, each of them becomes the other's complement: "Jerônimo's sex had ferment, hers water and salt" (112). And sex is posited as a path to salvation, as Jerônimo asks: "did we not invade paradise?" (112). In keeping with such a mystical view of sexuality, Marta desires pain in order to be transformed, in order to attain transcendence. When Jerônimo says she is the whitest womb, the most illuminated one of christianity, Marta responds: "no, do not bring me happiness, Jerônimo, I want the ailments of the world, the leprosy that dissolves perfect features, I want disease, yes, to contaminate you too, happiness, no, Jerônimo" (116–17). Sex thus becomes a way of experiencing death, as is made explicit in the course of the narrative: "they must know death during the act" (114); "love is agony, the best death" (115). There is a need to die to be reborn and this erotic death becomes the experience of mortality, of the body, that is needed for sacrificial redemption: "the heat of the sun now invaded our sanguinary realm, they could live death without dying" (117). They can get beyond, they can go outside their bodies through sex: they can live death without dying.

Their coupling, violent and painful, involves Christian as well as other ancient mythological imagery, portraying thus a syncretic, erotic sacrifice.[38] This sexual sacrifice becomes explicit, for example, when Jerônimo's body is proclaimed the earth's savior: "'He saves the earth'" (114). Further along, the sexual act is referred to as "the rapture of the sacrifice" (117). Marta comes to see Jerônimo as an incarnation of the sun: "Man is my sun, she exclaimed" (114). Later she insists that the sun enter her as Jerônimo penetrates her: "let the sun enter into me when you penetrate my vagina, between pain and spasm, I on the cross, you the wood created in the river, now dry, in order to lacerate me" (115). There are several threads all being wound together in these images. Marta becomes an altar for the realization of this making flesh of the sun, for this embodiment of that which is beyond. As a Christ figure, she is a sacrificial victim that will in some way save the earth; in this case, that will return the earth to its most human origins through fertilization. Jerônimo, meanwhile, is also the altar in this rite: he is the wood of the cross upon which she is being crucified.[39] So, mutually each other's savior, each of them needs the other for the realization of his/her transcendence through a symbiotic transformation process. The desire for transcendence and continuity is often expressed, as Jessica Benjamin points out, through sexual eroticism rather than through religious experience: "Erotic masochism or submission expresses the same need for transcendence of self—the same flight from separation and discontinuity—formerly satisfied and expressed by religion."[40] Such transcendence of self and psychic transformation certainly seem to be Marta's and Jerônimo's goal in their erotic enterprise. Yet, contrary to the master/slave relations at work in sado-masochism, it would seem that both Marta and Jerônimo participate equally, neither of them consistently dominating the other, breaking down boundaries mutually.

Throughout the last section of the novel, however, even in its aspirations toward a mutual transcendence, profound ambiguities and ambivalences abound that seem to question the reciprocality of their sexual liaison and to suggest that the traditional symmetry where the man takes up his dominant position on the woman's body is repeated rather than resisted. For example, their coupling, this passion, will leave a permanent scar on Marta's body: "the passion was an ugly scar that the woman would have to bear her whole life" (119). The passion they share thus hovers between a necessary step in her *bildung* where she loses her innocence and gains knowledge ("he let her breathe, because that face had suffered passion and knowledge" 120) and an unfortunate and somehow inevitable error on her part. The encounter has a profound effect on Marta and seems to be the source of a vital corporal and epistemological transformation, but this first earthly sexual liaison ultimately proves unsatisfactory for her:

antes que o homem controlasse a respiração em desvario, para recuperar-se e viver de novo, a mulher arrancou violenta seu membro da vagina, tampou com a mão a sua área predileta, e como se uma farpa dolorosa ainda estivesse ali e era-lhe sofrida a locomoção, foi levantando, o homem que pedia seu corpo debaixo do seu, buscou evitar a partida, a mulher o encarou severa, mais do que o amor, a sua exigência (120).

[before the man had controlled his wild breathing, in order to recover and live again, the woman tore his member from her vagina, covered her beloved area with her hand, and as if a painful barb were still there and movement caused her to suffer, she began getting up, the man who asked for her body under his own, tried to avoid her departure, the woman faced him severely, more than love, his/her demand.]

She gets up and, imitating Antônia, sets about fertilizing the earth with "the sacred ejaculation of the man" (120). She goes about feminine rituals and, although Jerônimo tries to accompany her, excludes her earthly lover from her activities. He reasserts her bodily function, reminding her that she is "the sacrificial altar" (121). But Marta, engaged in her ritual with the sun, seems to reject him: "Marta pediu: Nunca, Jerônimo" / "Marta asked: 'Never, Jerônimo'" (121). Indeed, throughout the final chapter, the narrator reveals Marta's ambivalence about her sexual union with Jerônimo. And, similarly, the reader's confusion as to Marta's position seems to mirror this waffling on the part of the protagonist. In this labyrinth of desire, Marta's acceptance of Jerônimo as the sun is narrated as a careless lapse in her sense of caution; she lets down her defenses and is seduced: "Marta was losing the caution she had maintained until the arrival of Jerônimo, she acted as if the sun were Jerônimo" (116). Marta is afraid that, for all the passion and eroticism she shares with Jerônimo, he will virtually suck her dry:

Jerônimo, ela falava, meu homem, meu desespero, ela calculava
que ele estivesse lambendo suas tetas formosas, . . . bebendo
seus líquidos, mas não beba toda minha água, Jerônimo, meu
bicho, Jerônimo . . . (116).

[Jerônimo, she spoke, my man, my despair, she reckoned that
he would be licking her lovely breasts, . . . drinking her liq-
uids, but do not drink all my water, Jerônimo, my animal,
Jerônimo . . .]

At once voicing the lover's discourse expected of her and yet
attempting to resist the pitfalls involved in such a position, Marta
expresses her reservations, effectively illustrating the duplicity and
ambivalence of her position.

In the end, Marta is disappointed by Jerônimo and troubled by
her new state. After she gets up and walks away from him, she
reflects that it is Antônia who will have to heal her, that it is only
this old representative of earthy femininity that has the power to
care for her wounds. Man, ultimately, is insufficient in this regard,
despite his desire to be all for her. Even though Jerônimo attempts to
heal her ("he kissed her legs, with his tongue he began to clean the
blood that the body in flames had set free" 121), his efforts are,
Marta realizes, insufficient and "Antônia would have to clean her
body, preparing her bath, when she arrived home" (121). Yet, ultimately her autonomy has already been neutralized and subsumed;
she promises "Sou sua mulher, vou para onde você quiser, ela prom-
eteu" / "'I am your woman, I will go wherever you wish,' she
promised" (122). Jerônimo welcomes this resolution, pleased at his
prominent role and his power over Marta's body: "Ele sorriu: Quem
cuida agora de suas feridas sou eu" / "He smiled: 'Now I am the
one who cares for your wounds'" (122). The sacrificial, solar sexual
liaison has been performed, the quests have reached their conclusion, yet Marta ultimately seems to surrender in her struggle for
the right to plot her own narrative.

Considering Piñon's text as a re-writing of the transformation
myth plot, why is it that Jerônimo's quest proves satisfactory while
Marta's is such a disappointment? According to Erich Neumann,
the hero narrative of self-transformation, whose pattern is taken up
as the "process of individuation in modern man," has the Osiris
myth as its archetypal repository (220). Understood as an archetypal
pattern, the Osiris narrative, among other hero myths, shows how
the hero crosses from the conscious to the unconscious realms in an

attempt to become a more fully developed individual or to attain a "higher level" of masculinity by "overcoming" his "lower fertility" associated with the feminine.[41] This is, in fact, the pattern of transformation set forth in *A Casa da Paixão*: both Marta and Jerônimo are involved in such a quest for psychosexual overcoming. Yet the heroic transformation model holds different promises for male and female heroes. Neumann himself characterizes the transformation hero myth (exemplified by the Osiris cycle) as entirely predicated on the male ego's agency. While in mythic sources it is Isis that finds Osiris after he is killed and dismembered by Set, and she who restores him to life, Neumann identifies as the heroic/transformation phase of the myth the versions that depict Osiris' resurrection as being an act of self-transformation undertaken by the hero himself, muting Isis' role completely (254–55). This subsuming of the feminine, explicitly enacted in the heroic, patriarchal versions of the Osiris/Isis narrative, are common to most heroic myth structures for, as Annis Pratt points out, the crux of any hero's struggle is with the "powerful feminine component of himself; his goal is to absorb her import, master her autonomous control over his impulses, and then return, a reborn psyche, to everyday life" ("Spinning Among Fields" 102). This is an appropriate description of Jerônimo's transformation. He strives to come into contact with and assimiliate the most bodily, sensual side of himself (according to traditional archetypes, his *anima*). He finally absorbs that (feminine) bodiliness through Marta in order to attain transcendence and to become one with the sun, and in doing so he usurps Marta's autonomy and subjectivity.[42]

Feminist reworkings of mythic narrative structures often script the female as the hero to be reborn, with the male figure or the "green world lover" as means to that end (Pratt "Spinning" 101–103).[43] The conflict arises in these women-centered rewritings of mythic narrative when the women heroes cannot assimilate the male figures (these "*animus* constellations"), which, in fact, "embody proscriptions against women's maturation" (Pratt "Spinning" 104). Indeed, Jerônimo is Marta's hope for an *animus* figure (as Moniz has pointed out); yet he embodies certain proscriptions against her autonomy in that his own quest involves mastery over her to enable his ascent to full subjectivity. My contention is that, ultimately, Jerônimo embodies proscriptions against Marta's subjectivity because he is allowed his own quest and its structure is the hero transformation myth. Piñon's narrative strives to give subjectivity, to give a certain plotting prerogative to both Marta *and* Jerônimo, rather than to either/or.[44] In other words, it is as if Piñon were trying to re-write the Osiris/Isis myth, returning to Isis the agency taken away from her through the heroic narrative plot, without completely muting Osiris' story of transformation and resurrection. And yet this involves a sticky business of what to do with the male hero model, which requires the conquest of the female/treasure within the (male) self. As we have seen, Jerônimo's quest definitely leans in this direction, with Marta functioning as his treasure to be conquered and subsumed. At one point, for example, responding to the authoritarian claims of the patriarch, Jerônimo's heroic ambitions regarding Marta are laid bare: "I am this woman's man. I decide for her" (99). Such a usurpation of Marta's subjectivity is in direct conflict with Marta's insistence that she decide for herself. So we could say that the ambiguity of the the closing scenes is symptomatic of a conflict of quests. As Pratt observes, "the discrepancy between what women desire and what society prescribes is reflected (perhaps unconsciously) in strangely acerbic tones, ironic overtones, ambivalent attitudes, and uncomfortable endings" ("Spinning" 116). When Marta tries to be the subject of her own quest, we are left with just such ambivalence and discomfort at the end of the narrative where Jerônimo's quest seems to determine the outcome.

In many ways, the ending of the novel seems puzzlingly conservative. While Marta and Jerônimo seem to have been striving toward a new sexuality that embodies a revolutionary reciprocity, Marta's complete surrender of her autonomy as well as Jerônimo's gleeful appropriation of her body bespeak the repetition of patterns that are entirely familiar. The final lines offer a less than satisfactory outcome:

> Mudar o estado do corpo era alterar todo o pensamento, ela viu a sua desdita. Aquele corpo o primeiro de todos. Não sou mais ingênua. Sou mulher de dois homens, ela argumentava convencida do sol, convencida de Jerônimo (122).

> [To change the state of the body was to alter all thinking, she saw her misfortune. That body the first before all others. I am no longer ingenuous. I am the woman of two men, she argued, convinced of the sun, convinced of Jerônimo.]

Surely these lines invoke a sense of narrative epiphany, some realization on Marta's part. Yet, her tone is one of resignation and she seems to be rationalizing and convincing herself of the viability of this solution. Her words ultimately suggest a profound ambivalence as to the significance of her realization. So, we might ask, what is Marta's realization? What is the "desdita" she perceives, the "misfortune" in the resolution of her quest?

The nature of this "misfortune" is highly ambiguous. One reading of these lines is that, indeed, this sexual union changes the state of the body and also changes the state of the mind, that this is true: in coupling with Jerônimo, Marta changes her body as well as her mind and can, consequently, no longer maintain her independence and sexual autonomy ("I am your woman, I will go wherever you wish"). In realizing this fact then, Marta sees her "misfortune," sees that she is now doomed to repeat the role of her mother: that of sacrificial victim doomed to die so that others might live. There is textual evidence that Marta views her actions as a repetition of preordained patterns; for example, as she lays with Jerônimo she is suddenly aware of their activities as a repetition of the relations between her mother and father:

> Meu homem, arrastava-se Marta sobre um campo minado, respirava o verde, que parecia um sorvete, lambia a terra, as mãos de Jerônimo, iguais às do pai, o mesmo teria feito a mãe com o pai, para que ela nascesse (114).

> [My man, Marta dragged herself over a minefield, she breathed in the green that seemed like an ice cream, she licked the earth, Jerônimo's hands, the same as the father's, the mother had done the same with the father, so that she would be born.]

Her seemingly enigmatic use of the term of "campo minado" ("minefield") betrays, to my mind, the danger inherent in entering into such a union with Jerônimo, implying as it does the sense of repetition of an entire series of rites and traditions.

On the other hand, we could read the "misfortune" she refers to at the end of her story in an opposite way. Marta's realization could be that, contrary to her expectation, she has not made significant epistemological or ontological changes through this bodily experience. The bodies have been changed, even permanently marked, but it was erroneous to think that this could effect a transcendent change. The structures and the sacrificial symmetry remain the same, and the idea that she could achieve salvation through sex, could revolutionize all modes of thought through the body, enacts a repetition of the same ("she saw her misfortune").

Either way, the results of this revolution of the flesh are a disappointment and signal a repetition of—rather than the hoped for resistance to—dominant gender patterns. As Rachel Blau DuPlessis shows, endings are places of ideological resolution, sites where "text meets values" (19). Indeed, *A Casa da Paixão* seems to run aground amidst heterosexual norms as well as, perhaps, the restrictions engendered by censorship. Regarding the latter, we could read the reestablishment of the law at the end of Piñon's text as having to do with the political circumstances under which the text was written. The contradictions and ambiguities could be read as emblematic of the difficulties of textual/sexual innovation under the restrictions of state censorship. Certainly, in spite of the radical feminine erotics througout the text, the ending barely differs from traditional endings of marriage and/or death for the female hero.[45] Reading in context, we could interpret such recapitulation as the marks of the authoritarian censorship in power in Brazil at the time which exacerbates the need for ideological resolutions in keeping with traditional sociosexual norms. And yet the contradictions involved here, in my opinion, well exceed the constrictions and tribulations of censorship.

The sex/gender system constitutes an even more complex and contradictory set of restrictions and proscriptions regarding sexual and textual "resolution." One of the most basic ideas held about sexuality is that it is somehow natural, outside of history, only needing to be freed through the breaking down of repressions.[46] Piñon's narrative both undoes and reinscribes this view of sexuality. In many ways, Marta questions the gendering process and refuses passive acceptance of the dominant script. She manages to lead Jerônimo to an acceptance of his body and only accepts him as a lover after he becomes less univocally masculine and more sexually ambiguous, as we have seen. On the other hand, Marta also views the masculine and feminine as essences to be dipped into as one bathes in a river or absorbs the sun's rays. And as we have seen, sexual union, for Marta, offers vast possibilities for a utopian reconciliation. In this way, *A Casa* does not escape the view of sexual categories as ontological, as essential aspects of being.[47] This basic conflict between resistance to the sexual norms that script sexuality as essential and unchangeable and the repetition of those very ideas is at the root of *A Casa da Paixão*'s contradictory ending.

So, as we reach the end of *A Casa da Paixão*, we are forced to reevaluate the novel's entire textual and sexual project. Rather than mimetic representations, the "protagonists" of the novel are incarnations of psychic qualities ordinarily deemed masculine and feminine, as Naomi Hoki Moniz has pointed out.[48] According to Moniz this text uses sexuality symbolically; that is, the sexual categories of masculine and feminine as well as the process of sexual relations are used to explore the polarity of consciousness and unconsciousness, of the different qualities of the ego (131). Certainly, sexual union becomes here a figure for a joining of opposite forces, a communication with that which exceeds the body and language, and a harmonization of conflicts. Sexual relations in *A Casa da Paixão*, seen this way, become part of an allegory of transformation and transcendence, a way of re-imagining the act of creation. That is to say, the transformations of the text portray the rituals involved in creating a new consciousness, a new sexuality, as well as a new textuality.

And yet, *A Casa* is not only a psychic allegory (as Moniz would have it) or an allegory of creation, but also a sociosexual fable where the protagonists incarnate the abstract scripts of masculinity and femininity such that the text lays bare the power relations inherent in the gendering process itself. Indeed, in many ways, the father is a virtual incarnation of the "law of the father" and Antônia a composite of "feminine" forces. Both of them remain constant and neither is involved in the process of gendering but rather are fixed forces representing the gendering scripts themselves. Marta's and Jerônimo's narratives of feminization and masculinization, meanwhile, tell the story of gender as a becoming, as a "doing," ultimately showing the process to be politically and culturally charged and by no means natural. In this way the novel becomes an allegory of sexual politics. While sexual categories are used to work through notions of the emotional versus the spiritual or the conscious versus the unconscious (the more abstract psychic realities Moniz talks about that ultimately form part of the transformation/quest myth so important to Jungian psychology), it is not that the figures of masculine and feminine innocently "represent" or refer to other abstractions. On the contrary, these categories themselves are culturally loaded and using masculine/feminine symbolically also remits to the politics of sexuality itself. In this way, *A Casa da Paixão* simultaneously projects sexuality as psychic allegory and enacts an allegory of sexual politics.

As an allegory of sexual politics Piñon's text certainly opens new perspectives. It both repeats and resists the cultural categories that have been used to keep women relegated to the immanent, the irrational, the emotional, the bodily. For example, while, as Moniz observes, Piñon utilizes the polarity of the sexes such that the emotional is feminine and the spiritual is masculine (131), the text, to my mind, also confounds that polarity in the processes undertaken by Marta and Jerônimo. Marta's sun worship represents not only a sexual but a spiritual activity, and Jerônimo's spirituality is pushed to include a sexual and even mystical exaltation of his body. Moreover, Piñon appropriates traditional constructs and succeeds in defying the way these traditional patterns dole out passive roles to women. Marta resists and defies her father, puts Jerônimo through a series of "exercises" to transform him into a masculine figure who accepts his more bodily, "feminine" side (his *anima*, in Jungian terms).

But Marta's quest is derailed by the other narratives in which she is inevitably a player. Even if Marta tries to rearticulate gender as socially rather than ontologically determined, she is also part of a social system that persists in thinking ontologically.[49] A pessimistic reading (a "negative hermeneutic") of the ending would see Marta as finally "domesticated" by Jerônimo, having adopted the feminine position of mediator between Jerônimo and the divine, the position of sacrificial body used to keep the system intact. As such, the novel becomes a fable of how a woman is femininized, how she comes to assume her role in the social realm, and how phallic law ultimately gets what it wants. Yet, for all the ambivalences and final "misfortune" of the text, Marta's attempts at "re-authorizing" the law do, to a degree, succeed in that through these efforts Marta manages to write her voice, her erotics, and her desire into the story.

We can also read the text not only as an allegory of sexual politics but also of the repressive political situation in Brazil at the time the novel was written. As I have noted, this period in Brazil was marked by a tightening of repressive tactics on the part of the authoritarian regime. The military crackdown was specifically responding to public protests that denounced human rights abuses and demanded more freedoms (Alvarez 8). These attempts at social transformation were checked by an intensification of authoritarian control that actively sought to reinforce traditional notions of womanhood.[50] Given this sociopolitical context surrounding the novel, the problems confronted in re-writing the heterosexual text portrayed in *A Casa* could be read as emblematic of the frustrations encountered in trying to transform the politically authoritarian text dominating Brazilian society. In other words, while the daughter defies the patriarch, challenging and critiquing his dominance, her failure to undo the patriarch's hold over the social order can be read allegorically as the failure to unseat the patriarchal regime in place in Brazil.

All things considered, while we could certainly say that Piñon's text is an allegory of trangression, of transformation, of sexual politics, or even of the political situation, it can also be read—within the context of feminist analysis—as an allegory of women's writing, of the "desdita" of trying to refashion a female subjectivity against and through the societal prescriptions of Woman, against and through the images and myth patterns women writers necessarily inherit and inhabit as (even ambiguously nonhegemonic) social subjects. Within such a reading, "She saw her misfortune" becomes, in a sense, the prime allegorical moment of the novel: the moment where the text literally reads itself, where the "misfortune" of Marta's quest tells the "missed fortune" of the textual project itself. As Marta sees she is doomed to repeat established patterns, so the narrator sees her confinement by the social nature of authorship, sees that she cannot—at least not now, not yet—write Marta's story of becoming a woman outside the constraints and contexts of the story of becoming Woman. Indeed, as Teresa De Lauretis matter-of-factly observes: "women continue to become woman" (*Alice Doesn't* 186). Yet, as she points out, denial of such seeming contradictions, or trying to completely reconcile them, should not be a goal, for "only by knowingly enacting and re-presenting [these contradictions], by knowing us to be both woman and women, does a woman today become a subject" (186). These are, perhaps, the contradictions and dualities of Marta's ending: "convinced of the sun, convinced of Jerônimo" she ends up both subject to social norms and subject of some new interventions, neither entirely her own woman nor reduced to the normative representations of Woman. In this way, then, we can read Marta's partial triumph and her incomplete transformation of the social script as the emblem of an ongoing struggle to open a textual space where women's agency can at least be glimpsed, a female erotics more fully imagined, and a woman's writing read, if only as writing on the wall.

2

TREASON AND TRANSFORMATION: RE-WRITING THE MARGINS IN DIAMELA ELTIT'S *POR LA PATRIA*

El origen de cualquier tragedia es siempre una traición.
Vivimos en un país arrasado ¿Qué traición pesará sobre nosotros?

[The origin of any tragedy is always a betrayal.
We live in a ravaged country. What betrayal must hang over us?]

—Raúl Zurita
from an interview in *La época* (1987)

La Bandera de Chile es usada de mordaza
    y por eso seguramente por eso
    nadie dice nada

[The Flag of Chile is used as a gag
    and therefore surely therefore
    no one says anything]

—Elvira Hernández
La Bandera de Chile (1991)

¿Podremos algún día limpiar tantas manchas,
tantas heridas, tantas huellas?

[Will we some day be able to clean so many stains,
so many wounds, so many marks?]

—Marco Antonio de la Parra
King Kong Palace (1990)

For Chilean writer Diamela Eltit, any profound sociocultural change must be undertaken at the linguistic and symbolic level.[1] Her narrative thus aspires to a symbolic transformation, attempting to "open language towards the places oppressed by official culture," and not to fall into what she sees as the flaw of so many politically committed literary productions that, "without altering or questioning the legitimacy of the codes they use . . . , rest their potential only on the messages they communicate."[2] These views have led Eltit to a radical experimentalism that includes disruptive linguistic innovation (such as syntactic modification, use of neologisms, and wordplay) as well as the disarticulation of the authoritative symbolic systems that produce cultural identities (racial, class, national, etc.). Her textual practice actively works to defy the authority of prevailing structures by breaking dominant codes of gender and family identities, by violating class boundaries that keep certain social groups muted and certain linguistic forms out of print, as well as by refusing to comply with narrative expectations of "readability" or "intelligibility." Needless to say, such tactics did not win her a wide acceptance in her native Chile, whose already small reading public originally received her work with a mixture of horror, fascination, and/or irritation at its "difficulty."[3] In this way, her experimentalism actually increased her marginality, a fact which could be viewed as genderically coded since, as another Chilean writer Agata Gligo has pointed out, such radical experimentalism is perhaps even less acceptable coming from a woman writer.[4]

Yet, Eltit's defiance of expectations is deliberate, the marginal—whether political, aesthetic, or genderic—embraced and articulated in her narrative production. As Eugenia Brito has pointed out, Eltit's texts attempt to "recuperate the most elided zones of Chilean and Latin American culture: the marginal, the indigenous, the feminine" (*Campos minados* 171). From within and through the highly repressive regime of Augusto Pinochet's dictatorship, Eltit's narratives, as both politically and aesthetically preoccupied, practice literary experimentalism as a means to disarticulate dominant discourses where the plurality of meanings has become a "security risk." Her experimentalism is thus a political as well as a literary transgression; and this innovative literary practice is, as she herself has put it, her militancy.[5]

Writing itself is, not surprisingly, a prime preocupation of Eltit's narrative. In *Por la patria* [For the Fatherland] (1986), for example, the protagonist's struggle is to forge a collective memory and, furthermore, to write that marginalized history as "una toma colectiva del habla" / "a collective taking of speech" (199). This concern is not limited to *Por la patria*; Eltit's third novel, *El cuarto mundo* [The Fourth World] (1988), also foregrounds the writing process. At the end of that novel, the unnamed protagonist of the story is suddenly transposed into the author as we read the last lines of the narrative, "diamela eltit . . . gives birth to a girl" (128), thus shifting the entire focus from the gestation and birth of a child to the engendering of the text itself. Writing plays such a principal role in these texts because it is quite self-consciously through the process of writing that Eltit manages the symbolic transformation she seeks. It is through a transgressive writing practice that this author can give voice to what has been muted by authoritarian discourse, to what has been censored and obscured by the prohibitions of the "law of the father."[6] Indeed, as we shall see, through tropes of sexual treason, Eltit's text becomes a "talking cure" of narration from and through the silenced periphery, thus reimagining and transforming the margins into a site of resistance, empowerment, and renewal.[7]

In many ways, the novel I examine in this chapter, *Por la patria*, traces its narrative path between two impulses: between trying to write the violence of the national tragedy and attempting to get beyond this victimization, transforming it from a state of pain and marginalization into a space of solidarity and power. This text both recognizes and tries to mobilize the margin's symbolic and political force, attempting to draw into the symbolic realm what has always been most hidden, most negated, most repressed. Traditionally, what is most marginalized by culture has been conceptually or symbolically relegated to the realm of the feminine.[8] For this reason, as Eltit sees it, the feminine, rather than linked only to women, must be conceived as more generally "that which is oppressed by the central power," and as an entire series of *meanings*, "a collection of mobile nuances" ("Cultura" 2). In *Por la patria*, Eltit tries to rearticulate this feminine, attempting to write the repressed and privatized realm, inhabiting its muted and marginalized position, and, *from there*, daring to make the most intellectually rigorous literary intervention possible. She thus works to transform the margins from a space of silenced subalterity into a site of epic possibilities.[9] To Gayatri Spivak's famous question "Can the Subaltern Speak?" Diamela Eltit might well respond: she can and she will, but for that to happen we must create a new, transgressive subjectivity in femininity and rethink the very bases of our symbolic structures.

Por la patria: Writing on the Dark Side

It seems a particularly difficult task to give a synopsis or "plot summary" of Eltit's second and perhaps most ambitious novel, *Por la patria*. We can begin by saying that, on a most basic level, this text provides a virtual counter-discourse to what has been called Pinochet's discursive "espectáculo de la chilenidad" / "spectacle of Chilean-ness."[10] As recent Chilean scholars have shown, the official, authoritarian discourse of Chile's military regime sought to construct a Chile made up of "todos nosotros los chilenos" / "all of us Chileans" whose attributes include "faith," "hope," "responsibility," "cohesion," "integrity," "sacrifice," and "loyalty" among others.[11] These "true" *chilenos*, supporters of the 1973 military intervention that installed the dictatorship, are cast as the polar opposites of the *others*: those that Pinochet calls the "pocos otros no-chilenos" / "few other non-Chileans" (i.e., the marxists and their collaborators) who are excluded from sharing either the qualities or functions of the "true" nationals (Munizaga and Ochsensius 73–79). In many ways, Eltit's *Por la patria* writes the symbolic dark side of this equation. Her text documents, on a symbolic level, the victimization, the suffering, and the poverty, of these "no-chilenos" who have indeed been sacrificed "por la patria" / "for the fatherland."

While the novel defies traditional ideas of setting and character, it does delineate particular, symbolic spaces and re-present the voices that inhabit them. The space that is indeed evoked and intermittently traced in the first half of the book is the urban periphery: a poor, sub-urban Santiago neighborhood; a bar that serves as a hideout or refuge during military incursions into the *barrio*; the even more privatized sphere of the bedroom; and then also a virtual abstraction of the margins: a deserted area called merely "el erial" (literally "untilled or uncultivated land"). These marginal spaces are populated by "other" Chileans, abstract or composite figures of the excluded "no-chilenos": the father (a political militant), the indigenous mother (alcoholic and promiscuous), and various female figures (Berta, Flora, La Rucia), all social pariahs of some sort (as one of them says, "My brothers, my sisters were Christian and I a Moor" 113). The protagonist/voice, Coya/Coa, is not a conventional character, but rather, as Eugenia Brito points out, "a sign subversive of any dominant order . . . the sign that makes possible a new mental landscape, in which 'the Indian,' the 'marginal,' and the 'delinquent' will be the productive semantic fields for a Latin American liberation" (*Campos minados* 206). Coya becomes the medium (a "machi," a type of visionary healer in indigenous culture) created to give voice to the periphery and its inhabitants. In many ways, Coya/Coa is a personification of language itself; she is "dual and bilingual" (22), an incestuous blend of regal language (Coya as "Quechuan nobility" 258) and vulgar language (*coa*).[12] Furthermore, as language, Coya's struggle for survival becomes a resistance to the violent silencing of the margins; she describes the attack launched against her as "un plan de rapto al habla" / "a plan to abduct speech" (246). Thus, the figures in *Por la patria* are the "CHILE-NOS" (118) who have been abandoned by the official "Great Chilean Family" and who have been made not only marginal but "mad" as well.[13] Indeed, while the regime casts as perverse or "mad" any disconformity, Eltit embraces madness, abbreviating the multiple "Madres" / "Mothers" of her text to "MAD 1-2-3" etc. (103) and rewriting the national catastrophe through six mystical "visions" included in a section of the first part of the book titled "El cerco, el delirio, el cerco" / "The Enclosure, The Delirium, The Enclosure." *Por la patria* takes up madness and delirium, turning it into a place of resistance as the "slogan," reflected by Coya at the end of these visions, demonstrates: "Ne Im Sisatxe On Arbah Nodrep Arap Solle"; that is, "en mi éxtasis no habrá perdón para ellos" / "in my ecstasy there will be no pardon for them" written backwards, thus emitting a rallying cry of resistance to the military—"ni perdón ni olvido" / "neither forgiveness nor forgetting"—from within the aphasic "other" side of madness.

Indeed, *Por la patria* responds to the official discourse on many levels, transgressing its boundaries, inhabiting the margins it creates, and refusing the silent acceptance, the "sacrifice" "for the fatherland," demanded by the regime. If, for example, the manifesto of the authoritarian regime, the *Declaración de Principios* [Declaration of Principles] declares that the proletariat will be eliminated by making Chile a nation of proprietors (Vidal "La *Declaración de Principios*" 68), Eltit's narrative directly challenges this formulation by writing an epic of the dispossessed classes and refusing propriety and proprietorship on all levels. If, furthermore, the military's *Declaración de Principios* elides the body in favor of spiritual transcendence, Eltit's text brings corporality back with a vengeance in *Por la patria*, as evidenced beginning with the cover photo that depicts an X ray of a human hand superimposed on a map of the Americas.[14] If, in 1986, the regime rounded up all the residents of the marginal neighborhoods who had any sort of prison record and sent them to a concentration camp in Pisagua, Eltit's narrative re-writes such a conflation of marginalizations, condensing images of political subversion, delinquency, and drunkenness in the "militants of wine" (21) of the bar and *barrio* of part I.[15] While the regime attempts to depict the military as a force of spiritual light, of firmness, of goodness, of national loyalty, Eltit envisions the soldiers as cruel rapists, as forces of destruction and terror, as "OSCUROS, MORENOS, CHILENOS, ESCURRIDIZOS Y TRAIDORES" / "OBSCURE, DARK-SKINNED, CHILEAN, SLIPPERY, AND TREASONOUS" (84). In sum, in the face of the official discursive formulation of the "no-chilenos," of those others to be excluded, *Por la patria* launches the battle cry "CHILE-NO," which, like the famous "NO" of the 1988 plebiscite that it anticipates, rejects the authoritarian regime. Indeed "CHILE-NO" effectively deconstructs Pinochet's "no-chilenos," showing the otherness (the "*no*") to be *within* the very construction of "chile-*no*," thus appropriating that otherness and making it a politics as well as a poetics.

It is through the process of giving voice to these muted areas of Chilean cultural life that *Por la patria* transforms the pain and passivity of victimhood into the power of the margins. But, that is not to say that Eltit unduly glorifies victimhood. José Joaquín Brunner has analyzed the danger of occupying and writing the margins, pointing out that "Repression . . . triumphs when, in addition to excluding, it also internalizes a glorification of the margins. So then, one thing is the response, the metaphors that assume and 'name' the repression, un-masking it; and another thing is the 'celebration' of repression practiced as a rite of the margins, happy captivity of the excluded, that no longer names the repression but enacts it" ("Campo artístico" 65). I would contend that Eltit does indeed enact the repression of the margins, her text forming more of a metonymical relationship to its context, rather than the metaphorical relationship that Brunner prefers. However, her text does not, to my mind at least, "glorify" or "celebrate" the margins in the way Brunner suggests, but rather "sublimates" the margins so as to reclaim a viable subjectivity for its inhabitants.

But even in "sublimating" the margins, as I suggest, Eltit does indeed write compellingly of the pain, isolation, and terror of the margins, avoiding any idealization: "Aquí estamos más muertos que vivos, más asustados que nadie, más inseguros, más animales mestizos" / "Here we are more dead than alive, more scared than anybody, more insecure, more animals of mixed blood" (142). The violent repression and terror of the margins of the Chilean scene are symbolically set forth in part I in the form of an allegorical narrative of repeated abuse by soldiers, constantly approaching military tanks, and roundups by police forces. The allegorical nature of these scenes lies in their repetitive, abstract quality; they are not mimetic representations of military violence but rather reflect the *idea* of violence, of institutionalized terror, of displacement, of abandonment, of the fragmentation of the city's periphery.[16] Throughout part I, tanks and soldiers close in upon the residents of the *barrio* in scenes of impending, mechanistic terror until Coya's arrest at the end of the section:

Los camiones, con los caballos de fuerza de sus motores, parecían en estampida por praderas lejanas y gringas, aunque de verdad que era el barrio que lo cercaban, custodiaban que nadie saliera indemne de la redada.

Estábamos presos por máquinas en movimiento (43).

—Ay que vienen, dijo la madre (109).

Afuera los camiones buscaban, cercando la cuadra precisa cuando ya los motores se detenían y la multiplicidad de pisadas definían el augurio (109).

SOLDADO ENTRA, EL BAR SE ENCOJE (117).

Cuando entra al bar los corazones suenan como tambores y frenéticas cajas de resonancia. Los pechos que tum-tum suenan, que tum-tum laten, que tum-tum no hay nada que los dilate (118).

SE HA DESATADO LA PRIMERA LIMPIEZA A LAS BARRIA-DAS CHILENAS (118).

Camiones, tanquetas, instrumentales variados, unidos por operación unitas criollas, con soldados rasos, paquitos, piquetes de boinas negras imitando, copiando desenfrenadas potencias y ya se siente el ejército nacional que dilapida sus proyectiles, tirando sobresaltados cuando volados, drogados se animan (151).

Me empujaron con violencia hacia el lado, para el lado de los camiones y subí formando parte del rebaño (152).

[The trucks, with the horsepower of their engines, seemed to be stampeding through distant and foreign meadows, even though in truth it was the *barrio* that they surrounded, assuring that no one escaped unscathed from the roundup.

We were taken prisoner by machines in movement (43).

"Ay, they are coming," said the mother (109).

Outside the trucks searched, surrounding the precise block when the motors stopped and the multiplicity of footsteps defined the omen (109).

SOLDIER ENTERS, THE BAR COWERS (117).

When he enters the bar, hearts resonate like drums and frenetic sound boxes. The chests that pound pum-pum, that beat pum-pum, that there is nothing pum-pum to give them away (118).

THE FIRST CLEAN UP OF THE CHILEAN SLUMS HAS BEEN UNLEASHED (118).

Trucks, tanks, varied instruments, united by operation *unitas criollas*, with private soldiers, street kids, squads of black berets imitating, copying unchecked powers and now the national army is felt, squandering its projectiles, jerking in shock when exploded, drugged they become exhilarated (151).

They pushed me violently toward the other side, toward the side of the trucks and I got in, forming part of the herd (152).]

These fragments exemplify perhaps the most politically testimonial aspect of part I: the military violence, the terror of the inhabitants, the rhetoric of the regime are all set forth without resorting to a linear, traditionally mimetic narrative.[17] Indeed, it is precisely the allegorical nature of this representation of violence that perhaps best captures not only the violence itself but also the difficulty of *any* representation of such terrorific circumstances. Through such means, Eltit manages to give voice to these events, finding militancy and heroism in this victimization, indeed in its most abject and bodily manifestations. As the final roundup approaches: "Hombres y mujeres estupefactos intentaban gestos heroicos: no gritar, no lamentarse, emanar agua del cuerpo. Por eso sudaban, vomitaban y menstruaban las mujeres" / "Stupified men and women attempted heroic gestures: no shouting, no lamenting, emanate water from the body. So they sweated, vomited and the women menstruated" (109). In this way, without patronizing or cleansing it of its most base aspects, Eltit articulates the terror and its toll, resemanticizing signs of fear as signs of bravery. Her goal is distinctly not to write the *victimario* of the margins only as a site of pain, worthy of commiseration. Indeed, she expresses disdain for this sort of approach:

Nada puede ser para mí más irritante que leer un libro que trata de los márgenes sociales desde una perspectiva compasiva. Ese tipo de aproximaciones me parecen clasistas y reductoras. Voy a usar una expresión; me parece que lo que pasa allí es que le 'roban el alma' a esos espacios, a esos habitantes. Mi proyecto fue restituir la estética que pertenece y moviliza esos espacios y dar estatuto narrativo a esas voces tradicionalmente oprimidas por la cultura oficial y estropeadas por una narrativa redentora" (interview with Ortega 232).

[Nothing could be more irritating for me than reading a book that treats the social margins from a compassionate perspective. That type of approach seems to me classist and reductive. I'll use an expression; it seems to me that what happens there is that they 'steal the soul' of those spaces, of those inhabitants. My project was to restore the aesthetic that belongs to and mobilizes those spaces and to give narrative enactment to those voices traditionally oppressed by official culture and damaged by a redemptive narrative.]

Rather than only a place of victimhood and suffering, *Por la patria* operates from the margins as radical feminist bel hooks conceives of it, as both site of pain and sign of repression and yet also site of resistance. In her article "marginality as a site of resistance," bel hooks rejects the sympathetic, othering discourse that tries to make her speak only of her pain in order to pity her and to then turn and try to "tell it back to her" (343). Rather, she demands to meet not in the center, not in the mainstream where her colonizer can have his or her discursive way, but in the marginal space where the marginalized subject will have the upper hand. Calling her interlocutor to move to the margins for this exchange, hooks writes: "This is an intervention. A message from that space in the margin that is a site of creativity and power, that inclusive space where we recover ourselves, where we move in solidarity to erase the category colonized/colonizer. Marginality as site of resistance. Enter that space. Let us meet there. Enter that space. We greet you as liberators" (343). The epic tone as well as the sentiment expressed in this incantation seems especially apropos to Eltit's narrative strategy. Indeed, the very "difficulty" of Eltit's prose also forces the reader to meet her on her own discursive turf, in her own marginal place. *Por la patria*, too, is an "intervention," a political performance, an uncompromising and epic convocation where the reader is subjected to both the pain and the power of the marginal. The margins as written by Eltit are more than a place of mere survival; indeed, she strives to write the margins as populated by "characters not only surviving, but combatant" (interview with Ríos 30). Eltit advocates and attempts to write a marginality its own aesthetics, its own voice, its own particular brand of heroism; in short, a marginality that involves the activity of a true social subjectivity rather than merely the passivity implied by "survival" or "victimization."

Superimposed on these visions of terror on a state level are other elusive and confusing glimpses of the relations between the protagonist and her parents. The predominant sense of these familial relations is one of orphanhood and separation: "I don't see my mother. I don't see my father" (14); at times, her sense of abandonment reaches powerfully poetic proportions: "hace todos los días que no te veo" / "it has been everyday since I saw you" (87). The loss and orphanhood inscribed by the text is intimately wrapped up with the political situation, with a distinctly Chilean crisis of representation. After the "primera pesca," the first roundup by the police, Coya chatters in fear: "I managed to do nothing but name them. No, to shout them, knowing that it aggravated the danger for me, but it is the usual thing, it is completely normal in those cases, yes, I believe it is, to call for the mother, to name your father" (17). Likewise, when Coya is forced into a military vehicle, her last words in the *barrio* are "I don't see my mother" (152). The stammering search for the parental figures repeated throughout the novel becomes a *mise en scène* of the profound sense of loss and abandonment of a people driven to a state of abject terror, forced into a forgetting of their collective past, severed from their traditions by a regime bent on rewriting history in its own image. Indeed, with regard to the modus operandi of the authoritarian regime, Nelly Richard explains that the first phase of the dictatorship (1973–77) was concerned with erasing the past, attempting a *"total obliteration of the collective memory* of the previous government and its achievements." In the second stage the regime then tried to refound Chilean culture according to its own totalitarian value system (*Margins* 105). Thus, the radical sense of orphanhood and rupture in *Por la patria* could be seen to respond to the collective crisis of violent separation from the "parents" of cultural traditions and memory.

This orphanhood is perhaps most powerfully inscribed with regard to the death of Coya's father. In one of the "roundups" by the military, Coya bears witness to his murder by the regime: "they broke down the door with their rifle butts, and without giving it a second thought, they dealt the fatal blow to my father. I did not miss a single detail, as if my eyes were the punishment and for me the execution" (43). Yet even before this decisive scene, through Coya's fragmentary and ellusive visions of isolation, confusion, and impending danger, the father had been symbolically dying. Near the beginning of the novel, allusions are made to the fact that the father had been mortally wounded by the military. Coya realizes his impending death and immediately begins mourning "Coa, Coya crucé la calle y mirando tras la ventana iluminada, vi crecer como matico el duelo" / "Coa, Coya I crossed the street and looking through the illuminated window, I saw grief grow like an herb" (27). At this point she begins preparing for his death as well as for the military's shakedown:

> Transformada, cerré la puerta y el desorden se hizo pasado recuerdo cuando rompí todos los papeles, las fotos, las cartas, la montonera de cosas ardía en la fogata y más allá otra y otra en cada casa, en todo el barrio se sabía que mi padre cruzaba el atajo y que los camiones y séquito venían como materia ensordecida (28).

> [Transformed, I closed the door and the disorder became a memory of the past when I tore up all the papers, the photos, the letters, the pile of things was burning in the bonfire and further along another and another in every house, in the whole barrio it was known that my father was crossing the short cut and that the trucks and entourage were approaching like muffled matter.]

The loss of the father here thus implies much more than a personal loss, coming to involve the loss of a documented past, a past that is not completely destroyed in the flames but that now occupies the space of memory alone ("pasado recuerdo"). Indeed, the death of the father with his "vaguely famous face" (191), represents the failure of a mythic, heroic ideal. Coya's father represented the revolutionary hero par excellence: "Lo vi armado, amado por mí como ninguna de las otras. El más bello de la cuadra, el más lúcido del barrio, el alma más ardiente del país" / "I saw him armed, loved by me like no one else. The most beautiful man on the block, the most lucid in the barrio, the most ardent soul of the country" (191). Yet, as Coya later says, this ideal—like the father figure—fails and perishes at the hands of the military: "Falla, fallece" / "He fails, he perishes" (193). In this way, then, the father's death and absence as reiterated throughout the novel recreates an overwhelming sense of loss, of orphanhood, of grief that extends beyond the family romance to signify the loss of a mythic, national history or of a transcendent, unknowable ideal.

This is not to downplay Eltit's very personal experience of mourning. She has explained that she wrote this novel while grieving her own father's violent death ("Duelo" 27). This private loss undoubtedly serves to intensify the overpowering sense of bereavement that is so evident throughout *Por la patria*: "I accept, I accept all the charges against my father: the jail cell was his destiny, not the cemetery. . . . As a last resort, Pisagua was his path: not the cemetery" (150). Furthermore, beyond the thematics of grief, Eltit sees the ruptures in syntax, the stuttering, fractured language of *Por la patria* as directly related to her own personal sense of mourning: "Crushed, then, by the death of my father and the violence of his death, I continued writing, but the writing I produced was contaminated by the closeness of mourning, affecting my syntax to great extremes and I came to write the most limit-reaching novel I have produced so far" ("Duelo" 27). Yet, as Eltit explains, the loss she writes in this novel goes well beyond her own grief to become an inscription of a sense of national mourning: "The title of that novel is *Por la patria*, epitaph encoded to my father and social epitaph in solidarity with the numerous deaths in the country due to the violence of the system, which has extended a clandestine mourning throughout the territory" (27). In this sense, the title of the novel is not only a denunciation of the victims sacrificed "for the fatherland" but also a commemoration of the loss of that father(land) as well. Eltit goes on to note that literary production always participates in and dialogues with history as it has been internalized in the subject, suggesting that textual practice occupies the border where history and personal biography meet ("Duelo" 27). Nowhere does such an encounter between the personal and the political seem more intense than in *Por la patria*. The loss of the father here combines the personal significance of a daughter's bereavement with other more sociohistorically significant losses: the overwhelming, national loss of the disappeared as well as the symbolic death of a utopian Patria.

And yet, the pronounced sense of orphanhood in *Por la patria* also relates to the difficulty of formulating a sexual and cultural identity as bisexual and *mestiza*. The search for *parentesco* (or familial relationships) in the first part of *Por la patria* is intimately linked to the struggle for an effective subjectivity, for a voice capable of articulating the heterogeneity of the margins. The parental figures constitute an always deferred and ungraspable cultural model, seeming to offer access to origins and identification and yet always frustrating that possibility as well. At one point, Coya thinks she has found her parents, found her "identity": "son ellos, pienso, tan unidos que están, y cuando se me va a abrir la boca para nombrarlos me fijo en el pelo de él que es rubio y por eso mismo no es, y el de ella oscuro que tampoco" / "it is them, I think, as close together as they are, and when my mouth is about to open to name them I fix my gaze on his blond hair and for that very reason it is not him, and neither is it her with her dark hair" (13). Thus, her struggle is for a viable subjectivity, a way to name her parents/her past; but as she is about to speak, when she is faced with the cultural models available to her (blond Spanish father, "rubio," and dark indigenous mother, "oscuro"), she is frustrated, left without a firm basis, a coherent cultural identity, from which to articulate herself. In this way, the struggle to speak and make meaning (to assume an active subjectivity) is not only related to a crisis of representation caused by the violence of authoritarianism but also a wider social structure whereby heterogeneity (e.g., *mestizaje*, or bisexuality) confounds any sense of identity. The genderic obstacles to the formulation of subjectivity in heterogeneity are addressed near the beginning of the novel:

Basta que entre y sé cuál es la mesa que me corresponde: olfateo y ocupo la silla de mi madre y le hablo a él las cosas que ella le ha dicho. O a la inversa, elijo a mi padre, el sitial que tenía y gesticulo a su modo, miro, pienso, largo de la misma manera.

No me atrevo a tomar la tercera silla, ni puedo, sé lo que me dirían. Una vez me pasó y no me salió la voz, es decir, me salió, pero la de ellos: parte de una frase de mi madre y la otra mitad de mi padre (15).

[It is enough for me to enter and I know which is the table that corresponds to me: I sniff and occupy my mother's chair and I speak to him of the things that she has told him. Or the inverse, I choose my father, the seat of honor he had and I gesture in his style, I look, I think, I let go in the same way.

I do not dare to take the third seat, nor can I, I know what they would tell me. It happened to me once and my voice did not come forth, that is, it came forth but it was theirs: part of a phrase of my mother's and the other half my father's.]

In this way, cultural subjectivity is shown to be instituted through language and any culturally intelligible subject position to require a specific and exclusive gender identity. To become a subject implies adopting either a masculine or a feminine model of culturally sanctioned behavior. To write or speak outside such norms is problematic, risking a heterogeneous disidentity and incoherence.

The search for the parents thus involves a quest for a viable subjectivity. Intimately linked to this quest is the struggle for interpretative power that is central to *Por la patria*. Indeed, much of what concerns Coya throughout the text is memory, history, and resisting the forgetfulness that the official history of the regime seeks to impose. The figure of Juan is the prime voicepiece of the official incantation to forgetfulness. The only male character with a name, Juan is simultaneously traitor (*soplón*), seducer of women (like his namesake, Don Juan), and authoritarian agent. He represents a parodic masculinity that tries—unsuccessfully—to usurp the position of the "Symbolic Father," the position of supreme authority, the virtual source of all meaning. Juan's desire to take up such a position of absolute patriarch is revealed when he tries to become Coya's father who, as we have seen, represents an idealized, mythic father. Juan urges Coya, insidiously unctuous: "Háblame como si fuera tu papá" / "Talk to me as if I were your father" (45). Juan manipulates and tries to seduce Coya, attempting to reindoctrinate her by robbing her of her memory and her voice, all in an effort to impose his own signifying system both on Coya and, by extension, on the Chilean people. Juan coaxes Coya: "Entremos en diálogo, yo te voy a ir apuntando las cosas y te van a aparecer ordenadas otra vez" / "Let's enter into dialogue, I will start noting things down for you and they will appear orderly to you once again" (49). Juan thus represents the official history whose tragic flaw is its own absolute belief in its self-generated signifying power.[18] In the women's prison, Juan threatens Coya, not only showing his attempt to obliterate her memory but also revealing his belief in his own ability to be the source of all meaning:

—O te avienes o pierdes la voz.

—¿A qué costo?

—Al absoluto de ti.

—¿Qué es en mí absoluto?

—Toda, entera tu memoria.

—¿Cómo puedes tener mi memoria? ¿Cómo puedes robármela? rasarla más bien.

—Hablándome sólo a mí y en tono preciso. Así me entregas y yo te vacío (244).

["Either you come to an agreement or you lose your voice."

"At what cost?"

"The absolute in you."

"What, in me, is absolute?"

"Your whole, entire memory."

"How can you have my memory? How can you rob me of it? Or rather destroy it?"

"Speaking only to me and in a precise tone. Thus you hand yourself over to me and I empty you."]

Juan formulates this desire to be the source of all signification as a desire to be both mother and father to Coya: "Asumiré toda la parentela: madre, padre acecharé la partición" / "I will assume all parentage: mother, father I will patrol the partition" (243). He will thus give a new birth to Coya ("Coya I will give birth to you again" 244), erasing all of her memory except her imprisonment ("I leave you the confinement intact, but before that nothing" 244). Coya's struggle to resist Juan's erasure of her memory is by no means a personal issue; the capacity of the subalterns (represented by the female prisoners) to keep speaking, to keep producing meaning, virtually to survive, depends on *her* survival, since she serves as a figure for the language of the dispossesed (Coa): "Tengo que decidir una trampa a su impostado proceder para que hablen, para que sigan expresando y sobrevivan" / "I have to decide on a trap for his fraudulent conduct so that they may speak, so that they may keep signifying and survive" (245). Her "trap" thus works to save not only herself but the women prisoners and thus, symbolically, the margins at large.

But Juan's self-generating signifying mode, a figure for the official history written by the regime, is ultimately doomed to fail. While Juan continually tries to usurp the position of the Symbolic Father, he is, time and again, shown to be impotent, to not have what it takes. Coya tells him "no tienes nada que poner. Mírate . . . que no hay nada que me sirva, que me hierva" / "you have nothing to put up. Look at you . . . there is nothing of use to me, or that inflames me" (63); "Juan ¿por qué no puedes?" / "Juan, why can't you?" (64). Indeed, Juan's masculine power is predicated on her silence and negation; he tries to convince her that he can be a "real" man if she will only completely submit to him: "Espérate y vas a ver: si te callas, si no me miras, si no te mueves, se te dejas, si me chupas, si no crees que soy él voy a crecer y enardecido nos vamos" / "Wait and you'll see: if you be quiet, if you do not look at me, if you do not move, if you give in, if you suck me, if you do not believe I am him I will grow and inflamed we are off" (63). Likewise, in the face of his inability to cajole her into submission, he attempts to force her into a subservient sexual position: "He turns her over. Face down her face is buried in the pillow and he gets on top and speaks to her, he slowly explains to her how things work, how *coa*'s must receive affection" (63). But Coya insists on unveiling his impotence: "Coya slips away and laughs and points at him with her finger. 'You can't.'" (63). But, what all of these sequences also demonstrate is that while Juan's story on one level represents a tale of sexual seduction, masculine impotence, and betrayal, it also refers allegorically to the violent failure of the Pinochet regime's attempts at stripping the Chilean people of their memory and replacing that memory with its own official history.

The failure of the autonomy of Juan's narrative becomes increasingly clear. Indeed, in the end, it is Juan who confesses to Coya: "You are my mother, my father, my family. You are all I have. . . . You Coya my memory. Coya race. I do not love you, you are the open field that rules me and the memory of my origin" (271). No matter how much Juan—as a metonymic figure of the authoritarian regime—strives to be the supreme, autonomous source of meaning, neither he nor the regime can ever disarticulate themselves from the collective memory (Coya) and language (Coa) of the people. Juan is not, however, obliterated by the realization that he inevitably depends on the marginal, on the brutalized popular culture he tried to render insignificant. He is, in fact, Coya's countermemory as well, that "other" history that gives her history, her memory, its particular shape. Juan insists: "I am, I was, I will be your counter-memory and the veneer of reality that affirms you" (271). This history of the margins, the text of *Por la patria* itself, could not exist in its present form without Juan, without the official history that *made* Coya's story marginal, which virtually constructs the margins that engendered her. They are therefore, a priori and almost tragically, intertwined and interdependent such that one can never be considered without the other.

Nonetheless, the failure of Juan's story, the collapse of his attempt to rewrite history in his own image, signifies Coya's triumph. In spite of all the obstacles to her subjectivity, Coya's voice as "toma colectiva del habla" manages to survive. Indeed, she eventually writes the collective history of the margins from inside a female prison, the marginal space par excellence that predominates in part II of *Por la patria*. One of the sections of part I called "Testimonies, Speeches, Documents, Manifestos" (111) is precisely that: a collection of voices, a catalogue of the criminal victimization of the Chilean people, which we later realize has been written by Coya from within the women's prison. So, Coya not only comes to speak but to write as well. Through a series of what Josefina Ludmer has called in another context "tretas del débil" / "tricks of the weak," through "traps" and "great epic lies" (105), hallucinations and simulacra, treason and incestuous liaisons, Coya moves from the position of conquered to conqueror ("Seré de vencida en vencedora especie" / "From the conquered to the conquering species I will be" 275), until she is able to articulate a new epic of the margin: "Hay una épica. Surgida de la opresión y destello del linchaco" / "There is an epic. Arisen from the oppression and flash of the billy club" (273). Thus, the marginalization and suffering created by the violence of the regime and by the oppression of dominant symbolic systems at large, become a source of symbolic power and solidarity as she writes. Indeed, it is specifically the *writing* of the margins that becomes a practice with subversive and libertatory potential for, ultimately, what allows Coya to transform herself from subjected subaltern ("vencida") to subject of an epic of the margins ("vencedora") is, as I suggested in the first few pages of this chapter, textual transgression.

Por la patria's direct confrontations with authorities and conventions—linguistic, sexual, and political—enable the emergence of a subaltern subjectivity, symbolically allowing Coya/Coa to become subject of a national narrative. In fact, as Coya herself says, "He cometido traición por el habla" / "I have committed treason for the sake of speech" (248), thus explicitly confessing to the treason that her transformation into subject of the margins required. In the next few sections I explore the nature of the "treason" that works to break both authoritarian and patriarchal laws, that virtually makes such a feminine/subaltern subjectivity possible.

Literary Experimentalism:
Por la patria's Political Erotics of Language

The linguistic experimentalism of *Por la patria* to which I have alluded in the previous pages cannot be overstated. The frequent use of techniques such as alliteration ("Corrí Coa y Coya por la calle" 27), the ludic repetition of the same word ("La Luz, La Luz, La Luz, La Luz del Día" title of part I) or of phonetically similar words ("pariste," "partiste" 75; "lama, llana, llama"; "barrio," "barro"; "eslavos," "eslabones" 29) all, in some way, disrupt any sense of signifying security or univocality. The various manifestations of this experimentalism have been helpfully categorized and analyzed by Rodrigo Cánovas. One of the techniques he mentions is the creation of neologisms in the text, citing, for example, "'langúándome la sangre' (30), 'obscenan entre ellos' (157)" / "'my blood languoring me' (30), 'they obscene between themselves' (157)."[19] The rupture of syntactical conventions (Cánovas 158) and nongrammatical usage are also prime features. In addition, *Por la patria* mixes popular, oral expression ("¿Pa dónde sale con ese cuero y con esas quiscas en la cabeza?" / "Where're you going with that bod and with those pins in your hair?" 9), written, highly cultured language ("L'amor se me iba mucho" / "Love flowed ever away from me" 31), lines that appear repeatedly, evoking Spanish epic poetry ("Vagarás por las calles, llorando" / "You will wander through the streets, crying" 274), as well as words derived from indigenous roots ("chuqui", "machi").[20] Indeed, we could say that through the experimentalism of *Por la patria*, Eltit works to write what lies on the margins of culture, not by making this sphere coherent and hence manageable but by inscribing the periphery in all its heteroglossic chaos; a chaos that is due, moreover, not to a dearth of discursive codes but rather to an excess of language. As Eltit herself observes with regard to this text: "In *Por la patria*, something quite strange happened to me, unknown to me and that was a type of excess of words, of language" (interview with Ortega 234). Furthermore, as Eltit's own comments cited earlier attest, such a writing of the margins has not only political concerns but aesthetic ones as well. The textual project of writing the margins is also, for Eltit, intimately involved with textualizing the desires that inhabit that realm.[21]

Such a confluence of textuality, sexuality, and politics is clear from the first page of *Por la patria*, which virtually enacts what could be called a political erotics of language. The novel opens with the following lines, which evoke a textual and libidinal play without a mimetic function:

ma ma ma ma ma ma ma ma ma ma ma ma ma ma ma ma ma ma
ma ma ma ma ma ma ma am am am am am am am am am am
am am am am ame ame ame ame ame dame dame dame dame
dame dame dame madame madame madame dona madona
mama mama mama mama mama mamá mamá mamá mamacho el pater y en el bar se la toman y arman trifulca (9).

[ma ma ma ma ma ma ma ma ma ma ma ma ma ma ma ma ma
ma ma ma ma ma ma ma me me me me me me me me me me
me me me me imme imme imme imme imme gimme giveme
giveme give me madame madame madame dona madona
mama mama mama mama mama mamma mamma mamma
mamacho the pater and in the bar they grab her and start up a
brawl.]

These disconcerting and disruptive first lines, with their aural and
visual effects, their ludic yet troubling qualities, are a prime example
of the experimental aestheticism of Eltit's text. In all their playfulness and ritual, these convocatory lines refuse the notion of language as referential vehicle used to denote something else, to make
sense in a traditional way. Rather, language here is performed as
itself, its own materiality as utterance moving center stage. The
rhythmic "ma ma ma . . ." leaves mimeticism by the wayside, suggesting instead the idea of language as at once emancipatory and
foundational act: a transgressive freeing of a primordial preverbal
realm—associated with the maternal and the erotic—which has been
repressed by linear, denotative discursive norms. This break with
traditional prose form could be understood as the writing of what
Julia Kristeva has called the semiotic: that realm of language which
retains its original libidinal relationship to the maternal body, that
which has been repressed and driven under by paternal, the institution of the "Symbolic" according to Lacan. For Kristeva, the semiotic
reasserts itself in language as a subversive element, disrupting the
"Symbolic" and its univocal meanings through poetic language with
its sound plays, repetitions, multiplicity, and "undecidability." The
experimental techniques prevalent throughout *Por la patria* certainly disrupt univocality in this way.[22] Indeed, the first lines of the
novel quoted earlier suggest an impulse toward an original, libidi-
nally charged language, a somatic subjectivity not predicated on the
rejection of the maternal but rather on the search for the indigenous
mater, on a restoration of her symbolic power as forgotten and
repressed source of *mestizo* (specifically Chilean) cultural identity.[23]

Yet even as it attempts to break down the repression (discursive
and otherwise) of maternal desire, this initial appeal seems at once to
search for origins and identity and to recognize the difficulty of such
a quest. The originary and foundational "ma ma" metamorphoses as
it is born into the social realm of the text, twisting its way parodi-
cally into culturally coded forms such as "madame" and "madona,"
disrupted further by the insertion of the *pater*, only to arrive (in the

line that follows those quoted earlier) at the inauthentic substitute "mamastra" / "stepmother" (9). Thus, even as the opening gesture of Eltit's text invokes the idea of a refoundation of language, an inauguration of a new voice, a self-engendering voice in search of its own origins, this same act simultaneously shows the problematic nature of such a quest. Access to any prediscursive maternity, to any "origin," to any pristine "original" indigenous culture, is barred by the numerous cultural discourses that have overwritten such origins.

These convocatory lines also immediately insert Eltit into the novelistic tradition of the Latin American neo-baroque.[24] In his essay on this phenomenon, Severo Sarduy shows how the erotic plays an important part in the textual practices of the neo-baroque. He describes this element of desire as it operates in neo-baroque textual play: "Play, loss, waste, and pleasure, that is, erotism insofar as it is an activity that is always purely ludic, that is no more than a parody of the reproductive function, a transgression of the useful, of the 'natural' dialogue of bodies" (182). Likewise, Eltit's linguistic playfulness in these opening lines and, indeed, in *Por la patria* at large, enacts a sort of textual eroticism—a textual and libidinal play without a mimetic, reproductive function—thus transgressing traditional notions of usefulness and denotative signification. Such transgressive ludism and eroticism, constitutive of the American neo-baroque, are seen by Sarduy as including a certain political component. At the end of his article he alludes to this textual play as having affinities with revolution: "baroque that rejects any establishment, that metaphorizes the disputed order, the judged god, the transgressed law. Baroque of the Revolution." (184). Of course, regarding Eltit's work, such transgression has a specifically generic component, which is ellided in Sarduy's formulation. In any case, there is a clear affinity between Sarduy's idea of the political efficacy of neo-baroque linguistic play and Kristeva's assertion of the politically transfomative power of textual transgression.[25] We could certainly see Eltit's narrative project as erotically transgressive and "revolutionary" in both senses, complicating Sarduy's conceptualization of the "transgressed law" with a rupture of specifically paternal, masculinist authority. Yet, to my mind the political practice of Eltit's work also goes beyond this sort of "textual" revolution.

The transgressive linguistic play employed by Eltit not only serves to break textual codes or laws (à la Sarduy and Kristeva) but at times works to inscribe, to represent or, perhaps more precisely, to reenact the political violence perpetrated on the Chilean social body.

On the level of political contingency, these opening lines—and others similar to them that virtually embody rupture—could indeed be read as the marks, the stigmata of the disarticulating punishments of the authoritarian regime. As Eltit herself has said in interviews, the history of Chile since 1973 has wreaked a violent rupture on both political and linguistic levels.[26] The stuttering, disrupted discourse of *Por la patria* effectively stages the very real crisis of representation operated by the authoritarian regime. In the second part of the novel, for example, Coya searches desperately for her mother among the other women who have been rounded up and taken prisoner: "nn o v e o aa mm i mm a má" / "I I ddo on't ssee mmy mm a mma" (165). The aphasia at this point in the text is the result of torture; she has been given mind-altering drugs and has suffered the application of electrical shocks (158–68). The fracturing of meaning in this case has a sociopolitical referent. Coya wants La Rucia to speak to her, to explain her incoherence to her: "I want her to talk to me, to make some sense of my words" (166). When La Rucia specifically asks her what drugs they have given her, Coya responds: "dd i ss t i n tt a" / "dd iff f err entt" (166) and La Rucia pronounces, "that's it, that's what has you like that" (166), thus providing a contextually specific "reason" for Coya's incapacity to make sense. In such a context, Eltit's playful, deconstructive language is neither outside the law nor a liberation of some "natural" *écriture féminine* anterior to the law but is an aggressive, imaginative, and subversive deployment of the very language that has been both generated and controlled by political repression. Working through and against existing codes, Eltit's text takes up the disarticulated language of a country and a cultural consciousness under siege and turns it into an aesthetics and an erotics. By writing the aphasia symptomatic of authoritarian violence, Eltit's text inhabits the linguistically marginal, the ruptured language that is a by-product of political repression. But in rearticulating this denunciation through a neo-baroque aesthetic, her text works to creatively transform this language of marginalization from a testimonial of victimhood to a poetically powerful epic of the margins.

In addition, the very concept of linguistic play is often enacted within the text as a strategy that Coya uses to combat various coercive interrogations. For example, another woman prisoner, Berta, accuses Coya of having an incestuous relationship with her parents: "'They told me that your father kissed you on the mouth'" (25). Coya responds evasively: "¿En la bo, en la boa dices?" / "'On the mo, on the mout you say?'" (25). Coya resists Berta's interpretative agression by disarticulating "boca" into "bo" "boa," deliberately deconstructing the linguistic crux of Berta's question. On another occasion, Juan is interrogating Coya in prison, trying to evoke a confession:

> Paciente, entrenado, continúa el informe delativo, aumentado por la extrema situación: que nosotros, que las chicas también y el bar, el reservado completo como arsenal.
>
> —¿Cómo arenal? le digo de adrede.
>
> —Como arsenal, me corrige. (185).

> [Patient, trained, he continues the disclosure report, augmented by the extreme situation: us, the girls too and the bar, the entire reservation as an arsenal.
>
>   "As an arenal?" I say on purpose.
>
>   "As an arsenal," he corrects me.]

Coya deliberately ("de adrede") resists Juan's accusation with a word play on *arsenal/arenal*. This intentional and distinctly linguistic confusion is a weapon of the dispossessed, a "treta del débil," a taking of the master's discourse and disarticulating it as an act of resistance. In this way linguistic play or deconstruction also occasionally has its use as a specifically *political* strategy within the text. And, as we shall see further on in this chapter, it is specifically language and writing that enable the epic of resistance, which virtually allow the articulation of the margins as a potential source of power.

Finally, the experimental excess of language and the disarticulation of syntactic and linguistic conventions become a key component of the liberation of the women prisoners in part II. The women are finally granted an amnesty: "Salimos al atardecer, ateridas, aterradas: [. . .] Multiplicadas en veinte coas de raza coya y yo Coya en el incesto total de la patria" / "We got out at dusk, numb with cold, terrified: [. . .] Multiplied into twenty coa's of coya race and I Coya in the total incest of the fatherland" (277). As the reference to "veinte coas" (a reference to the protagonist but literally twenty street slangs) indicates, their deliverance is most definitely a linguistic one. Indeed, the text of their liberation reads "Libertas hablamos" / "Liberated we speak," followed by a catalog of word play that is attributed to three of the women, La Rucia, Berta, and Flora. Finally, through this linguistic emancipation, the "yo" or "I," which had been confined by the proprieties of linguistic/literary convention, can emerge triumphant: "Se levanta el coa, el lunfardo, el giria, el pachuco, el caló, caliche, slang, calao, replana. El argot se dispara y yo" / "The coa, the lunfardo, the giria, the pachuco, the calo, the caliche, slang, calao, replana rises. The argot takes off and I" (278).

Sexual/Textual Transgression:
Writing the Other Side of the Oedipal Drama

Subjectivity and a coherent, univocal gender identity are intimately related in *Por la patria*, and bisexuality or androgyny is, as Coya relates, a treacherous option: "I do not dare take the third seat" (15). Coya does, nonetheless, strive to defy the cultural injunction to assume a single, coherent gender identity, claiming herself "andrógina" / "androgynous" on several occasions, and often speaking from a bisexual, heterogeneous position, "a punto de hombre, a asomo de mujer" / "on the verge of man, within a trace of woman" (148). When she is interrogated by the maternal authority figures, "the mother general" demands, "Define yourself" (149). Coya responds defiantly:

—No, no puedo. Yo soy mujer cuando me conviene y hombre cuando lo necesito. Me gusta mucho aparentar, les contesté.

Me quedé callada y antes que se pusieran a hablar, completé mi idea:

—Yo soy todas las cosas.

—No seas farsante, me retó furiosa madre general (149).

["No, I cannot. I am a woman when it suits me and a man when I need to be. I very much like to pretend," I answered them.

I remained quiet and before they started to speak, I finished my idea:

"I am all things."

"Don't be a charlatan," the mother general, furious, upbraided me.]

But while she refuses to surrender access to masculinity and her liberation has very much to do with a "retorno a la androginia" / "return to androgyny" (273), Coya retains a specifically feminine-inflected identity (i.e., she is never *andrógino*, always *andrógina*) right to the end of the novel, which, as we shall see, entails a partially glimpsed, distinctly feminine geopolical refoundation: "We saw the continent and we were again combatents and sisters, human almost" (279).

Perhaps the most emphatic and disruptive sexual transgression enacted in *Por la patria* is incest. From the very beginning of the text, incest reveals itself to be one of the dominant tropes of the novel. Given the centrality of the incest taboo for both the formation of gender identity and the organization of the social realm, it is perhaps not all that surprising that incest serves as a key metaphor for enacting a political as well as a sexual transgression in *Por la patria*.[27] Coya's relationships both with her father and with her mother are highly eroticized and sensual, continually reenacting the incestuous desire that the law works to repress. The relationship between Coya and the mother is eroticized right from the beginning of the text: we read, for example, "the glasses where she has put her mouth on mine and occasionally we have drunk together permeated by saliva and love" (16); "Her fingers run along my spine" (18); "I accept her hand around my waist and her breasts press against mine" (19). Likewise, her relations with the father, as we shall see, are profoundly erotic. She attends to her wounded father: "I cleaned his enlarged lip . . . I kiss and kiss and my mouth became red" (29). On a very basic level, these incestuous relationships are attempts to break, textually, the sexual taboo that separates the child from the parents', and especially from the mother's, body. In this sense, then, incest operates here as a metaphor of transgression, a textual lever by which Coya jeopardizes the psychosexual order. Furthermore, since both the father and mother in *Por la patria* are simultaneously personal, cultural, and political figures, such a sexual transgression not only denounces the rules governing the gender system but also remits to the sociopolitical realm. Indeed, these sexually transgressive relations are portrayed as ritualistic acts with a political or collective function. Incestuous transgression in this text serves to break the law on many levels specifically as a means of symbolic transformation.

The ritualistic and even sacrificial overtones of sexual transgression in this text are perhaps most evident in Coya's incestuous union with the father, which evokes a powerfully erotic and utopian bodily mysticism. Coya's intensely erotic encounter with her wounded father near the beginning of the novel is a manifestation of an ideal, divine, yet sensually erotic, love. Heavily laden with intertextual references to the "Song of Songs" and to the mystical poetry of San Juan de la Cruz, this scene articulates a Christian, sacrificial love where the body functions as a vehicle for expressing that which excedes language: "Mi pecho oscuro, sangrante en mí su corazón, mi pezón escarlata, él la sangre mía, la herida mía mamó" / "My dark breast, his heart bleeding in me, my scarlet nipple, he my blood, my wound he suckled" (30). As Coya's body bears the stigmata of the father's suffering ("sangrante en mí su corazón"), he thus becomes a divine figure, his blood and wounds likened to those of Christ: "Reventada la boca suya y mi amado no me decía palabra una, noticia l'amante mío, solo, sin disputa o rival que lo tomara y levantara la sangre suya seca, secada en la boca" / "His mouth split and my beloved said to me not one word, tidings beloved of mine, alone, without dispute or rival that would take him and lift up his dried blood, dried on the mouth" (30). Her incestuous love for the father—erotically, religiously, as well as aesthetically powerful—can only be called a passion (with all its connotations of desire, obsession, and suffering), a force that takes hold of the subject from the outside, making any rational control impossible. Coya has virtually been driven outside of herself by this passion, by both pleasure and pain. Indeed, at several points Coya refers to herself as "mí" as in "Mí lloró" / "Me cried" (30), emblematically showing the subject "yo" / "I" to be displaced by the more passive object, making her literally an object of this love. Yet the "passion" of this incestuous liaison functions in the sense of the Christian Passion, the torture Christ suffered in order to redeem humanity. Coya details the pain and punishment suffered by the father, a pain that she shares through their sexual coupling: "Sí, con la lengua mía limpiándolo, los dos plenos en la herida" / "Yes, with my tongue cleaning him, both of us complete in the wound" (31). The mingling of Coya's and the father's blood, the consumation of their love, is a sacrament, an act of communion with both erotic and mystical overtones.

The linguistic conceits and syntactical ruptures also align this encounter with the Spanish baroque. Indeed, the distinct formal aspects of the paternal and maternal models (Spanish Golden Age poetry and indigenous culture respectively) bring to mind Eltit's own characterization of incest in her work as having to do specifically with literary/linguistic concerns. According to the author, incest has a textual component in *Por la patria*, implying a transgressive joining of discourses (high/low, for example) usually prevented from coming together by traditional literary codes. Eltit herself has spoken about the importance of incest in this novel, explaining, to some degree, the use of incest as metaphor. Her comments are worth quoting in full:

> Hay una represión cultural que te empuja hacia el padre y hacia la heterosexualidad, pero yo pienso que ese deseo primigenio es también hacia la madre y quise salvar esa pulsión. Sabía que iba a llegar al incesto como metáfora. Leyendo un libro me topé con la existencia de la jerarquía Coya en la cultura incáica. Coya era la hermana del inca y a la vez su mujer y la madre del futuro inca. Eso por una parte. Por otra, estaba el coa, que es el lenguaje delictual que excede ese ámbito para traspasar los estratos más desposeídos. Fue ahí donde encontré el pivote para la construcción de Coya como la generadora de una estirpe que se va pervirtiendo porque tiene su origen en el incesto, hasta llegar a esa especie de hampa proletaria. (Interview with Claudia Donoso 47–48).

> [There is a cultural repression that pushes you toward the father and toward heterosexuality, but I think that original desire is also toward the mother and I wanted to salvage that drive. I knew that I was going to come to incest as a metaphor. Reading a book I came across the existence of the Coya hierarchy in Inca culture. Coya was the sister of the Inca and at the same time his wife, as well as the mother of the future Inca. That was on the one hand. On the other was the "coa," the language of delinquents which excedes that field and penetrates the most dispossessed social strata. That was where I found the fulcrum for the construction of Coya as the engenderer of a lineage that is becoming perverted because it originates in incest, until arriving at a type of proletarian underworld.]

Thus, Eltit's use of incest in this novel has simultaneously social, textual, and sexual intentions and functions.

Returning specifically to the paternal incest of *Por la patria*, besides the erotic and aesthetic aspects, it has a political function as well. The betrayal implied by an incestuous liaison with the father has the effect of exorcising and thus alleviating the burden of the brutal filial relationship between the Chilean subject and the "fatherland." In another ritualistic encounter with the father after his death, but in a vision where "the dead one was alive" (97), Coya

is at first violently searched by the father, summoning up the suspicion, arrests, and violence enacted repeatedly "for the fatherland" in
Pinochet's Chile. Coya then engages in a traitorous love scene with
the dead father:

> El amor que te tuve explotó como una bomba de dinamita y fui
> profundamente infiel a todo otro cariño, insanamente traidora,
> radicalmente desleal y perversa cuando empinamos el vaso y el
> peso del país se desvaneció en su final y fue argentino quizás y
> yo también argentina y perdí nacionalidad en esa alucinación
> (97).

> [The love that I had for you exploded like a bomb of dynamite
> and I was profoundly unfaithful to all other affection, insanely
> treasonous, radically disloyal and perverse when we lifted the
> glass and the weight of the country vanished in its finality and
> he was Argentine and I also Argentine and I lost my nationality
> in that hallucination.]

In this passage incest works to undo not only the narrative of "family" but that of "nation" as well. Their incestuous love is subversive,
obliterating all other allegiances, even exorcising any sense of
national identity. Incestuous desire enacted this way serves a sacrificial function: the burden of a violent, violating nationality is virtually expunged through transgressive ritual. In the textual configuration of *Por la patria*, then, incest performs a ritual of transgression,
representing betrayal, guilt, and intrafamiliar violence only to do
away with it in a final hallucinatory act.[28]

The family romance portayed in *Por la patria* thus rewrites the
Oedipal crisis, representing the destabilizing desire produced by the
law rather than just the repressive aftermath. By giving voice and textual form to a forbidden desire, to heterogeneity and to sexual transgression, the novel effectively writes a marginal space, a place that
has not been obliterated but that has been made unspeakable by
dominant cultural discourses.[29] But, in addition, the foundational
family romance has a particular resonance in the Chilean scene. As
Munizaga and Ochsensius point out, the authoritarian regime
worked to create a mythic family romance through its discourse
whereby:

> Al clamor de las mujeres y los jóvenes, en su lucha y resistencia
> frente al marxismo, acuden las fuerzas armadas venciendo al

invasor. Se realiza aquí la concreción de un acto mítico: esta trilogía, cual sagrada familia, vuelve a gestar la patria. Las mujeres dan a la luz a la patria y la entregan a las fuerzas armadas para que cuide de ella como un padre protector, procurando su crecimiento fuerte y sano, su grandeza futura (98).

[To the clamor of women and young people, in their fight and resistance to marxism, the armed forces respond, defeating the invader. The concretization of a mythic act is here realized: this trilogy, like the holy family, returns to bring forth the nation. The women give birth to the fatherland and turn it over to the armed forces so that they may care for the child like a protective father, securing its strong and healthy growth, their future greatness.]

Corresponding to as well as parodying these formulations, *Por la patria* also effectively collapses the realm of the family with that of the nation. But the decidedly dysfunctional family romance in this novel becomes not only a way of deconstructing the sociosexual foundational fiction but also of imagining and representing the national pathology. Eltit's text thus writes what has been made marginal, what has been excluded in order to consolidate a coherent social body, the official social identity of the Chile of Pinochet's regime. That is, incest in *Por la patria* fits into an overall textual project of writing transgression from "the other side," articulating what is fully within the authoritarian regime but what is inscribed within that regime as being "outside" it. As cultural critics Stallybrass and White point out: "the exclusion necessary to the formation of social identity at one level is simultaneously a production at the level of the imaginary" (193). Likewise, Eltit's text is ultimately a writing of the underworld (or X ray–like innerworld) of the cultural imaginary produced by the very Chilean authoritarian dogma that seeks to create a clean, coherent social body—or better yet, as Vidal points out, a social spirit with no body at all.

　　Por la patria is thus the infra-history of a nation literally beside itself, made marginal within its own borders, made unintelligible, unsayable, unthinkable in order to consolidate the power of the ruling regime. And yet, in the face of such coherence and repression, this text effectively manages to represent what has been relegated to the margins ("Love of wine, of idleness, of gambling, of the inner thigh, of the gaze, of punishments, of the uncommon fraternal caress" 120) because giving voice to these repressed and censored realms can mean survival on a psychological as well as a physical level: "Successions, waterfalls of images: and the activity of thinking, the gift of evoking, the power of transfiguring and fixing marked them as alive, as neurologically sane, as bodily individual" (120). In this way, *Por la patria* enacts what Rachel Blau DuPlessis calls "displacement" by giving voice to the silenced perifery and drawing attention to the cultural margins created by authoritarian sociosexual law. In her survey of the oppositional narrative strategies of twentieth-century Anglo-American women writers, Blau DuPlessis posits two related ways of revising mythic or traditional stories: displacement and delegitimation. For DuPlessis, "displacement" involves directing narrative attention to "the other side of the story," giving "voice to the muted." "Delegitimation" of the story line itself takes place when the narrative pattern is completely disrupted, putting "the last first and the first last," thus rupturing "conventional morality, politics, and narrative" (*Writing Beyond the Ending* 108). Eltit's narrative could indeed be seen to combine both of these tactics, displacing attention to what has been repressed by authoritarian social and sexual law as well as calling into question (and "delegitimating") dominant narrative patterns used to legitimate that law.

Nonetheless, within such a textual project, the transgression of incest cannot be an end in itself but rather becomes both symptom and cure, a way to take the pathology of such a sociosexual system to its limit, to write it from "the other side," and to refuse the replication of a narrative pattern where transgression is punished and contained. Sexual transgression becomes a means of textually exorcising repressive structures from the national consciousness in order to envision or imagine a new psychosexual and social order. The national pathology is indeed often represented in the text as a collective sexual stigma, incest being portrayed as a sign of the guilt imposed on the Chilean people, as a sign of their "original sin," which La Rucia describes: "The whole *barrio* was infected, affected by the same error, almost from the cradle onward" (134). When portrayed from the side of law and order (not from "the other side," to use Blau DuPlessis' term), incest represents a profound sense of collective guilt. The nation's catastrophic situation is often referred to in terms of this sexual transgression, with accusations, confessions, and interrogations metaphorically revolving around Coya's incestuous liaisons. When one of the women prisoners (la Rucia) is interrogated by Juan, Coya asks her what information he wanted. La Rucia responds "That damned relationship with your father and every one of your postures" (252). In the section titled "Testimonies, Speeches, Documents, Manifestos," Berta (another of the detainees) tells her mother:

> Algo habremos hecho, habré hecho para perder su favor y debemos con resignación soportar el sufrimiento. . . . Algo muy grave ha pasado: tener aquí amparada, a Coya, lesiva, lascivia mayor del universo (126).

> [We must have done something, I must have done something to lose his favor and we must resign ourselves to putting up with the suffering. . . . Something very serious has happened: having sheltered Coya here, injurious, largest lasciviousness of the universe.]

Berta's comments echo a refrain from the collective imaginary, a refrain heard reverberating throughout Chile as citizens tell themselves that something must be profoundly wrong for such punishments to be necessary, that the disappeared must have somehow sinned to deserved their fate: "Algo habrán hecho" / "They must have done something." But what could this "sin" possibly be? As Chilean poet Raúl Zurita muses, "El origen de cualquier tragedia es siempre una traición. Vivimos en un país arrasado ¿Qué traición pesará sobre nosotros?" / "The origin of any tragedy is always a betrayal. We live in a ravaged country. What betrayal must hang over us?"[30] Much of the Chilean literature that engages the social context of the dictatorship seems to ask itself this same question, often writing the origins of the national situation through tropes of betrayal and transgression.[31] In *Por la patria*, the betrayal that has caused this fall from grace, this national catastrophe, is represented as Coya's lasciviousness, her incestuous transgression. By the same token, Berta's polyvalent comments parody the sense of guilt that pervades Chilean society due to the brutal punishment of the regime. Watched, carded, controlled, and pursued, the Chilean citizen during Pinochet's regime has been interpellated as an *always already guilty* subject.

But rather than search for a lost innocence, *Por la patria* enacts its guilt with a vengeance: "'I was never innocent,' said Coya, 'nor ingenuous either'" (103). In this way, transgression is the path to transformation in the novel: in accepting and reveling in her "guilt," Coya perversely transforms a state of guilt into a state of grace and a site of resistance. This is displacing the perspective to "the other

side" of the incest prohibition; a strategy that is portrayed, furthermore, as symbolically and politically powerful. As Coya moves
through paternal and maternal incest, ritualistically enacting a transgressive sexuality against the father's law, taking up paternal and
maternal discourse each in turn, she progressively empowers and
frees herself. As Coya repeatedly reenacts that incestuous guilt, as
she writes this victimhood, she engenders a spectacle of transformation. In this way, even as the text represents a profound sense of
transgression and residual guilt, it is as sacrificial, ritual act: incest
operates as both representation and exorcism of an original, originary
betrayal.[32] That is, it enacts a set of violent practices as a way to
exorcise such violence as well as to create a collective victimhood
from which to launch a new order.

Re-Writing the Margins:
Transgression and the Maternal Body

We have seen how both linguistic experimentation and sexual
transgression work to transform the margins into a site of power
and resistance, thus enabling Coya to articulate a viable subjectivity
from and through those margins. *Por la patria* writes the symbolic
underworld (*hampa*) created and muted by the official discourse and
transgresses virtually all of the boundaries marked out by such
norms. Throughout this text, the body plays a key role in this deconstruction of dominant structures, both patriarchy (which is predicated on the repression of the maternal body for the installation of
the symbolic order, as Lacan and Kristeva explain) as well as authoritarianism (which is bent on preserving the Chilean spirit, seeking to
elide the material body altogether, as Vidal has shown). Indeed, the
maternal body plays an especially important role in the transgressions enacted in *Por la patria*. We have already seen how the maternal operates in the convocatory lines of the text (ma ma ma ma ma
ma, etc.). The scenes portraying maternal incest, however, are perhaps where the maternal body is most sexually and transgressively
imagined. Indeed, in interviews, Eltit has professed her concern for
rehabilitating the figure of the mother, for rethinking her in terms of
desire, that is, as a sexual being. Regarding *Por la patria*, Eltit states:
"I wanted to work on the mother as a sexual entity. The first sexual
drive of a child has to be toward the mother, not toward the father,
because the physical contact, in gestation and the first years, is with
her. We must rethink the problem of the mother" (interview with
Ríos). *Por la patria* indeed does just that, rethinking the maternal

against the authoritarian invocation of the mother as moral base for the regime as well as against more generalized prohibitions and limitations on female sexuality.

By rethinking the maternal and reenacting a desire for the maternal body, *Por la patria* breaks taboos on many levels. But, while the maternal body certainly plays a key role in the transgressions and transformation of this text, it is never written as an innocent, utopian, prediscursive body, never simply the paradise lost of the womb. Even though, as we shall see, Eltit's view of maternity certainly includes the idea of the maternal as potentially subversive to patriarchal law, she does not conceive of the maternal body as prelinguistic, as somehow outside the law or the social system. The subversive power of the maternal in Eltit's text rests not on the idea that the maternal lies outside the law, but rather that the mother's body *within* the patriarchal structure is a site of cultural and sexual reproduction. While we could certainly say that the traditional models of Latin American cultural foundation, authoritarian political systems, and subjectivity itself all depend on the prohibitions of the "law of the father" and the symbolic order that it generates, it is through the instrumentality of the feminine in its specifically maternal capacity that these systems are reproduced and maintained.[33] Eltit describes this culturally reproductive function of the feminine, as it has traditionally been conceptualized: "The feminine . . . has been constituted as a receptor and reproducer of this central power through the mechanical procedure of moving linearly from her bodily nature—the capacity of reception and human reproduction—to an identical cultural functionality" ("Cultura" 1). For this reason, rethinking the mother can simultaneously question sexual, politicocultural, and textual codes; and the drive toward rewriting the maternal body becomes a socially, sexually, and politically resonant quest. My goal in the pages that remain is to take a closer look at the role of the multifaceted mother figures in *Por la patria* and to examine how the transgressions regarding the maternal body are related to the overall project of the text.

From the very beginning of the novel, the maternal figure represents the nostalgic, primarily indigenous model, the almost unimaginable other and yet also the repository and mediator of memory and language. Throughout the first few scenes, the desire for the mother is for the indigenous mother, a pure, unadulterated maternal body that, as it turns out, cannot be found without the marks of colonialism, without the racist rewriting of her body:

Cuán desafora la rubicunda con su teñido pelo rubio y gringo
mientras cimbrea su ambivalente figura. Caderas amplias de
buena madre y mancha ese centímetro de raíz negra de mamá
mala, su pelo grueso y tosco, no como arriba que es rubiecito:
ondas y crespos de su infinita bondad (9).

[How excessive the ruddy one with her dyed, gringo blond hair
while she sways her ambivalent figure. Ample hips of the good
mother and stain of that centimeter of black roots of the bad
mother, her hair thick and coarse, not like on top where it is
blond: waves and curls of her infinite goodness.]

With her straight, dark hair that has been dyed blond and curled,
the mother virtually embodies racist prescriptions of beauty. The
mother's original indigenous features are only barely accessible
through a discourse that casts her racial specificity as negative, as
"ese centímetro de raíz negra de mamá mala" / "that centimeter of
black roots of the bad mother." There is a double impulse here:
desire for an overflowing, maternal sensuality ("desafora"; "caderas
amplias") and parody of the colonizing discourse that scripts the
indigenous in negative terms. Such an impulse represents a quest for
an original cultural identity that has been forever lost, a search for
that which, as Chilean anthropologist and writer Sonia Montecino
has shown, has been most obliterated from the cultural consciousness: the indigenous mother.[34] In this sense, then, the drive toward
the indigenous mother connotes a nostalgic search for cultural roots
that have been denied to the postcolonial subject; and Coya's desire
for the mother, while certainly sexually coded, also constitutes a
social, cultural, and political transgression as well.

Yet, the maternal figure, while in some ways portrayed as a
primordial object of desire, is also a source of fear, of betrayal, of
death. By no means a univocal figure, the maternal is written in *Por
la patria* as a virtual chorus of voices, a dizzying *mise-en-scène* of the
culturally coded scripts of the maternal. Here again, Eltit turns the
regime's discourse, with its refoundational script, on its head. Where
Pinochet's mythic narrative sought to invoke mothers as "honest,"
"defenders of spiritual values," "unselfish," "formers of conscience,"
indeed as beings who possess the necessary qualities of "faith," "fer-
vor," and "dignity,"[35] the maternal voices in *Por la patria* deconstruct this official version of motherhood, including the "Madres
1–6," who portray the mother as prostitute, as collaborator, as traitor,
unfaithful, murderous, accusing, moralizing, and sexually perverse

(pages 19–42). Contrary to the spiritual and patriotic motherhood invoked by the Pinochet's official discourse, in Eltit's text the mother's sensuality and sexuality come center stage:

> —Yo me pasaba de vieja cuando nació. Apenas me corría el hilito y después cuando me hicieron un favor pagué con éste la vergüenza.
>
> —Un favor, dijo la madre 2, yo fui la que hice un favor.
>
> —Yo tuve también un vecinito, murmuró la madre 3.
>
> —¿Quién no ha tenido un jovencito?, preguntó la madre 1.
>
> —Varios, muchos vecinitos en cada casa, dijeron casi a coro (42).

> ["I was too old when he was born. My blood a mere trickle and afterwards when they did me a favor, I paid for my shame with this one."
>
> "A favor," said mother 2, "I was the one who did a favor."
>
> "I also had a young neighbor," murmured mother 3.
>
> "Who hasn't had a young man?" asked mother 1.
>
> "Several, many young neighbors in every house," they said almost in chorus.]

This bawdy discussion of sexual desire and bodily functions works to undo the official version of motherhood that, as Munizaga and Ochsensius point out, "is essentially spirit and not body," "belonging to a nature, although not biological but rather principally social" (74). Furthermore, as should be clear from the segment just quoted, these maternal voices have a very theatrical function;[36] they are the performance of maternal sayings and admonitions, serving as voice-pieces for the popular, corporeal language absent from not only the official discourse on Chilean motherhood but also from much written, literary discourse as well. Clearly, the language of the Madres 1–6, of the "Mads.," is a prime element of Coya's "toma colectiva del habla" / "collective taking of speech."

In many ways, Eltit strives to inhabit and write from this multiple and protean otherness of the maternal. In the six versions/visions/passions (82–108), the narrative performs six different mystical visions by which Coya attempts to re-write the national catastrophe, to render accounts of the Chilean scene, to write the burden, the pain, the violence of the love "for the fatherland." As Cánovas describes this sequence: "These visions are those of a woman of the underworld and *also, literally,* those of a *machi* in trance, and *also,* the illuminations of a poet (à la Rimbaud) about a community. The feminine (narrative) voice appears inhabited by the American tradition (*machi-mapuche*) and European (visionary French poets of modernity)" (150). Throughout these visions, the mother is a protean, polyvalent figure, sometimes benign, sometimes malignant. The second of these visions for instance contains several tableaux titled, for example, "TO THE HAIRS OF MY UNSELFISH MOTHER" or "TO THE TONGUE OF MY INSATIABLE MOTHER", which are attempts at reembodying the maternal, recuperating the mother's corporality and sensuality, as well as figuring the materiality of language itself. One of the most powerfully and transgressively erotic of these sequences reads:

mama de mí que se me sale la leche del pezón y te cedo la punta para la sed. Chupa mi leche posparida y luego, cuando te llenes, te empiezas a bajar y a hundir en lo que tanto te gusta: te regalo el abajo, te ahorro el atajo y con la lengua me vas lamiendo y yo desde arriba te miro mamá, te estoy viendo de qué manera la lengua tuya se esgrime, me eleva, me calienta todo el cuerpecito el hueco. Claro que te apuras sí, ya sabes que los chilenitos morenos obedecen a los eslavos y reverencian la masacre, mamá, la sangre que se vulcaniza el alquitrán del hampa en fin mamita
tu lengua
            me lleva
        al suelo (89).

[suckle mother of mine, the milk runs from my nipple and I yield the tip to you for your thirst. Suck my postpartum milk and then, when you have your fill, you start to go down and to bury yourself in what pleases you so: I give you the lower part, I save the short cut for you and with your tongue you are licking me and I, from above, look at you mama, I am watching you how your tongue dodges in and out, it elevates me, it warms my whole little body, my hole. Of course you worry yes, you now know that the dark little Chileans obey the slavs and revere the massacre, mama, the blood that is vulcanized in the tar of the underworld, at last mama

> your tongue
>
>   takes me
>
>   to the ground.]

First of all, in envisioning a mother/daughter eroticism, the text undoes psychosexual models that envision the object of the mother's desire as always the male child. As Freud would have it: "The feminine situation is only established . . . if the wish for a penis is replaced by one for a baby, if, that is, a baby takes the place of a penis in accordance with an ancient symbolic equivalence" ("Femininity" 113). Furthermore, while he admits of the daughter's powerful pre-Oedipal attachment to her mother, and although these attachments are "important" and leave "lasting fixations," the main mother-daughter relation he sees is one of increasing hostility, rejection, and rivalry for the father's penis ("Femininity" 114). His "blind spot" has been denounced by Luce Irigaray who counters Freud's observation that "for a long time, the girl's Oedipus complex concealed her pre-Oedipus attachment to her mother from our view" by asserting that, rather, "*The desire of Oedipus* has misunderstood, repressed, and censored, the libidinal attachment between the growing girl and her mother."[37] In many ways, *Por la patria* attempts to make visible, to textualize these repressed libidinal attachments between mother and daughter, as is evidenced by the passage quoted above. Here maternal desire and the repressed mother/child eroticism is disruptively recast in entirely feminine, lesbian terms.

Yet given the previous sequence where the mother is also the the repository of all words ("te sabes todas las palabras" / "you know all words" 88), the "lengua" in the previous paragraph also remits to the materiality of the mother tongue, the primordial cultural tie that is quite literally here related to the (mother) earth ("tu lengua me lleva al suelo" / "your tongue takes me to the ground"). Further still, the reference to the mother's anguish regarding the murderous authoritarian regime causes the "madre" here to resonate as well with the *madre patria*, a term that can perhaps be best translated as "motherland" but that also carries within it the sense of fatherland (*patria*). While the official narration would have it that "the Fatherland-Woman is violated or raped by the action of those non-Chileans, that are the politicians and the marxists" and that "it is then that the Fatherland-Woman remains exposed to marxist attack and that the armed forces decide to save her" (Munizaga and Ochsensius 75), the sequence just quoted shows the ones who "revere the massacre" to be the armed forces themselves: the "slavs" (the blue-eyed, militaristic forces of destruction that appear throughout part I) and their followers ("the dark little Chileans" who obey them). Condensing the maternal body ("mama de mí") with the mother tongue (*lengua*) as well as with the motherland (*madre patria*), this incestuous and erotic sequence serves to disrupt both psychosexual and authoritarian codes in one multiply transgressive gesture.

Indeed, the violated maternal and/or female body is frequently conflated with the abused *madre patria*.[38] Likewise, rape serves throughout the text to denounce both sexual abuse and sociopolitical violence. Coya's rape by a group of soldiers in part II serves as an example:

> Ocurrió capote por la tropa: pasaron de todos los portes y se refocilaron a mi costa. Pude haber empapado praderas y engrudarlas. Ya después no resistí nada:
>   Yazgo con las piernas abiertas porque ya viene el otro y el siguiente:
> —Ahora tú, dicen.
>
> Yo mido cuántos movimientos les bastan, cuántos apretones y la descarga, mientras el suelo gotea rosáceo el líquido imbuido del rasgón por excesividad y brusqueza. (188).

> [A beating by the troops occurred: they exceeded all comportments and enjoyed themselves at my cost, at my coast. I could have drenched the meadows and turned them to paste. After that I did not resist at all:
>   I lie with my legs open because the other comes now and the next one:
> "Now you," they say.
>
> I measure how many movements are enough for them, how many squeezes and the discharge, while the ground drips pinkish with the imbued liquid from the tear caused by excessiveness and brusqueness.]

The double meaning of *costa* (both cost and coastline) and the reference to "praderas" / "meadows" work to superimpose the female body and the national territory, both of which are being raped by the military. The sociosexual taboo that works to silence rape is thus broken in Eltit's narrative.[39] Yet the ambivalence generated by such a violation is not easily exorcised and the tendency to "blame the victim" remains strong. The opened and violated female body is often inscribed in *Por la patria* as a sign of the national catastrophe, the culpability of the disaster ascribed equivocally either to the violated body or to the forces of violence. It is the voice of "madre 1" / "mother 1" who equates Coya's rape and the national collapse:

—Catástrofe y vergüenza para nosotras tú, perdida aquí tirada para gusto de zarcos, de eslavos, de toda ralea dura y nacional.

—Por fuerza madre, por dolor.

—Por costumbre bastarda, me dice.

—Por piedad, contesto, apiádate.

Me aplastan, me tapan la boca, la nariz, me asfixio casi. Madre 1 se aferra a mi ojo y el dolor intenso, izquierdo me vuela (172).

["Catastrophe and shame for us, you, lost here stretched out for the pleasure of blue-eyed slavs, of any breed hard and national."

"By force mother, by pain."

"By habit bastard," she says.

"For pity's sake," I answer, "take pity."

They crush me, they cover my mouth, my nose, I almost suffocate. Mother 1 clings to my eye and the intense, twisted pain explodes me.]

The battle here is between Coya and a distinctly maternal voice of the status quo that would affirm her responsibility and guilt for her own victimization. So while at times the maternal figure is portrayed as victimized by military violence, at other times she is seen as abetting such violence.

The maternal figure thus does not merely provide an ideal escape from patriarchal violence/violation, for she often operates as a collaborator with the regime or an empty space that serves as a conduit for any message the regime might wish to project. At one point, for example, fragments from the national anthem are voiced by the mother: "*el mar es salado*, helado. También es compatriota e *ilustre en nuestra patria* y enemigo crucial del barrio. Es un consejo, algo muy tierno que emana del hueco de tu madre" / "the sea is salty, freezing. Also a compatriot and illustrious one in our nation and crucial enemy of the barrio. It is advice, something very tender that emanates from the hollow of your mother."[40] At another point, Eltit parodies the official discourse where the mother serves as an ideal for the furthering of nationalistic sentiments:

AUDIENCIA Y PAZ A UNA NOTORIA MENTIRA CHILENA DE MI MADRE.
BUSQUEMOS A LA MAMA MEJOR DEL MUNDO QUE ESTA EN ESTE PAIS.

> la mía:
>> cayó parida del cielo por Dios Padre.
>> parada en el suelo (92-93).

[AUDIENCE AND PEACE FOR A NOTORIOUS CHILEAN LIE OF MY MOTHER'S.
LET US LOOK FOR THE BEST MOTHER IN THE WORLD WHO IS IN THIS COUNTRY.

> mine:
>> fell born of the heavens by God the Father.
>> standing on the ground.]

The maternal ideal is here mocked and regarded as a lie, a discursive invention. These formulations effectively unveil the maternal as not in any way essentially good or bad but as a social construction that serves as a vehicle for articulating a wide range of ideological positions. The maternal, ultimately a figure of the cultural imaginary used to reproduce social relations, is—more than anything else—a reproductive trope. Above all, then, "mother" here serves as a rhetorically adept reproducer of images.

As Munizaga and Ochsensius observe, in the official discourse the maternal function represents the propagation and conservation of the dominant power structures: "her task is thus to serve the government, understanding and supporting it, creating or rather perpetuating the mechanisms of its reproduction" (75). Indeed, as site of social reproduction par excellence, the maternal can wield immense repressive power. Likewise, the accusing, moralizing mother appears often in *Por la patria*, revealing just such a function of the mother as the guardian and reproducer of the social order. Berta's mother, for example, tells how she trained her daughter for passivity: "I prepared her for nothing, so that nothing would happen to her . . ." (125). Berta, however, does not follow her mother's instructions whereupon the mother's accusation is of a sexual and political transgression enacted specifically against maternal orders (125). The mother's reproach and judgment is harsh: "No. It will be a lesson for her. There is no signature or amnesty for her" (130). The maternal thus functions in certain places of *Por la patria* as a conservative force, as the voice of the status quo, undeniably on the side of law and order.

As keeper of society's foundations, the socially scripted maternal can also be a great source of betrayal. If something is profoundly wrong with society, it is often portrayed as a social disorder specifically generated by female promiscuity.[41] In several sequences near the beginning of *Por la patria*, this function of the mother's body is unveiled. Coya's mother, for example, is portrayed as unfaithful, as leaving the bar with a "zarco" (blue-eyed Caucasian), as collaborating in some way with the oppressors. Yet it is unclear whether she did betray her family or whether that is just the "official story." Juan, struggling to impose his version, would have the mother betraying her family: "'No,' said Juan. It happened this way, take note: The mother, who was a dancer and an expert, was seduced by the blue-eyed one who did not give up until he convinced her and squashed the whole family in telling her that she was above them" (48). There are various versions of the mother's role here as Coya and Juan battle for interpretative power. Coya insists that her mother is lost in the chaos of the military attack ("'My mother fell in the round-up'") while Juan counters her version with his own: "'Your mother got out before the round-up'"(49). But no matter which version one would accept, the various references to the unfaithfulness of the mother in *Por la patria* and the very use of the maternal figure as the site for such an interpretative struggle, testify to the mother as potential source of social disarray—a social disarray Eltit would seem to appropriate as a source of potentially subversive power.

Yet such an appropriation is not without its own problems due, perhaps, to the profound ambivalence associated with the maternal. The mother figure, albeit originator of life, often seems dangerous, even deadly. The Madres 1–6, appearing oneirically as black birds ("cuervos"), are sources of both life and death: "Tras la carroña llegó preparada de duelo al luto. Lujo traía lana para su expansión materna" / "In search of carrion she appeared prepared in grief for mourning. Luxury she brought wool for her maternal expansion" (39). Feeding on death and yet givers of life, the mothers in this section carry weapons, threatening to kill the son as they accuse him of incestuous desire as well as incite him to further transgression. This chorus of maternal voices, like the Fates, includes and controls all the possibilities for man's destiny.

Furthermore, even though the maternal represents a promise of refuge, a nostalgic drive toward a nurturing, all-encompassing love, this model is represented as imperfect, as a dysfunctional relationship where the mother is a source of violence and oppression. For instance, when Coya's mother pleads with her, "Love me," Coya responds: "We are at war" (144). Likewise, when Coya asks for the mother's love, she is similarly rejected: "'Love me,' I said. 'We are at war,' answered the rabid bitch" (146). The dysfunctional family in this way serves as a metonymical figure for the national siege, the political crisis. The maternal figure is often scripted as holding some hope for salvation, offering some type of relief, only to rise up against the already victimized child. One particular scene, a repetitive nightmare of Flora's, illustrates just this situation. The wounded child approaches her mother in the hopes of receiving some comfort, some healing caress, but, instead, just as she leans forward to receive the mother's comforting touch: "Her mother's hand rises up from her legs to hit her in the head: 'you are a stupid girl Flora, you're like an animal, you don't even look where you are going' her mother stands there and her head twists with the slap . . ." (229).[42] Thus, far from offering a viable alternative to the paternal utopia, maternal nostalgia is equally fraught with the difficulties, the violence, the frustrations of any formulation already inscribed in our social realm.

Ultimately, the maternal function is central in *Por la patria*, and also highly ambivalent, because it is the imaginary site of social and sexual reproduction. The maternal is both original object of desire as the child's first sensual attachment and source (collaborator, instrument) of social indoctrination and repression. In this way, the portrayal of the maternal function in *Por la patria* is polyvalent and protean because that is how the maternal has been socially inscribed. Never ascribing any original, presocial traits to the maternal, Eltit rather shows the maternal itself to be an *effect*, a production of social discourse. If the father has been the univocal subject presumed to know, the "I am who I am" of signification, the maternal has been the protean "other" used to prop up that univocality. Both inside and outside power structures, the mother is an "other," which has potential for becoming outlaw. Indeed, if the maternal is where the cultural imaginary reproduces itself, what better place to break current structures and reimagine new ones, what better place to launch a transgressive challenge to the regime.

In many ways, the textual reconnection to the mother's body in *Por la patria* implies both a rethinking of national roots and a new narrative practice that would entail a *re-membering* of the connections between body, memory, and language, connections that are dis-articulated and dis-membered by the reigning regime and its menacing, masculinist representative, Juan. The mother, as object of desire, seems to offer a means for rebirth, a return to origins, but a return that is continually frustrated. In an oneiric and evocative sequence titled "The Ecstasy of Maternal Love," there is an attempt to know and understand maternity, to reconnect with the maternal body, to reinhabit the repressed feminine/maternal realm. At the mother's urging, Coya tries to transgress the bodily division between child and mother:

Trató de meterme para adentro.

Traté de entrar y no cupe.

No pude el hueco excavar. Yo pujaba y ella contraía:

—Métete, me dice, empecemos esto de nuevo (180).

[She tried to push me inside.

I tried to go in and did not fit.

I could not excavate the hole. I would push and she would contract:

"Go in," she tells me, "let us begin this again."]

Yet, a return to the womb, to cultural origins, a rebirth of the nation, is impossible to accomplish by going back: "I butted with my head again and again and the intense pain to her who opened the hole with her own hands and the two of us were crying in the face of the impossible, the callousness of God" (181). This scene enacts the tragic impotence of nostalgia, representing and exorcising the nostalgic model of a return to the maternal. As ritual performance, it represents a desire for rebirth (which implies a rebirth of memory, language, and the nation) and yet tragically shows the irrecuperability of the lost paradise of the womb. This scene also has an erotic component, and when Coya dreams the encounter not as child but as mother, it takes on an especially sensual quality:

Me sube la falda y mi pierna se eriza engranujada. La niña brilla y sus dedos tiemblan cuando intentan subir, tocar en profundidad mi reducto heredado . . . (182).

[She raises my skirt and my leg bristles with gooseflesh. The girl shines and her fingers tremble when they try to go up, to touch deeply my inherited refuge . . . .]

This scene enacts a transgression of the incest taboo as an allegory of the transgression of the father's law, of the sociopolitical as well as sexual order. The force that interrupts this sexual encounter is none other than Juan, patriarchal imposter, jailer, and representative of the regime of law and order: "Juan . . . interrupts just when my thighs were opening to the spectacle. He pushes her reproaching her and with his tongue he starts cleaning the previous trail, erasing it . . ." (182). Nonetheless, in spite of the intervention of Juan and failure to consummate this act, the maternal remains a locus of potential transgression, a source of subversive possibilities, and the transgressive performance enacted here still represents, in some way, a step on the way to transformation.

Ultimately, writing is key to this movement between transgression and transformation. Indeed, Coya's transformation has mainly to do with language, with a collective *habla*, and with the possibilities of narrative. As she works through the dysfunctional family romance and the ruins of national collapse, Coya assumes the function of Madre General, a new source of an epic of the margins, remembering ties between motherhood, memory, and language to launch her own narrative of resistance. Coya moves—albeit intermittently—from desire for the mother to being the mother, repeating the maternal role but with a critical difference. Through a complex rite of passage, Coya becomes the mother of all mothers, assumes the position of mother to lead the epic battle. "Now Coya was queen and mother of mothers and she initiated her battle. In front of the pyre, the women humbled themselves, while the father and predecessor went up the flights of steps and confessed his offenses in full" (104). Through this confessionary ritual, this sacrificial rite, a redemptive epic is launched. The father places a ring on Coya's finger signifying, as Eugenia Brito has pointed out, her utopian union with him. The apocalyptic air ("hiroshima" 105) of the epic is center stage, yet it is all very self-consciously a "simulacrum" (105), a production put into play in order to show how the Chilean *pueblo* can resist oppression. This resistance is figured as simultaneously political and sexual: "En el pubis mío la comezón del acero y en el centro pubial y nupcial el odio contra la patria: CHILE-NO, grité el levantamiento. Y le largué una última mirada de deseo a mi madre la vasta bastarda. Partí" / "In my pubis the scratch of steel and in the pubial and nuptial center the hatred against the fatherland: "CHILE-NO," I shouted the call to arms. And I cast a final gaze of desire toward my mother the vast bastard. I departed." (106). The desire for the mother is worked through, inhabited, spent. The "NO" here is envisioned as a battle cry against both the national and the psychosexual order. Coya, as madre general, listens to testimony and takes on the role of a repository of collective memory. "'You,' I ordered him, 'are going to give a testimony,'" pronounces Coya and then describes her role in this testimonial act: "Mi ojo era una luz que imprimía de imágenes paternas la pared del fondo del bar. En el contramuro, desde los extramuros mi garganta le dio voz, le devolvió su vocalidad" / "My eye was a light that imprinted the wall at the back of the bar with paternal images. On the opposite wall, from outside, my throat gave him voice, returned his vocality to him" (107). In this way Coya/Coa becomes the medium for the transmission, for the projection of this voice of the victim of the regime. It is thus through Coya's giving voice to the margins that resistance can become possible.

But it is through the act of writing the margins that such a voice achieves its full potential. The reader soon realizes in part II that Coya has begun writing and that the previous section, "Testimonies, Speeches, Documents, Manifestos," is explicitly the product of Coya's visionary writings: "Elaboro parlamentos, me elaboro levitada" / "I elaborate speeches, I elaborate myself levitated" (194). As this expression reveals, Coya functions as both author and text, writing herself in an act of self-generation. Taking on the task of writing the passion play of Chile, Coya acts as mystical medium, memory incarnate: "Soy el último reducto mantengo intacta la memoria colectiva y metalizada" / "I am the last refuge I maintain the collective memory intact and metalized" (247). *Por la patria* is thus "todo una gran copia, un sustituto, una toma colectiva del habla" / "an entire great copy, a substitute, a collective taking of speech" (199). This "habla" is the voice of resistance, produced and yet not limited by the official demand of the torturers:

Habla, habla, habla.
. . .

                    Hay un zarco irónico y derrumbado
        habla, habla, habla (172)

[Speak, speak, speak.
. . .

                There is a blue-eyed one, ironic and down-cast
        speak, speak, speak]

Coya's "habla" / "speech" is a defiant response to this brutal demand for a confession: "Que hablen, que hablen, que hablen, llenando de voces la gran pieza y por la claraboya central . . ." / "Let them speak, speak, speak, filling with voices the great room and the central skylight . . ." (199–200). Coya's spectacle of common speech violently resists Juan's and the zarcos'/soldados' attempted erasure of the collective memory. Yet, it is Coya's writing that makes the re-production of such a spectacle possible. Writing becomes not only an act of individual resistance, but a vehicle for solidarity and collective action: "Sentada al borde de la cama voy ordenando cada uno de los parlamentos, para darles voz, preparando para ellas una actividad, otra oportunidad sobre el vacío del lugar abarrotado saturado de camas y de plañidos inútiles y reiterados" / "Sitting on the edge of the bed I am ordering each one of the speeches, to give them voice, preparing an activity for them, another opportunity over the emptiness of the crowded place saturated with beds and laments, useless and reiterated" (194). When she gives what she is writing to Berta, Coya observes that "I have given her sustenance, that Berta walks like when the icy barricades were set aflame by bonfires" (195). This writing of the national catastrophe is also a re-writing of the family romance: "Speeches, documents, manifestos. I always speak of the new things of infancy, of the amazingly decadent style of the fatherland" (199). The dysfunctional family romance, however, is not merely a metaphor for the national crisis. It is in the telling of this simulacrum, in the inventing of this allegory, that the women gain the force, garner the strength necessary to rebel against not only their political imprisonment but also against their sexual oppression. The allegory of the marginal neighborhood ("the allegory of the barrio" 185) that Coya writes from the prison has a galvanizing effect on the women prisoners. As she recounts her proposed allegorical narrative, "the other women begin to understand and they smile. . . . The consents multiply, one by one they commit themselves" (200). We could perhaps say, then, that *Por la patria* ultimately is an allegory of the powers of allegory, an allegory of the politicoethical capacities of fiction and of writing itself.

In the end, the maternal plays a key if ambivalent role in the liberation envisioned by *Por la patria*. Indeed, the otherness of the mother's body becomes, in some ways, the privileged site for the refoundation Coya seeks, a refoundation of Latin American culture and social subjectivity itself: "Widow of my father, widow of my mother, in mourning, I withdraw to my own origin, prior to the bar, enraged in the dark jungle of my mother" (260). Clearly, the goal in such a refoundation is not to establish a matriarchy in the place of the patriarchal, authoritarian regime that keeps the women imprisoned in part II of the novel. The maternal must also be exorcised in all its oppressive and opportunistic manifestations, as we have seen. After sexually coupling with both the mother and the father, Coya finally rends through both, becoming "widow" of both. Nonetheless, the maternal body does provide a base in Coya's vision of refoundation, as is evidenced by her reference to "the dark jungle of my mother."

It is perhaps the most bodily associations of the maternal that serve as an instrument in the liberation Coya seeks. Indeed, it is specifically an intensified attention to the body that Coya uses in order to unveil the phallic, disembodied power of Juan and, by extension, authoritarian power itself. At the end of the text, in "Memory," Juan's ruin and the fall of the regime become inevitable as Coya remembers and names the male body used to exercise his power: "I forgot that to which you cling and behind which you prevail: I forgot your body" (273). His body has been used to abuse her and control her: "I forgot the rhythm you had, the brusque movements you gave me: the saliva, the tongue, the bite, your head buried in me, looking for your father, for your mother, for yourself. I forget that to which you cling in order to contain me" (274). Since Juan's power depends on a disembodied transcendence to which he can never really lay claim, Coya's remembering his body finally topples his (always tenuous) hold on power, a power that has kept the women imprisoned and, by extension, that has maintained the Chilean people in a state of silence and terror.

Nonetheless, her denunciation is not limited to sexual oppression but applies to a more collective victimization; she tells Juan in her declaration, "no longer will you be able to retain me like you have done in this indescribable, incredible time for us" (274). While Eltit certainly denounces the oppression of women here, her critique is not limited to sexual abuse. It is in order to name the state of victimhood caused by Chile's political violence, in order to give voice to the margins (to which all others—not only women—are relegated), that Eltit reappropriates and rearticulates the feminine. Gender politics and sexual abuse thus refer metonymically to the victimization of the margins at large. Coya tells Juan:

Me has encerrado con mi corte desterrando.

Reduciéndome a las mujeres, privando mi horizonte para llegar tú y ocupar el lugar de los muchachos movedizos (274).

[You have enclosed me with my retinue, banishing.

Reducing me to the women, depriving my horizon in order for you to arrive and occupy the place of the shifting young men.]

In this way, *Por la patria* refers to how the authoritarian power held its own by virtually feminizing its subjects ("reducing" it to women), usurping all the power (a masculine prerogative), and taking the place of the only man (Juan, the singular and univocal male character).

But Juan and the authoritarian model fall as Coya finds her voice, as she declares this liberation, as the marginalized are transformed into a more regal and less subaltern "corte," refusing these set gender roles which would leave them powerless and voiceless: "You erred. You erred because my retinue has taken on all roles . . ." (274). Coya's liberation thus has to do not with installing a matriarchy but with breaking down the strict, hierarchical, sexually coded roles. She strives, rather, to remain dual, bisexual, double-voiced, neither entirely subjected nor supreme subject: "Yo erecta, erguida y doble soy: punzando y recibiendo, mojando y mojada, desmaterna y despaterna, desprendida ya" / "I, erect, straightened up, and double, am: pricking and receiving, wetting and wet, dismaternal and dispaternal, detached now" (273). Her call is not merely to reverse the patriarchal order and declare the maternal a new ideal. Coya serves, as we have seen, as a figure for language itself; hence her goal is not to remain isolated as a "maternal language" but to encompass all, reclaiming the feminine, but not limited to it. In this way, she seems to call for a new subjectivity that would not exclude the feminine but would transform the feminine and the maternal into sites of resistance and new sociopolitical possiblities. Coya tells her fellow prisoners, "women, we are leaving, we have amnesty" (276); and when they are finally liberated, they form a virtual army of mothers, but mothers who would lend new meaning to their maternal status: "Me sentí rodeada de un ejército de madres, caminando por calles extrañas. Somos veinte, pensé, veinte rangos en disputa por la carga que ganamos, por esa obstinada resistencia que tuvimos. Somos madre general y madre 1, 2, 3, 4, 5, 6, al destrone de las viejas y el nuevo símbolo de la parición invertida . . ." / "I felt surrounded by an army of mothers, walking through strange streets. We are twenty, I thought, twenty ranks in dispute for the charge we won, for that obstinate resistance we maintained. We are mother general and mother 1, 2, 3, 4, 5, 6, upon the overthrow of the old women and the new symbol of the inverted birthing . . ." (277). Thus, this new maternal, out to overthrow the old models, still functions as a subversive, productive trope capable of challenging what remains of the dominant social structure.[43]

Yet, the ending of *Por la patria* does not offer a utopian view of absolute transcendence. Rather, the final scene portrays the moment that a subaltern subjectivity finally becomes viable, albeit riddled with ambiguities and limitations:

> Vimos el continente y fuimos otra vez combatientes y hermanas, humanas casi.
>
> Hablé extenso, feliz, prudente y generosa:
>
> —Se abre el bar, mujeres. Lo abrimos, lo administramos con jerarquía (279).
>
> [We saw the continent and we were again combatants and sisters, human almost.
>
> I spoke at length, happy, prudent, and generous:
>
> "The bar is open, women. We open it, we administer it with hierarchy."]

Their freedom is by no means absolute; but they are finally almost human ("humanas casi"), and as they reopen the bar, coming full circle, they have taken possession of it, refounding a distinctly feminine structure that they will administer "con jerarquía," which they will in some way control. From the ashes of the national catastrophe a new epic surges forth: "The fire, the fire, the fire and the epic" (279). And in the face of the numbing, disembodied and mechanistic violence, this new birth implies a freeing and exultation of the somatic realm: "volvía a sentir: volví a sentir sobre el erial, superpuesta a mi niñez. Todas soltamos el cuerpo y las manos móviles y diestras" / "I was feeling once more: I began to feel once more upon the untilled land, superimposed on my childhood. We all let our bodies loose and our hands mobile and dexterous" (279). Thus, *Por la patria* ends with a vision of a new beginning, a new collectivity, defined and driven not by passivity and silent survival, but a lusty and insaciable thirst: "Y la sed se apoderó de ellas" / "And the thirst took hold of them" (279). In this way, the bar where they had been terrorized by the military and that once signified their marginalization and oppression now becomes a place of powerful possibilities, having been virtually re-written by Coya/Coa such that the solidarity, heroism, linguistic richness, and desire that inhabit that marginal realm are not erased. In the end, then, *Por la patria* succeeds in re-imagining and re-writing the margins. Through its transgressive linguistic experimentalism, its bitter indictment of political oppression, its reaffirmation of the feminine, as well as its insistence on the inclusion of the bodily realm, *Por la patria* effectively transforms the subaltern, the feminine, the *mestizo*, the social outcast into textual identities capable of assuming a social subjectivity of their own.

FROM SILENCE TO SUBJECTIVITY: READING AND WRITING IN REINA ROFFÉ'S *LA ROMPIENTE*

hay aquí un silencio oscuro
que nada tiene que ver con el silencio

[there is a dark silence here
that has nothing to do with silence]

—Liliana Lukin
Descomposición

Yo soy para mí misma una hipótesis,
una realidad en elaboración, una síntesis
provisoria. Soy mi propio esbozo.

[I am, for myself, a hypothesis, a reality
in production, a provisional synthesis. I
am my own sketch.]

—Liliana Mizrahi
La mujer transgresora

Argentine writer Reina Roffé's third novel, *La rompiente* [The Breakwater] (1987), is primarily concerned with breaking both internally and externally imposed silence, with producing a viable female subjectivity through the very processes of reading and writing. Such a project inevitably takes place at the very discursive boundary drawn between public and private, social and personal. The author herself characterizes the text as a personal recollection that inevitably inscribes and is inscribed by its sociopolitical context, that is, the "Process of National Reorganization" as the military regime called its authoritarian rule of Argentina from 1976–83: "*La rompiente* recovers a memory: the memory of a personal itinerary contaminated by the memory of a historical process (the years of the 'Process')" ("Qué escribimos" 213). Such a textual meeting of the personal and the political not only reflects a narrative strategy but also documents Roffé's own painful experience of the conflicts engendered as a writer who necessarily negotiates a path between the subjective and the social. In the prologue of *La rompiente*, called "Itinerario de una escritura" or "Writing Itinerary," Roffé gives a frank account of her narrative career thus far, providing a testimonial point of departure for *La rompiente*. In this preface she describes how her first novel, *Llamado al puf*, was criticized for its excess of subjective (and lack of social) content. Therefore, of her next novel, she says:

> La novela que emprendí después tuvo—ya que escuché con atención—menos "contenido personal" y más "contenido social". *Monte de Venus* fue mi novela "planificada", donde—traicionando el mensaje individual, subjetivo, "femenino"—pretendí hacer una pintura realista de los avatares de una franja social inmersa en y condicionada por las convenciones abso-lutistas que regían la sociedad en general. En apariencia, la pin-tura fue realista, y la intención desafortunadamente acertada, ya que a los pocos días de editado, el libro cayó en la mira de la censura que, de un solo plumazo, firmó la prohibición por inmoralidad y lo retiró de circulación (*La rompiente* 10).

> [The novel that I undertook afterwards had—since I listened carefully—less "personal content" and more "social content." *Monte de Venus* (Mons Veneris) was my "planned" novel, where—betraying the individual, subjective, "feminine" mes-sage—I tried to paint a realistic portrait of the avatars of a social fringe immersed in and conditioned by the absolutist conven-tions that governed society at large. Evidently, the portrait was realistic, and the intention unfortunately accurate, since a few days after appearing in print, the book came to the attention of the censor who, with a stroke of the pen, signed the prohibition due to immorality and withdrew it from circulation.]

Roffé thus moves from a primarily subjectivist story in her first text to a more social history in her second, only to be completely silenced by the authoritarian state.[1]

After being censored and subsequently ignored in Argentina,[2] Roffé spent the next ten years in relative silence and in exile. She has written (and spoken) in various contexts on the effects of this censorship and exile, on the "monsters" engendered by such an experience. In her testimonial prologue, she refers quite eloquently to the various censorships that affect women writers:

Advertí que al espectro de las censuras debía sumarle el de las autocensuras. Como mujer que escribe había recibido el bagaje de una serie de dichos y entredichos: que la escritura femenina carece de nivel simbólico, que está sujeta al referente, que abusa de interrogantes, repeticiones y detalles, que se caracteriza por un tono de enojo y resentimiento. Estigmas que, a la hora de escribir, aterrizan en la mesa de trabajo y se yerguen como sombras ominosas projectadas sobre la blanca superficie del papel. En este sentido, la autocensura que paraliza o anula también produce engendros . . . (*La rompiente* 10).

[I realized that to the specter of censorships I had to add that of self-censorships. As a woman who writes I had received the baggage of a series of proscriptions and expectations: that women's writing lacks a symbolic level, that it is tied to the referent, that it contains an excess of unanswered questions, repetitions and details, that it is characterized by a tone of anger and resentment. Stigmas that, at the moment of writing, land on one's desk and rise up like ominous shadows projected across the blank surface of the paper. In this sense, the self-censorship that paralyzes and de-authorizes also engenders monsters . . .]

Having been told she could not write what she wanted, Roffé was driven to ask herself what it was she wanted to write, only to find her "own" desires and creative impulses diluted and distorted through the series of discursive norms that had always mediated her self-representation. Her discovery is not unlike Irigaray's concerns about the inaccessibility of a feminine desire not determined by masculine parameters (and, consequently, a female imaginary upon/through which to build a female subjectivity). Irigaray laments in *This Sex*: "They have wrapped us for so long in their desires, we have adorned ourselves so often to please them, that we have come to forget the feel of our own skin" ("When Our Lips Speak Together" 218). The price for such a repression of the female imaginary, according to Irigaray, is steep: without access to a feminine desire, women's subjectivity is fragmented or lost, for if women cannot *imagine* what they want, they cannot *say* what they want either (*This Sex* 25; 30; 77). Likewise, Roffé directly addresses the dilemma of feminine desire (of concern to feminists of all persuasions) in a talk presented in Germany after the publication of *La rompiente*. With an oblique reference to Djuna Barnes, she laments that women writers are in a double bind: "As women writers we are in an uncomfortable place: we cannot integrate ourselves into our era; we cannot help but threaten it, but nor can we create another cosmovision. It is because our books, for the time being, do not definitively destroy the old myths about woman created by men" ("Qué escribimos" 208). Still subject to normative representations of Woman that make expressions of a feminine desire *not* determined by the masculine difficult if not impossible, not yet able to elaborate a system of representation of her own that would enable such expression, the woman writer struggles, in Sally Robinson's terms, between repetition and resistance. Roffé affirms in the same talk that the task at hand for women writers is not simply a question of "writing the body" but rather of finding new ways of writing women's experience not limited to the traditional representations of Womanhood: "it is not a question of 'writing the body,' but of woman being able to express femininity in a way different from the one imposed upon her, because otherwise it is a body masquerading as feminine that, undressed, reveals itself in relation to masculinity."[3] What Roffé is calling for, in effect, is the creation of a female imaginary, such that female desire and its expression become possible.

So, for Roffé as for so many contemporary feminist thinkers, women writers strive to write themselves as not only *subject to* socially determined representations of women but also as *subjects of* new, resistant representations. For the woman writing under dictatorship, this entails a double struggle since she works under a twofold silencing: one imposed on her by the normative representations of Woman and the other by the authoritarian state. It is from this conflicted and conflictive space of double censorship that Roffé launches her narrative. The impulse that drives *La rompiente* is, thus, the necessity of finding a voice or a subjectivity that could both document and break the censorships of the state as well as those of the normative representations of Woman, and that could resist (in Roffé's own words) "the internal fetters" and "the external fetters" ("Qué escribimos" 211). The strategy Roffé uses in order to find this voice of her own seems akin to the method Dennis Lee describes in his article about postcolonial writing in general: "The impasse of writing that is problematic to itself is transcended only when the impasse becomes its own subject, when writing accepts and enters and names its own condition as it is naming the world."[4] In a similar way, Roffé articulates the conditions of her writing: after being forced into silence, she inhabits that silence to the maximum and then, in turn, writes it as what both undermines and subtends her own writing practices.

While Roffé's project certainly involves such a search for a voice or language of her own, she does not, as we shall see, "find" an already formed subjectivity, but rather "produces" a gendered subjectivity through the act of reading and writing. As Sally Robinson has suggested, subjectivity is not a "being" but a "doing," both product and process at once.[5] Similarly, Argentine psychologist Liliana Mizrahi has detailed the importance of process, of "the subject as the task of subjectivity itself" (51), in her influential book, *La mujer transgresora* [The Transgressing Woman]. She points out that for women to assume both the "agent" and "actor" aspects of subjectivity, they must actively and transgressively engage with previous cultural representations of Woman (what she calls the "ancestral woman") in order for the necessary transformation to become possible. For Mizrahi, a viable subjectivity is dynamic not static:

> La mujer como creadora cotidiana de su propia identidad es un verdadero agente de cambio. La dinámica de este proceso de cambio no significa ni decapitar ni extirpar lo atávico sino reconocerlo y reubicarlo dentro de nuestro proyecto de vida. *Es del desarrollo reflexivo de la conciencia crítica sobre lo ancestral de donde surge la fuerza transgresora capaz de transformar nuestra historia* (86; emphasis added).

> [The woman as creator of her own identity is a true agent of change. The dynamic of this process of change does not mean decapitating or eradicating the atavistic but recognizing it and re-placing it within our life project. *It is from the reflective development of a critical consciousness of the ancestral that the transgressive force capable of transforming our history emerges.*]

For Roffé as well, subjectivity is both process and product at the same time, literally constituted through her critical engagement with the multiple narratives and discourses of her social context. In fact, Roffé achieves the effect of a subjectivity that encompasses both aspects of acting (that is, both acting as "actor"—subject *to a* social script—as well as acting as "agent"—subject *of* modifications and alterations in the script) through a delicate balance of transgressing and repeating norms on the levels of reading and writing.[6] Authorship is thus produced as a struggle, as always negotiated between repetition and resistance, as something formed in the space between writer and reader, speaker and listener. Indeed, it is primarily in the acts of reading and writing, in the various gestures of reading and writing performed in *La rompiente*, that Roffé locates the transformation she needs to construct a subjectivity of her own.

In this chapter I follow Roffé's readerly/writerly itinerary in *La rompiente* in order to show how she plots a path out of censorship toward a viable female subjectivity. Since the novel is divided into three distinct sections, I will treat them separately, finally discussing part 3 with regard to the transformations enacted in the text as a whole. Throughout the three parts, the subject of the story line shifts continuously creating a constant displacement of the narrative voice.[7] In the first part, an anonymous and ambiguous narrator (at once ideal interlocutor, analyst, and confessor) retells the protagonist's story to her, recounting her arrival in a foreign country as a political exile. In the second part, the narrative shifts and the former "listener" occupies the position of narrator (at the former narrator's urgings) in order to read aloud and comment upon the novel she wrote while in exile about the "years of silence" in her native country. This section thus constitutes a breaking of that enforced silence and an exploration of the possibilities of representing censorship and repression. In the third section the original narrator takes up the other's voice once again to retell the various and fragmentary events in the protagonist's native country which led up to her flight into exile.

The entire novel, in all its concern with reading and writing, also alludes allegorically to "another" story, glimpsed by a non-Argentine reader such as myself but patently obvious to the Argentine reader such as María Teresa Gramuglio who wrote the postscript included in *La rompiente*. At the end of her brief but suggestive analysis of the text, Gramuglio turns to the story that is not told in *La rompiente* but that can be read:

En los años del silencio, de las guerras sucias y los lavados de almas, una mujer se vincula con un grupo (¿de jugadores? ¿literario?) cuyo funcionamiento tiene vagas semejanzas con el de una organización celular. Uno de sus compañeros (¿el profe-

sor? ¿el ex-seminarista?) anuncia, una tarde, que se cree seguido
y vigilado. Poco tiempo después desaparece (¿muere?) y sus
amigos, asustados, queman, con rabia y con vergüenza, libros y
revistas que puede ser peligroso conservar. Hay razzias en bares,
sirenas policiales, miedo. Una serie de encuentros aparente-
mente casuales con 'el estudiante', un antiguo compañero de la
Facultad, hacen sospechar a la mujer que ella también es
seguida y vigilada. Un día ve al 'estudiante' dirigiendo un proceso policial. Acosada por sus miedos y por sus imposibilidades,
la mujer, finalmente, se va de su país (134).

[In the years of silence, of dirty wars and the laundering of
souls, a woman joins a group (of players? of literati?) whose
function has vague similarities with that of a political cell. One
of the comrades (the professor? the ex-seminarian?) announces,
one afternoon, that he believes he is being watched and followed. A short time later he disappears (he dies?) and his
friends, scared, burn, with anger and shame, books and maga-
zines that could be dangerous to keep. There are shakedowns in
bars, police sirens, fear. A series of apparently casual encounters
with "the student," an old classmate from the university, make
the woman suspect that she too is being followed and watched.
One day she sees the "student" directing a police operation.
Hounded by her fears and her impossibilities, the woman,
finally, leaves the country.]

While such a story can certainly be read, as Gramuglio has convincingly (and helpfully) shown, it is not the story Roffé has chosen to
tell explicitly. Rather, the author focuses on the interior transformations of the protagonist, the process of breaking the silences
imposed by both implicit and explicit social authorities. The story
Gramuglio retells is thus read (allegorically) as the "other" story,
the story told only as a trace of the more explicit narrative.

Such "reading between the lines" perhaps typifies the literary
experiences of readers and writers in the aftermath of authoritarianism. Later in her article, for example, Gramuglio observes, "So when
I read a scene with the tables of a sidewalk café facing a cemetery,
and someone says looking toward the other side 'I think I'm being
followed,' I can only ask myself how, by whom, from where, can
these enunciations be read. Is anything more even necessary for us?"
(135). It is worth pointing out, however, that Roffé's text makes no
explicit reference to the cemetery per se, only to a café in a fashion-

able area of the city where a religious procession passes by (55). And yet, as Grumuglio's reading demonstrates, for a reader familiar enough with the social milieu of the novel, this is clearly a reference to La Recoleta in Buenos Aires where there are two cafés frequented by literati directly across the street from the cemetery. This is, perhaps, a lesson in reading in context, showing how the referent and meaning are negotiated, partially articulated by the writer, picked up and completed by the reader, in the process of what amounts to the building of a collective memory.

Opting for a narrative that requires just such reading in context, Roffé resists the coherent, linear, "other" narrative read for us by Gramuglio. She explains:

> La resistencia al 'gran relato', al 'testimonio documental', a la 'historia completa', más que una opción deliberada de escritura y una imputación a la narración realista fue el resultado de mostrar los cabos sueltos del yo de la protagonista, la mujer fragmentada que va venciendo el silencio, que va encontrando la unidad a través de los lazos tenues de su respiración cortada, de sus pedazos dispersos ("Qué escribimos" 213).

> [The resistance to the "master narrative," to the "documental testimony," to the "complete (hi)story," more than a deliberate option of writing and an indictment of realist narrative, was the result of showing the loose ends of the "I" of the protagonist, the fragmented woman who is conquering silence, who is encountering unity through the tenuous ties of her disjointed breathing, of her scattered pieces.]

Indeed, the narrative strategies and the textual material of *La rompiente* could be seen as symptoms of the censorships women writers are subjected to and as a creative path plotted out of those symptoms. Yet, this is not to propose censorship as the only signified of the text. While Roffé's novel can certainly be read as a symptom of and a response to censorship, it also inscribes a desire to write the multifarious experiences and feelings that authoritarian discourse attempts to homogenize or to render superfluous. For Roffé, reading and writing respond to yet also *exceed* sociopolitical constraints, forming a type of self-affirmative "intimate resistance," a personal, yet powerful luxury that she views as a "a secret *power* that no one had the *power* to snatch away from me. . . . It was like saying: I can, in spite of everything."[8]

Subject to Censorship: Reading and Writing (in) Silence

In part 1 of *La rompiente* an intimate interlocutor (or analyst or "confessor") retells the protagonist's story back to her: the story of her arrival in a new country (certain traits of which suggest the United States) as a political exile, her missed encounter with an old friend or lover, her friendship and dialogue with "Miss Key." The narrator thus constructs the history of the protagonist, having evidently "listened to" her and read her diary ("last night I read your diary, the margin notes?—sorry—, what you call the *líneas de fuerza*" 27).[9] So the narrative discourse remits to another previous utterance on the part of the imagined protagonist, relating the story of her arrival in exile without yet narrating the political and personal events that provoked her departure from her native country. In fact, these events are not narrated until the third section of the novel. The effect on the reader of such an assault on the habitual temporal and spatial coherence of narrative is a sense of dislocation, of fragmentation, of confusion. This is precisely the desired effect, I would argue, in order to begin to narrate the rupture, the alienation, and the silence produced in the protagonist by her experience as a woman writing under authoritarianism.

The novel begins with a disembodied narrative voice: "Habló de una música de fondo, dijo: . . ." / "[He/she/you] spoke about a background music, [he/she/you] said: . . ." (15).[10] In Spanish it is acceptable usage to omit explicit reference to the subject of a verb if the subject has already been established. But by omitting explicit references to the subjects of the verbs "habló" and "dijo," the narrative begins by implying a previously established context whereby the subjects could be implicitly understood. Furthermore, the identities of the respective subjects of these verbs remain unclear at this point. As María Teresa Gramuglio observes, with this phrase the text immediately introduces an ambiguity: "did someone say that another spoke, or do 'spoke' and 'said' refer to the same subject?" (129). *La rompiente* further breaks with narrative conventions and exacerbates this ambiguity by introducing the use of "usted" (the formal "you," which takes the same verb form as "he" and "she") a few lines later. In this way, we find a constant undecidability of subject and object positions in the narrative as the novel metamorphoses in a complex game of ventriloquism where the positions of narrator, reader, writer, and listener are constantly conflated. *La rompiente* thus immediately produces a fragmentary subjectivity such that the protagonist occupies an object position (the narrator addresses him/herself *to her*) as well as a subject position (in that she has already told her story to the narrator). But that subject position has been, if not entirely erased, at least obscured almost beyond recognition. It is, ultimately, her story, mediated and controlled by an/other voice; a *mise en abîme* that serves as a virtual emblem of the effects of an imposed silence that disarticulates the subject, turning it in upon itself, at once multiplying, marginalizing, and obscuring its voices.

Such fragmentation and disidentity operate on many levels in the first section of the text: the lack of traditional temporal and spatial sequencing, the discombobulating question of who is speaking and to whom. The deliberate problematization of identity extends to generic ambiguity as well. Is the narrator/interlocutor male or female? No textual indicators point us in either direction, leaving it to the reader to imagine the sexual identity of the narrator.[11] Such generic ambiguity extends somewhat to the protagonist herself; on her arrival in the airport a stewardess approaches her, "confundiéndola quizá con un maletero novato o una discapacitada mental" / "confusing her perhaps with a new (male) porter or a mentally impaired (female)" (16). Certainly, the reader never doubts that the protagonist is a woman (after all, "confundiéndo*la*" / "confusing *her*" assures her sexual identity). This undecidability refers, rather, to how she is *seen* in this foreign place, to her status as displaced person as she arrives in a foreign country, to the disidentity generated by the state of exile. A much more acute generic ambiguity exists with relation to the person who was to meet her "on the other side." Referred to repeatedly as "esa vieja amistad o ese amor postergado" / "that old friend or that postponed love," both the affective identity (friend or lover?) and the sexual identity of this character are thrown into question.[12] The possibility that the "old friend" / "postponed love" could be a woman, and hence potential lesbian lover, is certainly not ruled out and indeed seems to be deliberately enhanced by so carefully eliding any reference to gender identity.[13] In many ways then, *La rompiente* transgresses narrative conventions having to do with "the absurd entelechy of identity" (17), enacting the crisis of identity produced by censorship and exile.

Indeed, this section of the novel serves as a virtual *mise-en-scène* of how subjectivity and identity have been torn apart, fragmented, or (at least) problematized due to the effects of the authoritarian regime. The protagonist has told her interlocutor: "There is nothing more vile than the violence of silence" (28) and, as such, the effects and aftermath of this "violence of silence" are explored at every textual turn. One such aftereffect is the overwhelming sense of discommunication and disconnectedness that the protagonist has described to her interlocutor. This discommunication is literally enacted by their lopsided, dysfunctional dialogue in part I where it always seems that one side of the sound is turned to "off," proof, in fact, that such disconnectedness is not only externally determined but has continued with the protagonist into exile. As the protagonist had observed, upon her arrival in what would appear to be New York City: "You were neither more nor less isolated than before and things were neither more nor less sordid in this place than in the one you had abandoned twenty-four hours ago" (21). The fact is that this incommunication, isolation, and fragmentation have been internalized by the protagonist, infiltrating and disarticulating any sense of inner, subjective coherence. She has mused to her interlocutor: "What was the use of scribbling ideas that stank of asphyxia, of speaking of self-absorption with pretentions of an inner life that, in reality, was the remains of an accumulation of waste" (24). While this certainly refers to the effect of the censorship and repression of the authoritarian regime, it also bears resemblance to how Luce Irigaray has described the plight of women in general: "The rejection, the exclusion of a female imaginary certainly puts woman in the position of experiencing herself only fragmentarily, in the little-structured margins of a dominant ideology, as waste, or excess, what is left of a mirror invested by the (masculine) 'subject' to reflect himself, to copy himself."[14] What both Roffé's protagonist's lament and Irigaray's analysis point to is the effects of censorship and repression on the imaginary.

La rompiente demonstrates from the first, then, that the "years of silence" wreak their havoc not only externally but internally as well, making the "doing" of subjectivity a nearly impossible task, paralyzing social agency through rigid proscriptions, fear of reprisals, and mandated pleasures and desires. Indeed, the discourse of authoritarianism sets up clear, intractable, and non-negotiable limits as to the accepted Argentine community, organizing an entire system of inclusions and exclusions.[15] By the same token, this discourse operates to obliterate an active or agential aspect of subjectivity, as Beatriz Sarlo explains:

El discurso autoritario . . . es transubjetivo, porque ni los grupos ni los individuos están en condiciones de pensarse respecto de los valores impuestos. Por el contrario, son pensados por ellos, son constituidos a partir de ellos y cualquier distancia supone, automáticamente, la exclusión de ese universo y, en consecuencia, la conversión en Otro, ante quien se abre la amenaza de supresión o aislamiento (38).

[Authoritarian discourse . . . is trans-subjective, because neither the groups nor the individuals are in any condition to think for themselves with respect to the values imposed. On the contrary, they are thought by those values, they are constituted through them and any distance supposes, automatically, the exclusion from that universe and, in consequence, the conversion into Other, before whom is opened the threat of suppression or isolation.]

For writers and intellectuals in general, then, the reduction of possibilities for social exchange (in cafés and bookstores for example) and the constant threat of being actively silenced and excluded, create a profound sense of isolation, such that the writer of this generation is "obligated to feel 'alone before his own voice.'"[16] Roffé in particular, through the censoring of *Monte de Venus*, was actively isolated and suppressed, virtually made into that "other" Sarlo talks about. Roffé describes the tactics undertaken when she was censored:

El periodismo me silenció; el editor no sólo hizo desaparecer del depósito los ejemplares que quedaban, sino que al libro y a mí nos eliminó del catálogo; los libreros apuraron las devoluciones, y hasta los amigos escogieron no mencionar la novela. Por otro lado, algunos señores se me acercaron para averiguar con mucha curiosidad cuán 'inmoral' era yo; y ciertas señoras se alejaron de mí ni bien se enteraron de que era una escritora prohibida, alguien que podía comprometerlas o contagiarlas de quién sabe qué rara peste ("Omnipresencia" 915).

[The press silenced me; the editor not only made the remaining copies disappear but also eliminated the book—and me—from the catalogue; the booksellers rushed to return their copies and even my friends chose not to mention the novel. On the other hand, some gentlemen approached me to see just how "immoral" I was; and some ladies retreated from me as soon as they found out I was a forbidden writer, someone who could compromise them or infect them with who knows what kind of strange plague.]

Rather than viewing her marginalization as a purely sociopolitical issue, or imagining her "true" self as beyond the censor's reach, Roffé recognizes a continuum between such experiences of literary censorship and other experiences of being subjected to and silenced by genderic norms.[17] Realizing that, as a woman writer, she had always been subject to censorship, albeit less explicit ("Qué escribimos" 210–11), as I pointed out in the introduction of this chapter, the question thus, for her, became not what she *could* write but what she *wanted* to write.

In short, as Roffé becomes aware of her subjection to multiple, contiguous forms of censorship, the objective of her quest shifts to a search for the shape of her own desire in writing, a desire that had been rendered inoperative, wrapped up under many layers of proscriptions, censorships, and normative representations. In *La rompiente*, Roffé textualizes that very inaccessibility and elusiveness of desire through the protagonist's "anhedonia," the diagnosis given for the protagonist's malady while she was still in Argentina and corresponding with her friend or lover. The symptoms of "la anhedonia," which she defines as "unhappiness and finding no pleasure in the things others enjoy" (22), are portrayed as a direct result of the violence of silence, of the imposed or permitted pleasure sanctioned by the regime. "Sentimientos de pesadumbre, de que nada vale la pena—me decía. Dijo, creo, que sin embargo había una dicha permitida de la que no pudo sacar provecho" / "Feelings of heaviness, that nothing is worth it—you told me. You said, I believe, that nevertheless there was a permitted happiness of which you could not take advantage" (28). This "dicha permitida" or "permitted happiness" refers to the way authoritarianism attempts to paralyze desire by dictating what may or may not be a source of pleasure, what may or may not be spoken about. Authoritarian practices of the state literally dictate norms, declaring certain pleasures or cultural discourses permissible and legitimate (the discourse of censorship deems them "legítimo, propio, nuestro, de adentro" / "legitimate, proper, our own, from inside") and others not only illegitimate but not Argentine ("ajeno, no-nuestro, de afuera" / "alien, not ours, from outside").[18] Such a determination and imposition of certain types of desire as permissible is also generically encoded. As an example of such a permissible pleasure, for example, the protagonist alludes to the traditionally feminine activity of discussing fashion. The narrator/interlocutor is unsure as to the significance of such talk: "Yo, simplemente, transcribo; por ejemplo, lo que usted un poco digregada puntualizó: hablaba de modas. Me pregunto de qué quería hablar o qué significaba hablar de modas. Dijo, equilibrando pesas, que el único conflicto posible era la felicidad" / "I, simply, transcribe; for example, what you, a bit off the track, described in detail: you were talking about fashion. I wonder what you wanted to say or what it meant to talk about fashion. You said, weighing your words, that the only possible conflict was happiness" (28). The dictates of fashion and the mandates of the regime are here conflated, effectively alluding to the double dictatorship to which women are subjected in this case. Furthermore, the "only conflict" involved here is "happiness," suggesting that within the realm of pleasures sanctioned by the regime, lack, desire, disconformity do not exist. Only happiness, satisfaction, conformity are legitimated.[19] The protagonist's comments suggest that the goal of authoritarian control is not only to delimit cultural production itself, but to marginalize and delegitimate the very desires which might provide means for questioning power relations as the military regime sought to maintain them.[20] The protagonist's *anhedonia*—her paralysis and lethargy, her inability to experience pleasure—results from this homogenization of desire. And likewise, access to desire becomes a political as well as a personal issue.

Certainly, in Argentina during the Process, the authoritarian practices of the state attempted to police specific desires and imaginings. Sexuality and sexual politics, for example, were at the forefront of the struggle to cleanse the Argentine national spirit of extraneous and "dangerous" influences (i.e., what the regime saw as Marxist ideological infiltration). Such "dangers" included, of course, cultural productions that depict sexuality outside of the marital/familial relationship.[21] Furthermore, the "dangers" in terms of gender and sexuality also included anything that might question the traditional roles for men and women.[22] So, policing the realms of sexuality and desire, attempting to construct and impose a single, homogenized idea of "Argentine" sexuality, was one of the explicit goals of authoritarian practices.

But, besides addressing such specifics, perhaps more importantly the regime also deployed repression randomly, deliberately obscuring the criteria for the application of sanctions, thus maximizing the potential for a generalized state of paralysis.[23] Such paralysis (symptomatically signified in *La rompiente* as the lethargy of *la anhedonia*) forecloses the possibility of forming a viable subjectivity which would enable the individual to act as social *agent*, not only social *actor*. This deadening of desire is undone in Roffé's text through the acts of reading and writing such that these activities become a means of reactivating agency. First of all, in general terms, reading involves in its very practice both aspects of subjectivity since it puts the reader simultaneously in positions of "subject to" and "subject of." Indeed, John Mowitt sees reading as an "instancing of agency" because "reading performs the mediation between the two poles of agency: activation and activism. Reading situates one within the experience of being empowered to oppose that which conditions one's experience."[24] Reading, as portrayed in Roffé's text, becomes just such an example of an "instancing of agency": the protagonist is quite literally reactivated and spurred to action (to writing) through reading.

On the one hand, a certain lack of creative power, a subjection to norms, is portrayed in this first part of the novel as a function of the position of reader. At one point, seeing some female university students together brings to the protagonist's mind her own youth as well as a similar situation she had read in a novel by Virginia Woolf: the point where Mrs. Dalloway recalls her sexually charged relationship with Sally Seton.[25] Suddenly aware of reading's influence on and determination of her psychic life, the protagonist proceeds to ask herself:

¿Fue tal vez cuando determinó que la literatura contamina? Si el tamaño de su alma o de los movimientos de su alma coincidían siempre o casi con lo que manifestaba alguna línea escrita, el deseo como la felicidad y la desdicha eran una invención. Esta idea, que sostuvo durante unos segundos, le planteó la disyuntiva de elegir entre quedarse tranquila o intranquilizarse por la carencia de originalidad para crear sentimientos propios. De la reverenciada libertad de las calles ya no podía salir indemne. Entendió—dijo—de qué manera se escamotea el deseo (27).

[Was that perhaps when you determined that literature contaminates? If the size of your heart or the movements of your heart coincided always or almost always with what was revealed in some written line, desire like happiness and misfortune were an invention. This idea, that you sustained for a few seconds, set forth the alternative of choosing either to be calmed or disturbed by the lack of originality for creating one's own feelings. From the revered freedom of the streets you could no longer emerge unscathed. You understood—you said—how desire slips away.]

Desire here is seen as produced, determined, and put into play by and through reading. Yet the response to such a "lack of originality" is ambiguous; while reading might determine desire, it also helps (re)produce a desire that has been under siege during the "lavado de almas" / "the laundering of souls" of the dictatorship.

Indeed, the letters the protagonist receives while still in Argentina from her friend or lover abroad reiterate this drawing together of reading and desire, showing how reading can provide an impetus or reactivation of repressed desire.[26] The letters from abroad excite in her a desire for contact with the pleasures prohibited to her, as she imagines herself a melodramatic "gagged hostage," languishing in an atmosphere of "weariness and exhaustion" (23). The letters (that "arrived imbued with woeful pantings, like perverse magicians") serve as an antidote for her *anhedonia*; causing her to imagine herself the subject of prohibited desires:

> Se figuraba visitando antros prohibidos. Gran *motion* y hebras de baba. En alianza con la excitada audiencia aplaudía el fabuloso strip-tease. Mineros, payasos, gangsters y cowboys se iban quitando la ropa al ritmo de sicodélicos bailes hasta lucir un minúsculo taparrabos—de oro o plata—, cuyos brillos resaltaban aún más la descollante naturaleza que apenas cubrían. Tantear, sopesar, acariciar las virilidades. Ah, se oía usted en incontrolable lujuria por el acceso público al manoseo. Oh, se veía usted dilapidando fortunas en los slips de los danzantes (23).

> [You imagined yourself visiting prohibited dens of iniquity. Great motion and threads of saliva. Along with the excited audience you applauded the fabulous strip-tease. Miners, clowns, gangsters and cowboys were taking off their clothes to the rhythm of psychedelic dances until they wore only a minuscule loincloth—of gold or silver—, whose brilliance emphasized even more the protruding genitals they barely covered. To handle, to weigh, to caress virilities. Ah, you heard yourself in uncontrollable lust due to such public access to groping. Oh, you saw yourself squandering fortunes in the g-strings of the dancers.]

Thus, the letters that arrive from abroad stimulate her to invent and fantasize, to imagine for herself what is most morally reprehensible according to the authoritarian scale of values: excess and sexual spectacle, a pornographic striptease. Furthermore, such desires are doubly transgressive, not only breaking the moral dictates of the political regime but also undoing gender scripts that usually cast the object of desire as female and traditionally prohibit women from taking up the position of spectator in such a sexual spectacle. Here the protagonist transgressively occupies the position of desiring, scopophilic subject.[27] There is an ironic distance, however, which shows that the protagonist and/or her interlocutor realize that such fantasies are those of a subject still *subject to* oppressive discourses (that is, of a subject "in wonder like the typical idiot of underdevelopment" 23). In other words, the desires provoked here are recognized as not free from the "wraps" of the cultural imperialism that scripts the inhabitant of the so-called third world into a position of lack. Nor are these imagined transgressions completely disengaged from traditional gender scripts; indeed, they seem the mirror opposite of the acceptable, thus in some way determined and generated by the very prohibitions they seek to violate. These fantasies are still, necessarily, engaged with currently available social discourses and do not represent the protagonist's "true" or "authentic" desires. And yet, such an authentic or essential desire is not the point at all. Her fantasies, inauthentic and overdetermined as they may be, are nonetheless exercises in subjectivity whereby the protagonist occupies a forbidden, desiring subject position as a practice, a rehearsal, an *act*.[28]

Reading and writing, as we shall see, serve throughout the text as practices that provide exercises in subjectivity. This function of reading as exercise becomes clear, for example, as the protagonist recognizes and describes the role of the letters from abroad: "That epistolary traffic redeemed, eroticized, disbanded your imagination bound by states of siege, dirty wars and the laundering of souls. That epistolary traffic—you finally recounted—took you away from the day-to-day mess of things" (23–24). This contraband of language becomes a means to escape not only the limits imposed by the regime but also the internalized sense of paralysis and lethargy that is the dictatorship's ultimate, "successful" infiltration of the social subject: "Habitually, you recapitulated, you lived overcome by indolence. The internal conflicts and the external circumstances pushed you toward laziness. You were unable to say or do anything. And your madness was not sufficient to marginalize you entirely" (24). This paralysis, an effect of the internalized conflicts of engaging both with the discourses of authoritarian control and with those that have historically limited women's participation in discourses of desire, can only be undone through processes of reading and writing.

After reading the letters from her correspondent, the protagonist is pushed into inventing a version of her life that could fit into prescribed molds:

> Entonces ponía a funcionar la achacada mitomanía de la feminidad en usted: inventaba personajes, descarrilamientos excepcionales, correspondía competitivamente a la receta vulgar que le enviaban. Sí, a la higiénica imprescindible sexualidad enriquecedora. Sí, al saneamiento mental. Sí, al panegírico del desarrollo. Sí, consentía usted en sacarse de encima esa daga de otro cielo (24).

> [So you set in motion femininity's imputed mythomania: you invented characters, exceptional derailments, you corresponded competitively with the vulgar recipe that they sent you. Yes, to an indispensable, hygienic, enriching sexuality. Yes, to mental sanitation. Yes, to the panegyric of development. Yes, you consented in freeing yourself from the dagger that was bearing down on another.]

The protagonist's search for a subjectivity that would include a sense of agency, a sense of being able to do or say *something*, leads her to write *anything*, to write a desire not necessarily her own ("de otro cielo"; literally "of another sky") as an exercise, as a cure for her lack of desire, her *anhedonia*, her lethargy, her inner life asphyxiated by censorships of many shades and forms.

The element of contradiction is important in such an exercise, in such an instancing of agency. Social change and the agency needed for it to occur are seen by many scholars as a function of contradiction between or among available subject positions.[29] Accordingly, we could read the letters from abroad as instances of interpellation of the subject according to certain ideological scripts (sexual freedom as healthy, "first world" culture as superior in terms of "development") that conflict with those of the authoritarian regime (sexual relations only in marriage, female passivity, the expressly "Argentine" as the only legitimate culture). Understood this way, the conflict or contradiction between scripts actually helps provoke the protagonist's resistance to each of these discourses, and therefore helps her to produce an active subjectivity that is not completely subject to either of them.

The nature of this exercise in subjectivity also determines the very narrative structure set up in the text. The disembodied voice of psychoanalyst, confessor, or friend could be read as "another voice," or alternative subject position, of the protagonist. Francine Masiello implies this when she observes that this doubling of voice is: "An indication perhaps of the double discourse sustained by every woman, insofar as she feels observed and the victim of an external, controlling voice" (167). In fact, this interpretation is supported by the protagonist's own testimony within the narrative (as well as, we shall see, the author's testimony in other contexts). For example, at one point during the course of this opening chapter of *La rompiente* we read: "'People who are alone talk to themselves,' says Miss Key who is now speaking with you. And you evoke those days, on the other shore, when you were thinking aloud and jumping from one imagined listener to another with an amazing facility" (25). The multiplicity of voices in these two lines is mind-boggling: evoked are the protagonist's imagined dialogue with herself ("on the other shore"), her (imagined?) conversation ("now"?) with "Miss Key," and the (also imagined?) dialogue with the narrator/interlocutor. As readers we ask ourselves, is the narrator/interlocutor a figure for Miss Key? Is Miss Key a fictitious voice invented by the protagonist herself or by the narrator of the text as a method of breaking the imposed silence? Such speculations are fueled at the end of the section when the narrator/interlocutor deliberately adds to the confusion, suggesting that these voices might indeed be carried within the protagonist: "acaso el viaje fue un simple traslado—le respondo a la deriva, como si la señorita Key fuese ahora su figurado oyente ¿interlocutor íntimo, voz imaginaria?" / "perhaps the trip was a simple transfer—I respond, adrift, as if Miss Key were now your imagined listener. Intimate interlocutor? Imaginary voice?" (30). What is clear is that the method of devising and giving voice to various, conflicting subject positions provides a path out of silence. The protagonist describes her conversations with herself, which frequently involve disagreements and lengthy arguments:

Lo asombroso—dijo—era que se pavoneaba despreocupadamente, alegre o casi. Desde que hablaba sola—allá, en la otra costa, me aclaró—se sinceraba con usted y los interlocutores que surgían para charlar o discutir. Le daban infinidad de puntos de vista y cada uno parecía contener su cuota de verdad. A veces se distraía horas pensando en lo que le decían, hasta que encontraba el punto de disentimiento; entonces reanuba la discusión (25).

[The amazing thing—you said—was that you were carelessly showing off, happy or almost. Since you began talking to yourself—over there, on the other shore, you explained to me—you were candid with yourself and with the interlocutors that emerged to chat or argue. They presented you with infinite points of view and each one appeared to contain its quota of truth. Sometimes you were distracted for hours thinking about what they said, until you found the point of disagreement; then you began the discussion all over again.]

These conflicts, however, are productive rather than destructive. Indeed, this strategy not only provides a way to break an oppressive, imposed silence but also becomes a method for finding a language of her own: "En esas pláticas me reconciliaba conmigo y el mundo, me quedaba henchida de satisfacción. De a poco iba uniendo los cables sueltos, desmenuzando la materia de su vida, construyendo—como en una tela en blanco—un discurso claro" / "In those talks I was reconciled with myself and the world, I ended up filled with satisfaction. Little by little you were tying up loose ends, analyzing the material of your life, constructing—like on a blank canvas—a clear discourse" (25). In this way, we can read the text of *La rompiente* as the textualization of just such dialogues the protagonist (as writer) maintains with herself; the progression of the text, as we shall see, replicates this trajectory as the conflicting, dissonant voices of parts 1 and 2 slowly but surely come together into a "clear discourse" in the third and final section.

In addition, Roffé's description of how she began writing *La rompiente* supports such a view. In the paper she gave in Germany—which also, interestingly enough, sets up a fictitious dialogue between the writer and a skeptical Argentine gentleman—Roffé describes the process of breaking the ten-year silence she maintained after the censorship of *Monte de Venus*:

A la mordaza de no poder expresar mis verdaderos deseos, le sumé (tal vez a manera de autocastigo) la mordaza de no escribir, quiero decir, de no publicar hasta tanto me atreviera a tener una actitud más sincera conmigo misma y con mis posibles lectores. Corrían los años del silencio—dije, tratando de que, por los menos, el tono de mi voz no fuese patético—*y yo no tenía con quién hablar. Institucionalmente se había convocado el silencio, a la vez yo me había llamado a silencio,*

pero empecé a hablarme y a transcribir lo que me iba diciendo.
Empecé a escribir La rompiente ("Qué escribimos" 211–12;
emphasis added).

[To the gag of not being able to express my true desires, I added
(perhaps as a form of self-punishment) the gag of not writing,
that is to say, of not publishing until I dared have a more honest
attitude with myself and my possible readers. The years of
silence passed by—I said, trying at least to keep at least the
tone of my voice from becoming pathetic—*and I had no one to
talk to. An institutional silence had been convened, at the
same time I had summoned myself to silence, but I began to
talk to myself and to transcribe what I was saying. I began to
write* La rompiente.]

So, as both Roffé's own testimony and her narrative show, a woman
writing under the censorships of social stigmas that obscure her
desires as well as under the authoritarian state that stymies her literary production can adopt contradictory subject positions as a
method of empowering herself, as a way to produce a language or
voice capable of textualizing just such an experience of multiple
repressions.[30]
    Such a method of forging a voice of her own from a constella-
tion of voices is no easy task, however, and must involve, as we
shall see, both writing and reading. The process of writing entails,
for the protagonist, an entire series of frustrations. She explicitly
complains, for example, that she feels plagued by the inevitable
"states of repetition" of writing, such that language seems incapable of signifying any material difference (30). Not the least aspect
of this sense of belatedness or repetition is the writer/protagonist's
feelings of postboom anxiety: "You told me that the pretentions of
your generation have gone down considerably in relation to some
previous generations. . . . Gone down? Who knows; what is true is
that you are not in Paris" (28). So, for the protagonist (as writer)
the process of writing as an attempt to find a language capable of
producing and representing a female subjectivity has proven frustrating and unsatisfactory:

Hartazgo dijo sentir cuando busca en los originales de su novela
algo ¿un lenguaje? que la recompense de los balbuceos maca-
rrónicos. Eufemismos, asegura, hay en cada página. Abstrac-
ciones, dispara, para que toda articulación fracase. Mentiras,

afirma. Miedos innombrables, coquetea. Lastre de un deseo despedazado. Me traba, dice, como este idioma que no termina de armarse en mi boca (30).

[You said you feel fed up when you look for something in the manuscript of your novel (a language?) that would make up for the macaronic babbling. Euphemisms, you assure me, are to be found on every page. Abstractions, you shoot off, so that every articulation fails. Lies, you affirm. Unnameable fears, you flirt. The weight of a desire torn asunder. It binds me, you say, like this language that never comes together in my mouth.]

But, as I argue in the coming pages, the viable female subjectivity she seeks lies precisely in the discrepancy between what she "writes" and what she tells her interlocutor, between her novel and her analysis of it, between the "lies" and her "affirms." It is by reading (("out loud") the process of writing her novel that she literally generates the voice she is looking for. The explicitly female subjectivity Roffé produces lies precisely between her writing exercise and her reading of this exercise.

In the Margins of Authorship: Subjectivity in Production

The protagonist of *La rompiente* (as well as, I would argue, the author herself according to her literary autobiography in the prologue and in essays) works to break a paralyzing silence as well as to construct a viable female subjectivity, seeking to bring about this transformation through writing, through her *traslado* into exile, through her (psycho)analysis, her confession, her conversation, and—most of all—her conversion into the narrator of part 2. Yet, such a transformation entails a delicate balancing act between repetition and resistance, in reading and in writing. As we have seen, this transformation process is initiated in the first part of *La rompiente*: the dialogue between this narrator/interlocutor and the protagonist becomes a method for opening the "reading" of the protagonist's novel, for opening a narrative space to allow another story to be told. Indeed, the narrator/interlocutor of part 1 portrays their conversation as an opportunity to "acercarnos al abismo de una historia" / "approach the abyss of a story" (29) and, at the very end of part 1, invites the protagonist to "tell" her "novel" to him/her: "Tell me the novel simply. My demons are permissive" (30). It is, perhaps, the margin between the written story (the "novel") and the spoken story (the "telling" of it) that virtually provides the "abyss," the textually deferred space where the elusive story of repression and censorship can finally be represented.[31] Furthermore, the protagonist's critical reading of what she had previously written shows meaning to be always mediated and negotiated and interpretation to be historically determined. Such a representation of the production of meaning explicitly challenges the monologic discourse of authoritarianism.[32] In addition, such a reading activity is, in some sense, a continuation of the methodology we saw outlined in part 1 of the novel: that is, the adoption of multiple, even contradictory, subject positions as a method of producing a voice capable of resisting censorships on various levels. The reading or retextualizing of the "novel" occupies the whole of part 2 and, indeed, the bulk of *La rompiente*, thus constituting a vital component in the process of breaking imposed silences, which is, as the title of the text indicates, of prime concern. My contention is that through this complex "reading" of the writing process, the protagonist produces the voice, and hence the active subjectivity, she is looking for.

The activities of reading and writing in part 2 can be seen as ways of setting subjectivity in motion again after its virtual paralysis through censorship. In a brilliant *mise en abîme*, the protagonist reads her own authored text and de-authorizes it, contradicting what she wrote, reading with a critical eye to the insufficiency of that "novel" vis-à-vis the "real events" that stimulated its writing. The story line of the "novel," as Gramuglio's reconstruction has perhaps already made clear, is that a young woman falls in with a group of gamblers, has an affair with one of them, and then, along with the other members of the group, becomes alarmed and fearful when one of the members is "disappeared."[33] Meanwhile, alongside the narrative of the "novel" that the protagonist is reading out loud to her (imaginary?) interlocutor, another story emerges that the protagonist terms the "verdadera historia" / "the real story" (38). This story relates the "real" events that the novelist had been trying to textualize in her novel, as she now "remembers" them and narrates them to her interlocutor in their conversation. In the "real story," the group is not made up of gamblers but of literary critics and writers.[34] Yet when writing the "novel," the protagonist had faced the censorship[35] of literary expectations and had decided to textualize her story differently:

La verdadera historia comenzó de otra manera. A ese hombre, ahora para usted llamado el ex-seminarista, lo ví por primera

vez en un salón de conferencias; este dato real me pareció
inverosímil, presuntuoso—como usted dice—, poco atractivo
para mis ingenuas ambiciones de originalidad. Preferí disfrazar
los hechos, rasgar las vestiduras, abismar la mentira, sucumbir
a la seducción del juego, edificar un casino de humo (39).

[The real story began in another way. I first saw that man, now
known to you as the ex-seminarian, in a conference hall; this
real detail seemed improbable to me, presumptuous, as you
say, not very attractive for my naive ambitions of originality. I
preferred to disguise the facts, tear away the garments, yield to
lies, succumb to the seduction of gaming, build a casino of
smoke.]

In search of the "originality" so valued in literary production, antic-
ipating and responding to the expectations of readers and critics,
the protagonist tells how she transformed her story into an/other
story, through what amounts to an allegorical gesture.[36] The ironic
distance taken in the passage just cited (39), the judgment that such
words as "disguise," "lie," and "succumb" imply, show that the
protagonist views her efforts as insufficient, as somehow inauthentic. Yet, as she says of her *historia* (which means both "history"
and "story") at the end of part 2: "No es cierta y tiene, sin embargo,
la utilidad de lo verosímil" / "It is not true and it has, nonetheless,
the utility of the probable" (91). Just what, we might ask, does such
a "utility" entail? I suggest that the utility of this nontestimonial
and allegorical narrative lies precisely in its insufficiency, its false-
ness, and its duplicity which ultimately augment its capacity to
gesture at the less accessible effects of authoritarianism, at the difficulty of reaching or articulating *any* repressed story, at the virtual
crisis of representation engendered by the many censorships to
which a woman writing under dictatorship is subjected.

Such censorships are intimately connected with gender politics, as becomes explicit as the protagonist meditates on her relationship with Boomer, the literary critic who, as the protagonist
ironizes, "put me in the hands of my destiny" (57).[37] It is with regard
to this relationship that the confluence of literary and generic
expectations emerges and the power relations involved become clear.
The expectations—simultaneously literary, emotional, and sexual—
involve the appropriation and stifling of the protagonist's subjectivity. The emotional and sexual expectations are expressed even before
the "love story" begins; the protagonist reflects, "El crítico me

adoptó inmediatamente y no crea que fue por mi bella cara ni por mis bellos versos sino por lo que yo prometía" / "The critic adopted me immediately and don't think it was for my beautiful face or my beautiful verses but for what I promised" (57). At one point in the "love story," which unfolds in ten brief sections, the protagonist realizes exactly what it is she "promises," what he expects from her: "Oh sí, ya entiendo, querés apropriarte de mí, no te alcanza con poseerme, necesitás que yo sea algo más que una simple pupila. Oh sí, ahora veo claro, deseas que también me convierta en tu doble bueno, manso y hasta en tu payaso" / "Oh yes, now I understand, you want to appropriate me, it's not enough for you to possess me, you need me to be more than a simple pupil. Oh yes, now I see clearly, you want me also to turn into your good, gentle double, and even your clown" (66). These attempts of absolute appropriation stifle her, producing a type of censorship that has everything to do with gender politics. For example, when he insists that they become "one" in their love, effectively subsuming her identity completely, she is effectively silenced:

> Él solía decirle: 'Cuando dos personas andan bien se funden una en la otra'. Ella acata las sentencias del hombre, casi todas. Sin embargo considera que ella es sola y necesita de vez en cuando estar sola. Y a veces necesita estar acompañada, sin dejar de ser sola. Pero calla porque esto la avergüenza (67).

> [He used to say to her: 'When two people are good together they fuse with one another.' She complies with the man's pronouncements, almost all of them. Nevertheless, she believes she is essentially alone and sometimes needs to be alone. And sometimes she needs to be accompanied, without ceasing to be alone. But she keeps silent because this embarrasses her.]

While she obeys much of what he says as law ("acata las sentencias"), she also resists what amounts to the annihilation of her autonomy. She manages her resistance by buying and mounting a mirror by which she can see herself "de cuerpo entero" / "full length" (66) and can thus form a complete image of her/self by which to establish a viable subjectivity.[38] Her other form of resistance becomes the "exercise in subjectivity" of imaginary gambling and card playing. Boomer attempts to override her autonomy here again, trying to debilitate her strategies and delegitimate the "plays" she makes: "He liked to make remarks to me, to contribute his knowledge; he impugned my strategies, he hindered my ingenuity, he laughed at my unctuous subtleties . . . he also criticized with cruelty my blind opening plays" (72). The protagonist finally escapes from her "love story" by rejecting Boomer's criticisms that consistently derail her attempts at self-determination.

Yet, Boomer's and his group's expectations have had specifically literary consequences as well, relating to the issue of the "voice" the protagonist searches for. As the critic accepts her poems for publication and pays her compliments, she begins to write not according to her own desires and impulses, but according to his expectations. She explains this to her "listener"/reader:

> Mi 'gratitud' se convirtió en servilismo. Fue cuando buscando aprobación, renuncié a lo que quería decir y tomé una voz prestada que al no pertenecerme, se volvió contra mí misma. La necesidad de responder a las expectativas y exigencias de los que yo creía eran mis interlocutores . . . y que funcionaban como marco de referencia, produjo un fenómeno extraño: me desvió de mi camino. . . . Ahora, salir de estas aguas estancadas y encontrar el curso de un torrente propio ¿me será asequible? La pregunta me llena de angustia (58).

> [My 'gratitude' turned into servility. That was when, in looking for approval, I renounced what I wanted to say and took on a borrowed voice which, since it did not belong to me, turned against me. The necessity of responding to the expectations and demands of those that I believed to be my interlocutors . . . and that functioned like a frame of reference, produced a strange phenomenon: it diverted me from my path. . . . Now, will it be possible for me to get out of these stagnant waters and to find the current of a stream of my own? The question fills me with anguish.]

This search for approval that plagues her protagonist in *La rompiente* is also the subject of Roffé's comments in her critical essay, "Qué escribimos" ("What we write"), where she even more explicitly addresses the sexual politics at play. When her gentleman interlocutor pronounces with regard to women writers that "the only ones that are more or less worth reading are the ones that write like men: in a clear, precise, and direct way," Roffé counters "they are the ones who look for approval" (206), revealing that this perpetual writing according to others' expectations cannot help but be generically inflected.

Nonetheless, in spite of the expectations that determine both the "real" events and her "novel," the protagonist also has her own agenda. Indeed, further along in the narrative the protagonist indicates that her "false" story had an allegorical function, that through it she aspired to refer to another, more obscure, less accessible story: "en el fondo de mi corazoncito intentaba valerme de agudos artificios para dar, mediante la gran metáfora, los oscuros padecimientos de mi época" / "in the bottom of my little heart I tried to avail myself of keen artifices to convey, through the great metaphor, the obscure sufferings of my time" (45). Linguistic play of an especially decorative sort ("the adventure of language with impeccable flowers and bows" 45) as well as the intimist mode of the love story ("I wanted to be ascribed to the current of intimist, subjective, lyrical writing" 44) are used by the narrator to gain a certain critical approval or to conform to particular, genderically inflected conventions, again showing how writing inevitably involves engaging with social and discursive expectations and practices. Yet through these literary conventions, the protagonist now sees that she had another agenda: to use this artificially constructed story (what I would call an allegory) to refer to the "obscure sufferings" of the sociopolitical situation: the stifling censorships and stagnating fear invoked by the authoritarian regime.

So, as the protagonist retells her "novel" to her interlocutor, the new narrative she is verbally reconstructing is primarily about the writing process itself. In particular, her resultant texualization of this process shows us how writing becomes allegorical in response to sociopolitical, genderic, and literary constraints. Allegory, as we saw in the introduction, has many properties that make it ideal for times of political oppression. But, rather than merely a way of avoiding censorships, it is also a mode of representing the crisis of representation engendered by political terror. At the German conference where Roffé gave the paper quoted earlier, Ricardo Piglia commented that a large group of texts produced outside Argentina during the dictatorship have allegorical traits. Disagreeing with the view that censorship engendered an entire series of "masks" or allusions that were specifically employed to skirt its oppression,[39] Piglia does, however, find such masking techniques in literature produced outside Argentina. The editor who compiled the proceedings quotes Piglia at length:

'En el exilio se hacía más alegoría que en la escritura que se realizaba en la Argentina. No digo que sean textos alegóricos; yo veo *rasgos* alegóricos, formas de expresar la situación de opresión.' Ello podría deberse a que 'en situaciones de terror político, uno tiende a una lectura alegórica, y que la situación de presión política genera una lectura alegórica. Esa relación entre terror político y lectura alegórica, me parece que es un modo de acercarnos a la problemática de la relación entre escritura y política' (Kohut *Literatura argentina hoy* 291).

['There was more allegory done in exile than in the writing produced in Argentina. I am not saying that they were allegorical texts; I see allegorical *features*, ways of expressing the situation of oppression.' That could be due to the fact that 'in situations of political terror, one tends toward an allegorical reading, and that the situation of political pressure generates an allegorical reading. That relationship between political terror and allegorical reading seems to me a way for us to approach the problematic of the relationship between writing and politics.']

What these comments show is that, while certainly related to political oppression in many ways, allegory denotes a mode of reading as well as of writing in its relation to the social context. In the authoritarian context in particular, not only do writers produce oblique references to the silenced social scene, but readers interpret all socially produced texts in an allegorical mode, thus bringing the social situation to bear on any text.[40] As such, it is significant that in Roffé's text the allegorical nature of the protagonist's "novel" can only be glimpsed through her own reading in context, her juxtaposing the "text" with the remembered "real story." In this way, allegory does not merely mask or "hide" a "real" story; rather, it evokes the complexities involved in representation itself, especially in the presence of restrictive social authorities. Thus, the allegorical gesture in *La rompiente* works not to avoid censorship per se, but rather to signify the allegorical gestures actually produced in writing under censorship, to gesture at the crisis of representation, the problematics of reading and of writing, provoked by repression (political, sexual, literary). By rereading her "novel" allegorically, the protagonist is able to glimpse and re-produce not necessarily a "real" story, but rather the very difficulties in telling any "real" story or even knowing what such a story might be. Furthermore, such techniques also undo the monological system of representation espoused by authoritarianism, denaturalizing meaning and showing the constructed nature of all narratives. In this sense, the fragmented, multiple forms of writing used in *La rompiente* are at once symptomatic of the oppression of authoritarian culture, as well as a form of resistance to the homogenization and univocality attempted by that same culture.

While, as Piglia suggests, allegory can indeed help us to comprehend the relationship between literature and politics, I am not, by any means, arguing that there is a one-to-one correspondence here between the allegorical "great metaphor" and the sociopolitical situation. There are at least three levels of narrative here: the "novel," the "real story," and the "reading" of these narratives of the past undertaken by the protagonist in the moment of retelling both stories to her interlocutor. The following enunciation on the part of the protagonist demonstrates quite succinctly what I mean: "Delirious alcoholic, Boomer's buffoon and lackey, Asius is a minor character in the fiction; I could say in reality as well. Now I see that he was more important than I thought" (82). Clearly, three levels of narrative, corresponding to the "fiction," the "reality," and the protagonist's "reading" of both ("now I see . . ."), emerge. But, as this very example also shows, these three stories are far from separate. One story tells the other, gestures at the other, bears the trace of the other. Yet the resonance between these stories does not reflect a simple one-to-one correspondence such that the "novel" can come to refer directly and exclusively to the sociopolitical scene. It is rather that both of these stories, both of these incomplete, inadequate, inauthentic narratives, trace in their very incompleteness the innermost effects of political terror, the "other story" of "the obscure sufferings" of authoritarian culture: fear, incommunication, guilt, and the concomitant crisis of representation. Such traces are, furthermore, only activated through the "third" level of the narrative (the "now I see"), that is, through the protagonist's *reading*.

So, true to the protagonist's observation in part 1, "literature contaminates" and each of these narratives implicates the other, all ultimately overlapping on the level of the unconscious. The protagonist herself characterizes the unconscious as an internal witness that will not let her forget: "To use a cliché, I will tell you that then (let's place this 'then' in the first years of silence) the unconscious exposed me" (48). Her comment, while establishing the sociohistorical parameters necessary for the reader to contextualize the narrative, reveals the unconscious as somehow outside her agency and yet nonetheless inscribed in her writing. Indeed, her dreams from this period make their way into the "novel," as the protagonist herself notes: "I jotted down my oneiric images in a diary to have them at my fingertips at the moment of my report from the couch. One of the dreams forms part of the novel" (48). Product of the unconscious during the "years of silence," inscribed in both the "novel" and the novel, recorded and told to the protagonist's psychoanalyst, the dream occupies all levels of narrative at once. Furthermore, the content of the dream reveals much about the exact nature of the "obscure sufferings" of her time, whether or not they were the ones the protagonist had wanted to textualize with "the great metaphor." In the dream Boomer, the protagonist, and the others are in the process of exploring and reconstructing a castle, symbolic of unearthing and re-membering the past, when suddenly: "Through a crack of the past emerges the memory of a box with three rats as the contents. . . . To find them dead, through our unpardonable negligence, fills us with anguish. Nevertheless, the possibility of finding them still alive, disturbs me" (48). Thus, the rats evoke fears of confronting the bodies of the disappeared, the guilt of having let these victims of the "dirty war" die, or the discomfort of finding them still alive. These sensations of guilt and fear become even more tangible as the dream becomes a nightmare of horrific proportions, the castle turning into a concentration camp, the dead ("los *muertos*") rising up against the living in revenge for their fate: "On the platform are all of us the *living*. . . . We are prisoners of the *dead*. The *dead* form a Tribunal. They have borrowed bodies. . . . I am sure that they anticipate our disintegration" (49; emphasis in the original). It is this interior (unconscious) story of terror, guilt, and death—all the effects of the violence of the regime—which the dream, embedded as it is in three contexts simultaneously, represents and will not let her forget. While she remembers wanting only to forget the terror ("what I wanted was to sleep" 51; "I didn't want to think about these things" 52; "one learns to forget and with the passage of time one forgets almost everything" 52), her unconscious—especially as manifested in her dreams—will not allow her to: "One gets hardened, you see, and if it weren't for the tricks concocted by bad dreams, not even the ghosts would come to us at night" (52).

Perhaps most importantly, it is in reading her own textualization of the "years of silence," in all its allegorical antimimeticism, that the protagonist regains access to the unspeakable fear that inhabited her dreams and, ultimately, her text:

> No era entonces, cuando evocaba fragmentos de mi vida y escribía que se me paralizaban los órganos y éste tan vituperado que llaman corazón, sino ahora frente a tantas artimañas para decir algo trabado por el miedo. Ahora, le decía, en el momento

de la lectura, de exponerme con un ridículo texto que apenas
testimonia todo lo que escondía: un recuerdo agazapado en lo
que no se quiso o pudo recordar. Una puede ser indiferente a la
realidad, pero no al recuerdo de esa realidad que está en con-
stante desenvolvimiento" (74–75).

[It wasn't then, when I was evoking fragments of my life and
writing, that my organs especially this much reviled one called
heart became paralyzed, but rather now before so many ruses in
order to say something bound up by fear. Now, I was telling
you, in the moment of reading, of exposing myself with a
ridiculous text that barely bears witness to everything that it
concealed: a memory camouflaged in what could not or would
not be said. One can be indifferent to reality, but not to the
memory of that reality which is constantly unfolding.]

She thus reads traces of her unconscious as written in her text. What
her writing has inscribed is not a mimetic copy of her life, not a testimony of political terror; rather it inadvertently bears witness to
the fragmentation and paralysis engendered by censorships. Thus
the act of writing is here portrayed as incomplete, because only upon
reading her own writing can she read the silences of her text and
hence remember what was (un)spoken by those silences. It is only as
the protagonist reads her narrative, tells the conditions that surrounded her textual production, recalls and contextualizes her night-
mares, and consequently activates her memory of what was so
untellable, that she begins to be able to re-member the subjectivity
fragmented and torn up by silence and repression.

Thus, part 2 of *La rompiente* becomes a highly complex performance of reading as well as of writing. By "making sense of the
conditions activated by the text," by making sense of the fear, the
violence of silence, the sense of guilt that both inhabit and are inhabited by the "novel," the protagonist produces a voice capable of narrating what had been repressed.[41] It is virtually in the contradictions
between what the protagonist "wrote," what she "remembers," and
what she "tells" that she is *enabled*, that is, that she can come to tell
the unspeakable, repressed story of the "years of silence" and that a
subjective agency becomes viable. Thus, the protagonist's reading
practice ultimately shows how reading can put agency in motion,
can actually become what Mowitt calls an "instancing of agency."

And yet, there is never any sense that *this* is it, that she has
come into a voice—singular and autonomous—of her own; she never

represents herself as "whole" or merely "one." Through this complex literary game, this intricate *mise en abîme*, the protagonist manages to posit an "authentic" voice by negation (that is, by positing each of these voices as not "it"), thus continuing to defer any "true" voice or any "true" narrative as not yet accessible. She concludes these exercises in reading, writing, and remembering thus:

> Ahora sé, por lo escrito y lo contado, que esta historia—aunque inconcluyente—terminó. No es cierta y tiene, sin embargo, la utilidad de lo verosímil. Aquí o allá, los accidentes y postales del camino difieren el fin de viaje (91).

> [Now I know, through what was written and what was told, that this story—although inconclusive—has ended. It is not true and it has, nevertheless, the utility of the probable. Here or there, the accidents and postcards of the road defer the end of the journey.]

Indeed, history (*los accidentes del camino*), writing (*las postales del camino*), and memory (inscribed and *read* in writing as well as in the unconscious), all make it impossible for the story ever to reach a definitive version or to truly conclude. And yet it ends. The double gesture embodied in this part of Roffé's narrative is not unlike Irigaray's formulations in that the latter also posits an essential identity of woman while continuing to deconstruct such an identity.[42] As Diana Fuss notes regarding this aspect of her work: "Irigaray works towards securing a woman's access to an essence of her own, without actually prescribing what that essence might be, or without precluding the possibility that a subject might possess multiple essences which may even contradict or compete with one another" (72). Similarly, Roffé's protagonist's multiple narratives work toward conceiving "a voice of her own," made up of a constellation of voices gathered from various, contradictory discourses, yet that nonetheless effectively breaks the silences imposed by social, sexual, and literary authorities.[43] Thus the focus in Irigaray's poetic theory as well as Roffé's theoretical narrative is on both process and product.

The Personal and the Political:
Re-Embodying the Social Subject

As we have seen, the constant textual play involved in part 2, the double- or even triple-voicedness of the *mise en abîme* employed, continually defers a definitive ending of the protagonist's narrative. Indeed, this becomes patently obvious in the third and last section of the novel, which terminates the story, paradoxically, with the beginning of the journey, with the protagonist's contemplation of her departure into exile in search of a voice of her own ("will I find, wherever I might go, the splendor of a voice?" 124). While part 3 of the novel in no way offers an essential, singular, "authentic" voice as the conclusion of the exercises in subjectivity rehearsed in the first two sections, it does, however, re-embody the disembodied voices put in circulation throughout the author's "Writing Itinerary." That is to say, this last section—with its memories of the protagonist's dying grandmother, its remembered smells and flavors from the protagonist's childhood, its testimony to the protagonist's daily existence in isolation and silence cloistered in her apartment in the city—virtually re-incorporates the various textual motifs that had been only gestured at and denounced in part 1 and variously textualized in the multiple and contradictory narratives of part 2.

In a sense, this last section achieves a certain antidote to the dispersion of censorships, silence, and political terror, through the telling of the most biographical or personal aspects of her story, involving as it does the narrator/interlocutor of part 1 rereading the protagonist's diary (what she calls the *líneas de fuerza*) to her. As the interlocutor/narrator reads this diary back to the protagonist, the past is reactualized and repersonalized, even though the voice of the protagonist is, admittedly, still mediated. It seems as if *La rompiente*'s function, through all of its exercises in subjectivity, had been to give voice to this most testimonial story. And indeed, between the lines, interspersed and "contaminated" by literary texts, the most untellable, personal, privatized aspects of the protagonist's experiences are finally told. Yet, the text does not posit this personalized narrative as the definitive version of events, for as this third section also shows, no matter how personal these experiences seem, they are always imbedded in and contaminated by the social realm and history: the internal as well as external "fetters," re-incorporated and unraveled in part 3, are both ultimately localized in the individual subject.

The terms re-incorporation or re-integration describe this third section in part because of the way episodes narrated in the previous two sections are picked up and given a more immediate focus and voice. The protagonist's activity of reading letters from her friends as a means to stimulate her own writing, for example, reappears in part 3: "She looks for refuge in the letters of a few friends in the hope that the re-reading might supply her with creative enthusiasm. Perhaps this epistolary exercise might be of some use" (100). We have already read the effects of this epistolary exercise, with more and different details, in part 1. The difference is that the "exercise" is narrated in part 3 without the ironic distance of part 1; in fact, in part 3 it is told in the present tense where in part 1 it is recounted in the past: "That epistolary traffic . . . took you away from the day to day mess of things" (23–24). Through the narrative of the third section we have, in some sense, gotten closer to the historical moment of these actions; the past, now rewritten in the present tense, somehow reactualizes the painful events held at a distance, that is, told in the past, all through parts 1 and 2.

Also recurring in part 3 are various remnants of the "novel" the protagonist recounts in part 2. The grandmother's feet are like those of a character in the "novel," "like the wide feet of Leonor" (105). The protagonist imagines herself fleeing to her home as "the vulnerable Rahab escapes" (103), "Rahab" being the name the heroine of the "novel" takes as her pseudonym in the gambling group. Spotting her friend Miri on the street in the city in part 3, the protagonist suddenly confuses her with Quenia, another character in the "novel": "That was Miri, it can't be anyone else. Is she asking for cigarettes in the street? Quenia, too. No, it can't be. Is it possible to confuse her with another?" (111). In this way, part 3 shows the path between "reality" and "fiction" to be a reversible one where "real events" not only get textualized in "texts" but also vice versa.

Overall, then, the narrative of part 3 re-integrates the various stories ("reality" with "fiction"), the spatial parameters (the "here" of the narrator's and the protagonist's conversation with the "there" of the diary), as well as the disjunctive temporal sequences ("past" with "present"), showing all of these discourses to exist simultaneously. So, in a sense, the text replicates not the teleological impulses of realist narrative, but the backward and forward, inconsistent yet repetitive movements of memory. Working less linearly and more cumulatively, *La rompiente* enacts its textual transformation (from silence to subjectivity) by taking up and accumulating contradictory discourses and subject positions, allowing these ambiguities to coexist. The resultant text, taken as a whole, is thus a series of exercises that begin to create a new textual space and new possibilities for a female imaginary through reading and writing. That the diary— or its "margin notes" as the narrator/interlocutor calls them in part 1 (27)—is called *"líneas de fuerza"* is very significant in this regard.

Clearly, *líneas de fuerza* explicitly aligns writing (*líneas* / lines) with power (*fuerza* / strength or force). But also, these lines refer not only to writing but rather to notes made in the margins of her own writing, that is her *reading* of her *writing*. Indeed, her diary, as an exercise in reading and writing, is a place of empowerment for the protagonist/writer; it is through this reading and writing that she finds the lever, the "force," to begin to break down the silences that are imposed on her and that she imposes on herself.

Another aspect of the "re-embodiment" theme of the third section is, of course, the way the diary of part 3 seems to recontextualize the protagonist's *anhedonia*—with its concomitant discommunication, isolation, and silence—in the most personal, private, bodily sphere. For example, the protagonist's discommunication is gestured at and denounced by and through the various narrative levels and the displacing of voices in parts 1 and 2. This alienation is now retextualized in part 3 in more personal, and even more physical, dimensions; that is, the impossibility of finding pleasure in any activity is now narrated in terms of the most quotidian details. In part 1, for example, we had read: "The internal conflicts and the external circumstances pushed you toward laziness" (24). It is a retrospective observation, somewhat distant and disembodied, bereft of biographical information. In part 3, the *anhedonia* is retextualized on a more mundane, bodily level, manifested in day-to-day occurrences. At one point, for example, the protagonist attempts to make herself some fried eggs as if it were possible to cure the symptoms of her *anhedonia* with such a meal:

Curar una enfermedad a la que llaman anhedonia con embriones fritos. Pero no era cuestión de curar sino de pasar el trance con una metafora sensual que le devolviera algo del placer perdido o del ansia de placer. . . . La metáfora ha ido a parar al tacho de basura. Su estómago ejemplifica de manera patética la sensación de vacío. Piensa tristemente en las galletitas que hoy no compró (104).

[Curing an ailment that they call *anhedonia* with fried embryos. But it wasn't a matter of curing but rather of getting through a tight spot with a sensual metaphor that would give you back something of the lost pleasure or of the desire for pleasure. . . . The metaphor has ended up in the garbage. Your stomach exemplifies in a pathetic way the sensation of emptiness. You think sadly about the little cookies you didn't buy today.]

Her *anhedonia* here is manifested on a physical level; her empty stomach and her pathetic attempt at remedying her lack of pleasure with fried eggs become symbolic (and symptomatic) of the overwhelming sense of emptiness and paralysis she faces.

The motifs of silence and isolation which contribute to the writer's *anhedonia* also recur in the diary of part 3, recontextualized in terms of the protagonist's daily life in the city "on the other shore" (95). Whereas in part 1 we had read in more abstract terms that "there is nothing more vile than the violence of silence" (28), the protagonist's silence is now re-written in the context of her family circle. At the beginning of part 3, the protagonist's grandmother complains of her lack of conversation: "*Ela* complains that you don't talk. . . . She serves tea and lets you take a sip and take pleasure in the freshness of the citron or mint. Afterwards she asks you if you will be that way, in silence. Are you silent with your friends as well?" (95–96). Later it is the grandmother herself who falls silent and depressed as she approaches death, and the protagonist who tries to get her to speak: "You put on the best face you can to go to her room, you have the intention of accomplishing what nobody has been able to do these past days: making her say a few words" (96). The protagonist is then interrogated by her family as to what she said to make the Ela think she was suffering: "They call to ask what is the matter with you. *Ela* has mentioned your name, she has said how much one must suffer. You swear that you said nothing that could be interpreted as a present, and much less future, pain. . . . You suggest that *Ela* is talking about herself, since both of you have the same name" (98). The unspoken or forbidden signified that circulates through all of these silences is pain, suffered as individual and exclusive and yet somehow shared through silent exchanges. In this way, part 3 repersonalizes and re-embodies silence, a dominant theme of the novel from the beginning, and by the same token shows it to belong to both the personal and the social realms at once.

The isolation and solitude that virtually imbue parts 1 and 2 are also refocused and re-embodied in part 3. Through the diary of part 3 we read of entire days spent trying to write, drinking coffee, eating cookies, and sleeping with the help of tranquilizers (102–03). After the grandmother's death, the protagonist refuses company in her mourning, preferring to remain cloistered in her apartment, exacerbating the silence and incommunication she suffers (107). Her seclusion has, in the narrative of her diary, several and perhaps overlapping personal motives:

Creí que la reclusión era necesaria para contar una historia—escribe—; la historia se ha convertido en el pretexto ideal para mantener las puertas cerradas: hacerme insensible al mundo exterior—quizás de alguna forma lo he logrado. En un principio, pensó que se enclaustraba porque la separación requería luto. El luto se lleva dos años y éste ha tomado más tiempo; abarca otras penas (113).

[I thought that seclusion was necessary to tell a story, you write; the story has turned into an ideal pretext to keep the doors closed: to make myself insensible to the exterior world—perhaps in some way I have accomplished it. At first, you thought that you cloistered yourself because the separation required mourning. Mourning is observed for two years and this one has gone on longer; it encompasses other sorrows.]

As this passage indicates, the protagonist has had varying interpretations of her own seclusion: the solitude needed for writing, the result of grief (mourning either her divorce from "el crítico Boomer" or her grandmother's death). But through her writing she comes to realize that she had been deceiving herself, that this isolation, as we shall see, has political as well as personal motives. Clearly, instrumental to this realization is the very act of writing, as this passage also drives home, with its blatant "escribe" / "you write" and the mixture of first and third person narrative due to the particular narrative mechanism the author has devised for this section (that the narrator/interlocutor is *reading* what the protagonist *writes* in her diary). It is, thus, through writing her diary that the protagonist realizes that her mourning and isolation indeed "encompass other sorrows," and ultimately have to do with larger, more social questions.

This realization of the sociopolitical aspect of her seclusion at first only drives her to further solitude and repression: "Now to realize that you are protecting yourself from something that transcends personal matters large or small, it seems to you another battle and among the most humiliating" (113). But as such isolation and inner exile take their toll, one of the protagonist's friends comes to a more historical consciousness of her pain and resolves to leave: "Your friend . . . seems to shake off a long sleep and, now that you are recuperating, says she is leaving soon. Having begun another decade breathing the same air gives her asphyxia. She makes you look upon '80 as if that were the determining year" (113–14). It would seem that taking such a historically aware view of her situation is what makes agency a possibility; it is what allows her to shake off the lethargy and paralysis (the "long sleep") she and the protagonist inhabit. Psychologist Liliana Mizrahi's comments are elucidating in this regard: "The fear of change has to do with the unconsciousness of the social significance of personal conflicts and with the repression of that consciousness" (64). Furthermore, according to Mizrahi, change and action become possible, indeed a sense of agency is activated, through an awareness of the social dimension of one's pathology (64). Extrapolating from Mizrahi's observations, we could say that in *La rompiente* the protagonist's friend is empowered and begins to strive to make changes and take action just as she realizes the sociocultural dimension of her situation. Her awareness encompasses not only the political situation of authoritarianism but also the social import of her condition as a woman. Upon telling the protagonist of her decision to leave the country, she observes angrily: "'Don't we women adapt easily to the vicissitudes of destiny; haven't we followed man to all corners of the earth, changing our home, our language, our God? Aren't we well trained for exile?'" (116). The protagonist is, on the other hand, still immersed in the traditional schemas that seem to virtually think for her: "You think, *as if someone were thinking for you*, that she is an angry woman; the symptoms: protest, overrating her sex, etc." (116; emphasis added).[44] Her friend responds to this unspoken criticism by viewing her anger as a product of her sociocultural situation and accepting it: "'I am resentful, how could I not be'"(116). As the protagonist herself gains more of such a historical consciousness, or as it becomes increasingly difficult for her to repress it, she also becomes more capable of imagining change, of undoing her lethargy, of beginning her voyage.

Such a historical consciousness begins to become inevitable for the protagonist of the *líneas de fuerza*. Indeed, as the protagonist's isolation and discommunication are exacerbated (her friend stands her up, failing to meet her at a bar [102–03]; her telephone stops working [117]; her indifference grows [117]), they also become more explicitly symptomatic of her political terror. She begins to fear she is being watched by a police agent/taxi driver/ex-fellow student whom she names simply *"the student"* and whose image "was a source of perturbation that had left you without will or strength" (118; emphasis in the original). The feeling that she is being followed and spied on by the "student" thus paralyzes her further. Through the episodes involving the "student," we see how the protagonist's experience of the military regime is mostly filtered or mediated through details of her personal life. Having decided to divorce her husband and discontinue her psychoanalysis, she is confronted by the "student" who lets her know that he is aware of these details of her personal life that she had discussed only with her husband and a close friend (118–19). This invasion of her personal life by political forces causes her great anxiety and provokes a reaction of denial: "In the face of an anguishing paranoia, you preferred to think that his comments were innocent and not a message to let you know that he knew a secret part of your personal story" (119). Indeed, since this character seems to signify an entire nightmarish sociopolitical system that is painful to confront, the protagonist resolves to "no pensar más" / "not think anymore" and to obliterate him from her memory (121). Just before resolving to undertake this willful forgetting, she had observed: "Pensar en un taxista–policía o policía–taxista no es una invención delirante sino un delirio de la realidad y el susodicho encaja, por sus características físicas y mentales en la categoría de estos personajes que el país ha engendrado" / "To think of a taxi driver–police agent or a police agent–taxi driver is not a delirious invention but a delirium of reality and the above-mentioned individual fits, due to his physical and mental characteristics, into the category of these characters that the country has engendered" (121). Yet, even though she glimpses the "big picture" of the authoritarian regime in moments such as these, a consciousness of which would help her see her "paranoia" as social as well as personal, she represses this consciousness, willfully attempting to forget it (121). Finally she is no longer able to ignore her sociopolitical situation and the "student's" status as police agent when she witnesses him commanding a police operation in a bar.

This scene provides a compelling account of the discommunication and self-censorship that political terror has engendered on the level of interpersonal relations. At a café with another friend, the protagonist converses with him solely through allusions, talking without saying explicitly what she means: "Su amigo . . . parecía no haber notado otra cosa que la manera de hablar sin decir lo que en el fondo él presentía que usted tramaba; sin embargo, usted estaba absolutamente convencida de que lo que decía era suficiente para un buen entendedor" / "Your friend . . . had not seemed to realize anything other than your way of speaking without saying what he, at heart, sensed you were trying to say; nevertheless, you were absolutely convinced that what you were saying was sufficient for a good listener" (122). While this conversation mediated by self-censorship goes on, the agent walks in and the protagonist silences herself further:

Calló que el hombre de civil que dirigía al grupo uniformado era de su conocimiento. La mirada de *el estudiante* fue recorriendo las mesas y señalando quiénes sí y quiénes no y se detuvo, por una milésima de segundo, en sus ojos que mantuvieron la mirada una eternidad hasta que por fin se desvió a otro rostro (122).

[You kept quiet that you knew the civilian that commanded the uniformed group. The gaze of *the student* was scanning the tables and indicating those who were and were not to be detained, and it lingered, for a fraction of a second, on your eyes which held his gaze for an eternity until at last it looked away to another face.]

It has become impossible for the protagonist to ignore her sociopolitical situation: as the *estudiante*'s gaze catches hers for a second, their mutual recognition makes it impossible to avoid or repress knowledge of his power and her subjection and silent complicity.

But as such a realization of her involvement in a political situation becomes impossible to avoid, it is this very realization, seemingly haphazard and admittedly reactive, that finally spurs her to action. Originally having climbed on the wrong bus in her rush to avoid the *estudiante*'s vigilance, she ends her trip in the cemetery, more in control of the situation than she had thought and more resolute in her decision to leave the country than she had anticipated: "Her uneven itinerary now seemed to have been planned from the beginning: in front of the tomb of *Ela* you realized that all of your dead were buried there, to whom you had gone to say a very long goodbye" (122). This comment could serve as an assessment of her textual itinerary as well: while seemingly random and exceedingly fragmented, as the writer/protagonist gains consciousness of what she is trying to do, and as the reader comes to the end of her text, it becomes clear that her itinerary of reading and writing has had a plan all along and certainly the journey has been a fruitful one. In both cases, driven by terror into fleeing her home, riding aimlessly into exile, she has nonetheless (at the end of her text/bus ride) recovered a sense of her past.

So, the personal or biographical details of part 3 re-embody the suffocation and discommunication referred to in parts 1 and 2, intensifying the correlation between the protagonist's ailments and her personal history, as well as between that personal story and social history. In this sense, Roffé's own appraisal of the narrative transformation plotted in *La rompiente* seems right on the mark: for her, according to her prologue, *La rompiente* is "the integration through writing of a personal world, alienated and in fragments" (11). Part 3 of *La rompiente*, especially, signifies just such a re-incorporation or re-integration of a subjectivity torn asunder by censorships, imposed silences, "internal and external fetters." Furthermore, it is an integration of the personal, inhabiting and inhabited by the political realm. Her isolation, paralysis, and *anhedonia* constitute both personal and political symptoms; indeed, as we saw at the outset, Roffé views her novel as "the memory (*memoria*) of a personal itinerary contaminated by the memory (*memoria*) of a historical process (the years of the 'Process')"("Qué escribimos" 213). And, just as a *memoria* also implies a written *memoire*, the text involves a re-incorporation of subjectivity achieved quite self-consciously through writing.

All along, I have purposefully referred to the processes of part 3 as rein*corp*oration, for it is through the body that such a re-integration is ultimately imagined. The role of the body in *La rompiente* as a whole, but especially in part 3, suggests that the protagonist's goal is to work toward a gendered subjectivity, *embodied* without resting on some essential biologism. The body, especially at the end of the text, functions as a means of imagining a productive solitude and as a point of departure from which to produce an active, explicitly female subjectivity. The last scene significantly relocates the protagonist's voice in her female body and sexuality, as she lies in bed awaiting the arrival of her menstrual period.[45] Her isolation has been converted from a hellish place ("a private hell where you debate with yourself" 113) into a space opened to the possibilities of throwing off alienation and converting isolation into a productive and temporary separatism: "Se ve fluctuando con la marea, haciendo lo indecible por deshacerse de todos los lazos: sentirse poseída de sí misma desposeída del mundo" / "You see yourself flowing with the tide, doing the unsayable to get rid of all ties: to feel possessed of yourself, dispossessed of the world" (123). Irigaray similarly advocates a strategic separatism in *This Sex*, primarily to give women a chance to fathom or perhaps imagine a desire that would be less false, less a masquerade of the desire of the other.[46] The protagonist imagines this productive isolation in the fluid, marginal, and inarticulate (*indecible*) space of the body. Yet, such separation from the external is never complete; her immediate context is her own body and her bed, but "the roar of motors locates you in the heart of the city" (123). There is, as we have seen, no complete protection against the external realm. Yet her isolation—now viewed as strategic—has indeed liberated her from the obstacles she had faced: she realizes with a thrill of fear, that "el vacío la ha liberado de las ataduras" / "emptiness has freed you of ties" (123). Similarly, Liliana Mizrahi ends her book with the following meditation: "From desert, solitude has been transformed into world. The vibrant resonances of history emerge in each of its memories, the generous flavor of plenitude, the depth of plot, the phantasmagoria of fears, the eternal youth of desire, the soft density of sadness. Subjectivity unfolds in intimate and multiplied certainties" (143). In the quest for a viable female subjectivity, solitude thus becomes not an escape from the social realm, but rather the place—not hermetic but infiltrated by desires, history, and memory—from where we ultimately experience the world. The solitude of part 3 of Roffé's text becomes just such a richly textured solitude. The memories of her youth, with the Jewish traditions and cuisine associated with her grandmother, the various sights, smells, and sorrows of the past that permeate her memory all keep her solitude from being a withdrawal from the world. These personal details also become intimately entwined with the historical realities of the "dirty war" and the fear of reprisals such tactics have engendered.

Indeed, Roffé's protagonist begins to experience her bodily solitude as marginalized, as fluid, and yet as *worldly*: "Now in your head all the water of the planet has been condensed" (123). *La rompiente*, thus, finally comes to a close:

> Oye una sirena quebrar la noche. Su cuerpo se repliega, sin embargo es inútil evitar el escalofrío y una puntada en el bajo vientre que las manos no componen con sus friegas. Respira hondo y exhala lentamente esa pregunta que la persigue: ¿hallaré, a dónde vaya, el esplendor de una voz? El dolor se disipa como si ese esplendor incierto contuviera una substancia benévola que pondrá otra vez su vida en juego. Ahora, sangra (123–24).

> [You hear a siren break the night. Your body retracts, nonetheless it is useless to evade the shiver and a stabbing pain in your lower belly that your hands do not soothe with their rubbings. You breathe in deeply and slowly exhale that question that hounds you: will you find, wherever you might go, the splendor of a voice? The pain dissipates as if that uncertain splendor contained a benevolent substance that would once again put your life into play. Now, you bleed.]

Moving from exterior to interior, her narrative is certainly re-embodied, articulating, as it does, the pain and fluids of the female body. Her characterization of this process suggests that reoccupying her body involves confronting pain and accepting certain physiological functions beyond her control. Yet, while her pain is perhaps necessary, as a possible way out of the anesthetized existence she had been leading, the hope and real possibility of finding a voice, of giving voice to her pain, dissipates it and will actually put her life back "into play," will reactivate her subjectivity that had been paralyzed by various, contiguous censorships: authoritarian, patriarchal, and literary. So, the much theorized and poeticized activity of "writing the body" is not here a goal in itself. The female body—envisioned not according to masculine desires, not wrapped in foreign adornments—provides the protagonist/writer with the space of her own that she needs in order to imagine a female subjectivity and, perhaps even more significantly, to imagine that female subjectivity in a politically inflected world.[47]

In this way, the protagonist/writer has not only embodied the subjectivity she was building but provided a new female imaginary, a new way of thinking through the female body in order to subtend that female subjectivity. The fact that she foregrounds her sexuality in this way, writing literally from the specificity of the female body and experience, rejects a type of subjectivity that would elide the body and especially its sexual "markings." Roffé's imaginary exchange with the Argentine gentleman in her critical essay provides some insight regarding her views on writing and gender. When her interlocutor points out that "your so often mentioned Virginia Woolf . . . believed, just like Coleridge, that the great minds are androgynous" Roffé retorts: "I disbelieve, for the moment, . . . the androgyny of literature. The person who writes has a sex that determines him or her and that socially applies its mark; as such, what that person produces has, without fail, the register of his or her sexuality" (206). Likewise, Roffé's novel strives not to erase the femininity from the subjectivity it engenders for the protagonist, but rather works to elaborate a subjectivity from a specifically female material existence.

Yet, all of this is not to propose the textual version of part 3 as an origin or as the "authentic" point of departure for the protagonist's textually, sexually, and politically inflected journey through censorship and exile into subjectivity. She has rather written—in a mediated, constantly deferred, tentative way—the marginalized, fluid, "other" space ordinarily left silenced, unwritten, invisible: the paralysis, suffocation, and nonproduction due to (self-)censorship; the female body and sexuality smothered under the wraps of masculine parameters of desire; the most private of spheres (the home, the body, interpersonal relations) as they were crossed and contaminated by political violence. We, as readers, have thus indeed read an intimate approximation of "the other shore." Yet, we never actually read the departure or any essential origin of her journey and as readers, we are actually discouraged from searching for such an origin. The protagonist observes: "Manía ésta de ordenar objetos creyendo que así uno puede encontrar nuevamente el punto de partida. Tarea ingrata, en realidad debería resignarse a empezar todos los días de fojas cero" / "This mania of putting objects in order, believing that in this way one can find the point of departure again. A thankless task, in reality one should resign oneself to beginning each day as a blank page" (109). As Liliana Mizrahi's words used in the epigraph for this chapter indicate, subjectivity is indeed a question of *elaboration*, of what she calls "el ser proyecto" or "the self as project."[48] Indeed, Roffé's protagonist virtually becomes her own creation and creator through her various "exercises," through her journey in search of a subjectivity capable of resisting censorships simultaneously political, literary, and generic. It is not a matter of returning to a previous originary identity but of imagining a new female subjectivity, continually "por hacerse," deconstructed and reconstructed through the processes of imagining, reading, and writing.

4

EXILE AND A NEW DREAM OF SYMMETRY: CRISTINA PERI ROSSI'S *LA NAVE DE LOS LOCOS*

Seres entre dos aguas, marginales de ayer y de
mañana: es esto lo que hicieron de nosotros.

[Beings between two waters, marginalized from
yesterday and today: this is what
they have done with us.]

—José Emilio Pacheco
No me preguntes cómo
pasa el tiempo

The ship of fools sails through a landscape of delights,
where all is offered to desire, a sort of renewed paradise
since here man no longer knows either suffering or need;
and yet he has not recovered his innocence.

—Michel Foucault
Madness and Civilization

The man who finds his homeland sweet
is still a tender beginner; he to whom every
soil is as his native one is already strong;
but he is perfect to whom the entire world is as
a foreign land.

—Hugo of St. Victor

Cristina Peri Rossi's novel *La nave de los locos* [*The Ship of Fools*] (1984) documents the wayward itinerary of the generic, contemporary everyman "Ecks"—part political exile, part postmodern pilgrim—in an attempt to speak from and articulate the place of the *extranjero*.[1] I say "place" deliberately because what this text most eloquently demonstrates is that foreignness is eminently positional, constructed, and reversible. As Peri Rossi has put it in an interview, playing on the two Spanish verbs to be, *ser* (essence) and *estar* (location or state): "Uno no se es extranjero, se está extranjero" / "One is not [essentially] foreign, one is foreign [in a particular place or time.]"[2] Similarly, exile involves not essence but position and point of view. In fact, Peri Rossi herself has lived in exile since 1972 when, due to the violent oppression of the Uruguayan military regime, she left Montevideo for Barcelona where she still resides. Yet exile for this writer has to do not only with sociopolitical circumstances and national identity but with sexuality and textuality, with urban living and the postmodern condition.[3] Indeed, as we shall see, in *La nave de los locos* exile is the textual place where sexual, political, and literary concerns converge. In this chapter I examine the multiple meanings of exile in this narrative, that is, how it is articulated as a contextual, textual, and sexual condition and how it comes to imply not only a powerful sense of loss that provokes nostalgia but also the opening of a new space of utopian possibilities.

By way of introduction to the novel and what I see as its ethical preoccupations, I would first like to discuss briefly the use of allegorical procedures in the text. Certainly, allegory plays a key role in this narrative, in an even more explicit and pervasive way than in any of the other novels treated thus far.[4] Ecks, a generic everyman protagonist akin to Kafka's own allegorical antihero Joseph K., seems to embody or personify the abstract qualities of the position of the *extranjero*. As a permanent outsider he moves from place to place, always observing the contemporary social context from a different, more critical perspective. Such perambulations are recounted using an almost essayistic technique, incorporating commentary by the narrator as well as by the protagonist himself. *La nave de los locos* employs such an essayistic discourse constantly: various characters act as virtual mouthpieces for expounding on ideas about the meaning of sexual and national identity and the nature of exile, as will become clear in the following pages. In this way, the narrative often seems to suggest its own interpretation, a frequently cited feature of what is most commonly considered allegory.[5]

Another aspect of the allegorical components of *La nave* is that the principal thrust of the narrative is Ecks's endless journey, a common allegorical topos, which takes him through a series of abstracted places such as "the city of A," "city B," "the Island," "the Earth's Navel."[6] In addition, interspersed with these contemporary meanderings is a description of a medieval tapestry that depicts the Creation, an allegory that strives to represent the origin of man, "a vision of the world that gives order to chaos, an hypothe-sis that is comprehensible and restores our faith" (14). As Paul Smith points out, allegory often makes such a gesture toward an original oneness or plenitude: "Allegory . . . resembles romanticism in that it attempts to counter and cover over the realization and effects of an historical fall from an original plenitude" ("The Will to Allegory" 120).[7] Certainly, the allegory of the tapestry, static and ultimately impossible, attempts such a reparation while, as we shall see, the other allegorical gesture (Ecks's travels and journey toward enlight-enment) strives not to cover over but to counter and somehow repair the "original fall from plenitude" in a very different way.

Indeed, the multilayered allegorical mode Peri Rossi uses in this text fulfills several key functions.[8] First of all, the allegorical mode used by Peri Rossi draws attention to what I have called a cri-sis of representation: due to the sociopolitical and literary contexts, the authority of the "world picture," indeed the very possibility of representing our world at all, has been cast into doubt. The nature of this crisis is brought into focus through the juxtaposition of the alle-gorical tapestry of the Creation, which depicts a fixed, closed repre-sentational order, and the counter-allegory woven by the series of tableaux of Ecks's journey through our imperfect, fragmented, vio-lence-torn contemporary society, which undoes the authority of the divinely "authorized" representation. Furthermore, on the allegorical function of the tapestry, Mabel Moraña points out, "it works like a backdrop and thematic counterpoint in the novel, creating that cor-respondence between microcosmos and macrocosmos particular to many allegorical constructions" (41). I would add that virtually all of the allegorical traits of La nave help to make such a correspondence between "micro" and "macro" levels or what I have frequently referred to as the personal and the political. For instance, by provid-ing Ecks with such a generic and synthetic identity, his personal transformations take on wider, more social significance and the text can thus continually relate the personal realm to a more collective struggle. Moreover, as will become increasingly clear, by allegori-cally staging both gender identities and national identities as simi-larly nonorganic, binary, and politically charged constructions, the blatant critique of oppressive gender relations at the end of the novel can become a critique with more far-reaching implications, suggest-ing an overall, "macro" denunciation of the dangers and violence of binary thinking.

La nave de los locos is a novel with a critical agenda, grap-pling with the alienation and social disintegration of contemporary society as well as searching for a way to subvert the restrictive binary operations that act violently to exclude so many "others." The "others" that populate the text include Ecks and Vercingetorix (political exiles and perpetual travelers), Morris (ex-centric, homosexual collector and writer who falls in love with nine-year-old Percival), Graciela (young feminist who escaped from her bureaucratic and authoritarian father), and Gordon (ex-astronaut "exiled" forever from the moon). While exploring the various oppressions that have acted upon and marginalized these expatriates and outsiders, the text also works to delegitimate such oppressive structures by rearticulating the relationships among these figures as mutually respectful, tender, and generously loving. As Gabriela Mora points out, the positive portrayals of what would traditionally be considered abnormal personalities and transgressive relationships are in stark contrast to the grim depictions of other much more violent and outrageous social phenomena that society accepts with more complacency: for example, the "disappearance" and torture of political opponents, Lucía's attempts to get an abortion, or Ecks's encounter with a prostitute who has been brutally beaten (Mora "Peri Rossi" 346–47).

The movement of the narrative primarily follows the perambulations of Ecks. Indeed, the majority of the tableaux portray Ecks ("A stranger. Ex. Estranged." 2) on an endless and seemingly aimless voyage that includes real places (Toronto, Madrid), unnamed sites ("the city of A" etc.), symbolic and imaginary spaces ("La Isla," "Pueblo de Dios"), as well as comical and distorted references to recognizable cities ("Old York, Merlin, Texaco, Ombu-Beach, Psycho-Aires, Asnapolis" 33). The intermetropolitan voyage thus primarily covers the urban centers of postmodern/postindustrial society. But the "referents" of this journey are perhaps of less concern than the symbolic nature of Ecks's quest. Indeed, the many references to his having "read of the journey" ("el viaje leído") and to the metaphor of the "ship of fools" emphasize the figurative aspect of his travels. In this way, Ecks's exile and journey tells the story of a perpetual traveler in order to gesture allegorically at the plight of the social subject of our times.[9] Yet while his condition is one of exile and marginalization, Ecks' journey also shows how such a predicament can be transformed into a search for a new ideal of plenitude and harmony, not based on an exclusion or marginalization of the other but rather on intersubjectivity whereby the other's subjectivity and agency is not obliterated or supressed but recognized and respected. Jessica Benjamin, whose book *The Bonds of*

Love: Psychoanalysis, Feminism, and the Problem of Domination is an extended exploration of how intersubjectivity could transform sexual and social relations, proposes that "the idea of intersubjectivity reorients the conception of the psychic world from a subject's relations to its object toward a subject meeting another subject" (20). Such a conceptualization as an ideal seems especially apropos to Cristina Peri Rossi's novel, which strives to imagine a new sense of community in the face of dispersion and marginalization.

Indeed, hovering between a nostalgia for a lost plenitude and a utopia that is, as we shall see, dynamically imagined through the breaking down of restrictive gender categories, *La nave de los locos* longs for "un equilibrio sin sacrificios" (" an equilibrium without sacrifices"),[10] for representation without the violence of exclusion, for a recognition of difference without the obliteration or subsuming of the other. In the context of such a textual project, the ethical dimension of allegory proves a valuable tool in enabling Peri Rossi's narrative to bring into focus—that is, to envision or imagine—a particular type of redemption, not as a definite program for a better future but a glimpse of how things could be transformed. Indeed, the properties particular to allegory help the text to reveal and articulate the "blind spot of an old dream of symmetry" and to try to imagine something different.

The Possibilities of Exile:
Loss, Otherness, and the Opportunity for Difference

I have used the notion of "an old dream of symmetry" to refer here to what Peri Rossi denounces as an oppressive, patriarchal logic whereby representation and identity are founded upon binary systems that exclude and marginalize the other, unable to account for difference in any inclusive, pluralistic way. I borrow the phrase (and conceptualization) from Luce Irigaray's "The Blind Spot of an Old Dream of Symmetry," her deconstructive reading of Freud's account of femininity (*Speculum* 13–129). Irigaray's contention is that Freud's model reflects the "blind spot" of Western philosophical discourse, incapable of casting woman as anything but a negative mirror image of man (see specifically pages 27–28). She critiques the binary thinking described and put into action in Freud's theory such that one term (the masculine) always stifles the other (the feminine) in its hierarchy, virtually making the other over, always in relation to the same. What Irigaray advocates then is an account of sexual difference that would not be merely a function of this "logic of the same." My

contention is that in *La nave de los locos,* Peri Rossi tries to undermine just such a "logic of the same," which is incapable of recognizing and embracing difference.

Ecks's quest is, in many ways, for a new dream of symmetry,
contrary to the "old dream" of binary thinking as manifested in traditional forms of representation, in sociopolitical systems, and in
the sexual economy. It is precisely with such an "old dream"—
arguably an "old dream of representation"—that the novel begins.[11]
The text opens with an oneiric reelaboration of the Fall of Man,
which can be read, in this postmodern context, as the Fall from the
kingdom of the illusion of innocent and unproblematic representation, from the prelapsarian realm where the realization of the master
narrative still seemed possible. The masculine, first-person narrator
is ordered by a voice of authority to represent his world: "You will
come to the city—describe it" (1). He immediately recognizes that
this order to represent will entail sorting, deciding what to include,
what to exclude. The first person narrator initially sets about this
sorting process in an orderly, straightforward way: "Later I found
myself in a field, winnowing wheat from chaff. Under a grey sky
and lilac clouds, the work was hard, but simple" (1). This is a staging
of what Irigaray would call an "economy of representation," a system whereby value and meaning are regulated and (re)produced, a
system that is, ultimately, authored and authorized by male subjects (*Speculum* 22). Yet, with the insertion of an active feminine element ("she") into the scene of representation, he suddenly finds
that it becomes impossible to sort the wheat from the chaff, to distinguish the significant from the insignificant, to make the decisions regarding inclusion and exclusion with the same surety as
before. This dream seems to fall into the genre of what Ecks later
describes as "los sueños de la representación" ("dreams of representation") (*La nave* 174), anxiety dreams in which he is somehow
always incapable of performing his role either as representor or as
spectator.

Gender politics clearly plays a key role in this crisis of representation, as the narrator's description of the "Fall" demonstrates:

> Trabajaba en silencio, hasta que ella apareció. Inclinada sobre el
> campo, tuvo piedad de una hierba y yo, por complacerla, la
> mezclé con el grano. Luego, hizo lo mismo con una piedra.
> Más tarde, suplicó por un ratón. Cuando se fue, quedé confuso.
> La paja me parecía más bella y los granos, torvos. La duda me
> ganó (*La nave* 9).

[I kept working in silence until she appeared. Stooping over the field, she took pity on a weed and I, to please her, added it to the harvest. Then she did the same for a stone. After, she begged mercy for a mouse. When she had gone, I was confused. The straw seemed more beautiful and the grain, unyielding. Doubt overwhelmed me. (1)]

In this way, the once straightforward and simple operation of exclusion/inclusion that representation involves has been complicated by woman ("she") who, in taking up an active position of author (here a "sorter"), takes pity on the excluded and pleads for compassion in this sorting process.

This opening scene puts the issue of representation at the fore, laying bare the way any representation implies exclusions and showing how the very possibility of representation has been thrown into crisis. Such a crisis and critique of representation are often portrayed as symptomatic of postmodernism.[12] Recent theorists draw attention to how representation inevitably involves a certain violence, a radical exclusion of what falls outside its gaze, thus implying the banishment of the other, the exile of what is other to it.[13] This violence of representation comes into focus in the opening dream sequence of *La nave* through the participation of the feminine. It is the woman that appears on the scene who takes pity on that which is excluded, marginalized, or banished (who "took pity on a weed"; "begged mercy for a mouse"). With her compassion she confuses the "simplicity" of the scale of values operating in the representational economy such that for the male narrator, "the straw seemed more beautiful and the grain, unyielding." So, the participation of the feminine causes or facilitates what can be taken as a figure for postmodern confusion, making the narrator's sorting of the significant from the insignificant increasingly problematic, throwing the emplotment of the master narrative into crisis, and ultimately shaking the confidence of the once divinely inspired author who, in the end, laments, "Doubt overwhelmed me." Loss of mastery and the crisis of representational authority, deemed endemic to postmodernism, are symptoms, as Craig Owens points out, not unrelated to gender politics. As Owens observes (following Heidegger), in many ways modern man has conquered and mastered his world (read the colonized, woman, nature) through the act of representation. The revolt of the "represented," the taking up of subject positions by former objects of representation, is both cause and effect of the current, postmodern crisis that has thrown into question Western man's view of himself as representer and hence subject and master of his world (Owens 64–70). It is in this way that the very first sketch of *La nave* can be read as an allegory of the postmodern malaise, as depicting the crisis of relative forms and shifting criteria, the confusion generated when the other ("she") takes an active and critical role in the construction of values, when man becomes an "other among others."[14]

It is this confusion that virtually initiates the journey and propels the narrative of *La nave*. Fallen from his position of relative mastery, the protagonist is lost: "Since then wheat and chaff have mixed. Under the grey sky the horizon is a smudge, and no voice answers" (1). This sense of loss, and of lostness, is emblematic of the whole book; after the initial scene, the first person narrative falls away and "Ecks" embarks on an endless maritime journey through various indefinite spaces.[15] In foregoing the position of divinely imparted authority, in finding the chaff beautiful and the grain harsh and uncompromising, Ecks takes up (or is cast into) the position of the excluded, the exiled, the other.[16] And yet, as Ecks tastes his own "national death" (see note 14) through this exile, as he is cast out of the paradise of fixed identities and sure things, he manages to make of his exile an opportunity for creation and transformation. The account of his journey, the supposed travel log that the narrator "reads," for example, is a direct product of Ecks's homelessness. Indeed, later in *La nave*, the narrator observes that exile can prove quite useful for writing: a "'stateless citizen' certificate" might be "inconvenient at borders, but very useful for writing poetry" (33). In interviews, Cristina Peri Rossi portrays exile as provoking an overwhelming sense of loss but also as constituting a potentially enriching experience. Here, she explicitly emphasizes the possibilities for forming new relationships with others, with oneself, and with language:

El exilio es una experiencia que siempre puede capitalizarse. Si uno no se vuelve loco. . . . Hay que reconstruir un mundo afectivo que no es sólo los amigos sino las relaciones que uno tenía con determinadas calles, el bar donde entraba a tomar una copa, el colegio al que había ido. Obliga a replantearse hasta las palabras. . . . Ya que [el exilio] obliga a replantearlo todo, la identidad o sucumbe o se ensancha. Si se ensancha es una experiencia capitalizable, rica (interview with Camps 47).

[Exile is an experience that can always be capitalized on. If one doesn't go crazy. . . . One has to reconstruct an emotional world that not only has to do with friends but with one's relationship with certain streets, a favorite bar, the school one went to. It requires rethinking everything, even words. . . . Since exile requires such a rethinking, either identity crumbles or it expands. If it expands it is an enriching experience.]

So, exile for Peri Rossi can be turned into a productive condition if one can become, somewhat at least, subject *of* the experience (capitalize on it), rather than merely subject *to* it. Indeed, writing itself involves, for this author, assuming the position of exile: "I think it was Kafka who said that the writer is always an exile. He was referring to the angle from which he observes reality" (interview with Montserrat Ordóñez 196). This is precisely the role that many of the exiles and foreigners of *La nave* take up, viewing society from the margins, able therefore to see its flaws, and then sometimes even writing their observations—like one of the characters, Morris, who makes a trip to the Gran Ombligo and subsequently writes a critical essay titled "The Metropolis According to Morris" (121–25) or another, Graciela, who writes scholarly essays on women's oppression from the nineteenth century to World War II (153).[17]

In this way, in *La nave de los locos*, exile from the grip of authoritative representation can be positive and productive, becoming an opportunity to search for a different type of representation which could avoid the violence of traditional inclusions and exclusions. Indeed, Ecks embarks on a journey that is not only an escape from the violence of authoritarianism but is also a pilgrimage, a quest for a lost order and harmony.[18] Further along in the text, for example, Ecks contemplates an engraving of Venice with a certain longing for order, for a symmetry that would not, however, involve a violent sacrifice of the other: "This small and seductive image of Venice comforted Ecks. The perfect harmony of the landscape, the structure of the palaces, the symmetry of the canals—all this was a manifestation of a possible order, *of an equilibrium without sacrifice, of a redeeming harmony*" (*La nave* 35; emphasis added, my translation). On another occasion, Ecks attempts to see this harmony in the face of an aging and obese woman. With her rolls of warm flesh, she is hardly the typical object of erotic contemplation; but she becomes under Ecks's gaze an aged and fallen angel, excluded from traditional representations, "one of those mature angels ignored by painters and theologians," whose smile nonetheless "partakes of grace and expresses the harmony and order of the universe" (75–76). What both of these segments show is that Ecks searches for a sense of unity or harmony that could have pity on the excluded, which could, in the terms of the crisis of representation depicted in the first dream, find the chaff also beautiful. In this sense, Ecks's search is for a harmony beyond the violence of binary oppositions where one always subsumes or excludes (in his terms "sacrifices") the other. Such a "critique of binarism," at the top of the postmodern critical agenda, is an urgent task, as Craig Owens cogently observes in "The Discourse of Others":

> The critique of binarism, . . . sometimes dismissed as intellectual fashion, . . . is, however, an intellectual imperative, since the hierarchical opposition of marked and unmarked terms (the decisive/divisive presence/absence of the phallus) is the dominant form both of representing difference and justifying its subordination in our society. *What we must learn, then, is how to conceive difference without opposition.*[19]

This, I would argue, is what Ecks's anti-epic, almost quixotic quest comes to involve: a utopian search for difference without violence, difference without exclusion or suppression, difference without sacrificing the other. In short, a new dream of symmetry, contrary to the "old dream" of the patriarchal sexual economy documented by Freud and critiqued by Irigaray, and contrary as well to the "old dream" the military regimes of the world attempt to install, persecuting all those who might threaten the homogeneity of the sociopolitical and cultural orders.[20]

The otherness of exile inhabited by Ecks and his dream of an inclusive, generous recognition of difference necessarily imply both a sense of loss of boundaries and also an enriching broadening of identities, that is, both loss and gain. The aspect of loss corresponds to the sense of aimlessness of Ecks's journey and to the very definite spasms of nostalgia Ecks feels for the "old dream" of order and identity. Ecks is, in many ways, still in the thrall of the "old dream," often trying to assume a position of mastery: "Like the Creator in the tapestry, who orders and watches over his creatures, already knowing their future, . . . so Ecks watched the girl who advanced toward him" (85). And yet this position is often foiled as Ecks is confronted with another, new reality that he must accept and that undoes the old patterns of order. For example, when the same young girl (Graciela) appears with her guitar case, Ecks ("ever the eager student of human behaviour" 91) ponders the necessity of studying the role of music among young people, persisting in taking the position of "Creator" who orders the world (91), only to find out that her guitar case contains not a musical instrument at all, but rather all of her possessions (including underwear, colored pencils, and a box of condoms), thus serving as her suitcase. Yet Ecks does not resist these confrontations with conditions that defy his old sense of order, but opens himself to them, allowing himself to be displaced from his position of knower and learning from that loss of mastery. After Graciela opens the guitar case for Ecks, for example, he gracefully accepts the unexpected: "Ecks found this a most discreet way of travelling" (92).

In a poem included in *La nave* titled "The Laws of Hospitality" we can read both the loss of identity (evoking nostalgia) and the hope for a new order (a glimpse of utopia). The transformations involved in becoming other (as *extranjero* or exile) make possible a true intersubjectivity, a "hospitable" meeting of the other without suppressing that other:

> Una vez, por cortesía, me enamoré de una extranjera.
> (Condición reversible de la extranjeridad:
> yo para ella también era un extranjero.)
> Su lengua, que picaba como un áspid,
> no era idéntica a la mía,
> y yo por cortesía,
> dejé que fuera la suya la primera.
> Amarnos fue comenzar por la letra *a*.
> Hube de explicarle las crónicas medievales
> y pronunciar, pausadamente, la palabra *aproximación*.
> [. . .]
> Como ciegos, tuvimos que amarnos
> en códigos diferentes . . . (39)

> [Once, for courtesy, I loved a stranger.
> (A reversible condition, this strangeness,
> I too was a stranger for her.)
> Her tongue, which stung like an asp,
> was not the same as mine;
> and I, out of courtesy,
> let hers come first.
> At the letter *a* our love began,
> I spelled out for her the old romances,
> and sounded out the word *approximate*.
> [. . .]
> Like the blind, we had to love each other
> in different codes . . . (34-35)]

Such an encounter, accepting the position of other (*extranjero*) as he meets the other, provides the opportunity for difference without opposition, indeed for an arousing reencounter with his own language and tradition, for an erotic *nearness* such that one term does not suppress the other. Yet this dream of difference where one would not merely subsume the other presents certain dangers, implied in her tongue/language that "stung like an asp." Furthermore, becoming "other," exiling oneself, in love has as its price a sure sense of identity:

> Cuando se fue
> me quedé muy solo,
> mi lengua ya no era la mía,
> balbuceaba palabras raras,
> vagaba por los aledaños
> de una ciudad vacía
> y en la hospitalidad
> perdí mi nombre (40).

> [When she left
> I was alone,
> This tongue of mine was mine no longer.
> I stammered strange words,
> wandered throught the outskirts
> of an empty city
> and in this hospitality
> I lost my name (35).]

To lose one's name is to lose a sense of proper identity, of ownership of oneself, for, as another character, a child wise beyond his years, points out, "to name something is to some extent to own it" (142). And yet, in spite of the risks involved in a loss of identity, the disruption of a sure sense of self, such displacement can actually produce positive effects. Names are, after all, of limited use value: "Ecks thought that names were irrelevant, as was gender, although in both cases people did their best to live up to them" (19). Ecks's own name implies an unknown quantity, a position, a name function, without the restrictions of a proper name.[21] This disdain for the proper name is seconded by one of Ecks's fellow travelers, Graciela, who pronounces: "I don't like being asked who I am and what I do. . . . The answer would be too complicated. Impossible to state briefly. . . . If you like you can call me Graciela, given our necessity to refer to people and objects by name." (87). So, the loss of a name, in the context of the novel, becomes a loss that opens possibilities for creating an identity instead of remaining subject to an already determined and imposed identity. Perhaps, as Cristina Peri Rossi's own comments on exile quoted earlier indicate, identity must be broadened beyond the limiting propriety/property of the proper name. In this way, the loss that is involved in exile, the destabilizing of a "proper" identity due to "The Laws of Hospitality," can provide an opportunity for the imagining of a new utopia: a new dream of symmetry, a generous and expansive intersubjectivity such that one "other" can greet the "other" on equal terms.

From National Identity to World Citizen:
Exile and the Sociopolitical Context

As we have seen, exile, becoming "other" as a loss of a sure (masculine) position of control, simultaneously evokes a sense of victimhood and opens a space for a new intersubjectivity, a mutual recognition that would not resort to an attempted obliteration of the other. Similarly, political exile operates in *La nave* as both a crisis of loss and an opportunity for transformation. While national identity is certainly thrown into crisis in Ecks's exile, sheer nostalgia for the country of origin does not take over. This is because, as the text shows, the very binary thinking involved in the formation of national identity is what subtends socio-political violence. In other words, national identity is found to be another instance of the rigid binary system the text denounces.

Sociopolitical violence and its dependence on binary logic take center stage at several key moments of Ecks's journey. For example, the ninth tableau, "The Cement Factory," recounts the "disappearance" of one of Ecks's fellow travelers, Vercingetorix. With clear references to an unfortunately typical scenario in so many Southern Cone countries, Vercingetorix disappeared "on a bleak, cold August morning" such that "to disappear is no longer voluntary, but acquires passive form: *'We are being disappeared'*, Vercingetorix had said on those few occasions when he referred to these things" (51; emphasis in the original). After his release from the concentration camp ("The Cement Factory") he goes into exile specifically because he is unable to stand the idea of the binary split between two worlds operating simultaneously: "two disinct worlds, parallel yet unknown to each other, remote and independent . . ." (56). This "world split in two" refers specifically to the violence enacted by the military in concentration camps ("[the world of] torture, rape and death" 56) while maintaining a veneer of goodness and justice ("[the world of] films, football games and school lessons" 56). In an essay on literature under fascism, Hernán Vidal has dubbed this phenomenon "daily life split in two: the visible nation / the invisible nation" whereby a vast, subterranean network (including secret detainment and torture centers) operates out of the view of the typical, depoliticized citizen unless he or she has the misfortune of falling victim to one of the many arbitrary roundups enacted by the regime ("Hacia un modelo" 29–30). This underground network and the very "naturalization" of the "routine" of such places, Vidal goes on to observe: "permits the torturer to experience his work as a simple office routine that he then leaves behind at quitting time to join an apparently normal family; he enjoys diversions and other everyday activities in such radical contrast that they become the virtual antithesis of the underground atmosphere he works in " ("Hacia un modelo" 30). In this way, the sociopolitical violence of the Southern Cone both enacts and is sustained by a dangerous dualism that has ultimately disappeared the "others" into clandestine concentration camps, exile, or death.

Such political persecution is encoded in *La nave* as both particularly South American and common to the world at large.[22] For example, Ecks converses with Morris, another fellow *extranjero*, about political oppression: Ecks "maintains that all periods have been periods of poverty and uncertainly for those who have no power: our days are no different from the past, except in the number of tyrants, their systematic methods and the cold logic with which they lead the world to madness" (100). Yet, when Morris suggests designating the sea as an oppression-free zone, Ecks reminds him of the chilling reality of the "ocean cemeteries," lately a particularly South American phenomenon: "their beaches, riverbeds and remoter shores yield mutilated bodies with some frequency nowadays; bodies which, tortured and thrown into the water, have become entangled like weeds among the reefs and sandbanks . . ." (101). In Argentina this is precisely what happened, for example, during the "dirty war": cadavers of prisoners that had been tortured and then dumped into the sea from helicopters began appearing on shore.[23]

Ecks's own exile, while multifaceted, nonetheless has a specifically sociopolitical component. When the ex-astronaut in Pueblo de Dios asks him, for example, whether he saw the moon landing, Ecks admits that he was sleeping: "You see, the times were bad, dangerous; we were being persecuted and were living in constant fright. That night we could sleep, because, in view of what was happening, we felt sure that even the police would stay at home to watch the television" (107). While the condition of Ecks's exile can be specifically traced to the sociopolitical situation of his home country, such an oppressive situation is by no means portrayed as unique to South America.

Although Ecks definitely bears the mark of a political exile, his dream is not to return to his place of origin. Any return to the origin is, perhaps, dubious, as Ecks himself observes regarding Gordon the astronaut, permanently exiled from his lunar paradise: "there are journeys from which one cannot return" (111), a sentiment echoed by Graciela later in the novel (184).[24] While Ecks's journey moves (albeit haphazardly) toward a redeeming harmony and a sense of deliverance, his goal is not to regain his sense of a national identity. His memory and nostalgia, for example, do not privilege his particular national culture to the exclusion of all else. He remembers, for example, verses by Dante, "unlike most exiles unable to recall anything but the odd folkloric and detestable song" (75). His nostalgia is provoked by diverse objects and representations: "an engraving of Venice" (34), a bar in a city he had often visited (41), or "dated, nostalgic music of doubtful origin" (3). Indeed, national identity often entails a restrictive and limiting binarism of us (nationals) versus them (foreigners), a binarism that Ecks confounds as expansive, unidentified everyman, "whose own conversation also frequently combined sounds of various tongues" (73). Peri Rossi herself reiterates the constricting and rigid aspects of national identity when she says, "There is only one country in the world where I am not a foreigner" (interview with Ordóñez 198), thus indicating the extreme exclusions involved in the very idea of national identity. The danger of such identities is plainly, if comically, exposed in an incident in the 15th tableau, "The Lost Paradise":

También vivía en Pueblo de Dios un famoso violador, el cual, luego de haber sembrado el pánico en tres ciudades, por fin fue capturado; descubrióse entonces que antes de dedicarse a esa profesión, había sido policía, por lo cual enseguida lo pusieron en libertad. Se casó y se instaló en Pueblo de Dios, donde lo dejaron vivir siempre y cuando violara fuera del perímetro del lugar, y todo el mundo lo quiere mucho, porque es un hombre muy simpático y de buen carácter, que ama a los perros. En los últimos tiempos sólo viola a turistas, por delicadeza (105).

[Finally there was a famous rapist who had been captured after sowing panic in three cities. When it was found that he had previously been a policeman, he was quietly released. He then married and came to live in Pueblo de Dios, where he was accepted on condition that he practise his activity outside the town perimeter. Everybody liked him because he had an attractive personality and a gentle nature, and he loved dogs. Lately he had taken to rape again, but only tourists, out of consideration for the locals (105)].

This episode, a virtual miniature allegory of identity politics, provides a biting satire of a system of blind legitimation by which certain identities lend impunity to otherwise criminal behavior. It furthermore shows how a system of insider/outside identity, paradigm for the way national identities usually operate, can allow atrocities to be perpetrated on "others" (here, on those outside "the town perimeter" or "tourists"). It was this very logic that worked with terrifying efficacy in the National Security States of the Southern Cone where "subversives" were discursively turned into "others," silenced, marginalized, and virtually disappeared from view, allowing precisely the type of world divided in two that proved so unbearable to Vercingetorix, the world divided in two that allowed generals and torturers to live peaceful, rich lives while condoning or actually perpetrating the rape and murder of those "others."[25]

So, while national exile would suggest a sense of loss, the productive aspects of this homelessness are actually many in *La nave*. The outsider, the exiled, the foreigner, gain a new critical perspective on the workings of the contemporary urban societies on whose margins they live. Peri Rossi makes it clear in an essay that she is well aware of these benefits of exile: "I owe to exile the possibility of looking at European reality . . . without the veil of its myths nor the nearsightedness of those who have never left" ("Genesis de 'Europa después de la lluvia'" 71). Likewise, Olivera-Williams points out regarding *La nave*: "Marginalization is compensated with a privileged, analytical eye that permits creation. . . . Imposed solitude impels a questioning of everything and converts the exile in the great dissident of the Great Navel" (87). As an example she points to Morris's trip to the Great Navel and the critical perspective he gains on the alienation and myopic views of the Metropolis (Olivera-Williams 120).

Indeed, the loss of a national or civic identity not only enables the adoption of a critical perspective, but can actually open a space for utopian possiblities. If, as both Ecks and Graciela affirm, *"Hell is not being able to love"* (153; emphasis in the original), surely the "Great Navel"—metaphor for contemporary urban society, where the loud noise of machinery "leads to a lack of communication and the need for psychoanalists" (125) and where "the favourite animal among navelists is the car, which they value above any family member" (125)—is hell. In this dystopia *par excellence*, a nationalist mentality is rampant and taken to its most satirical limits as a metropolitan chauvinism, an excessive and ridiculous devotion to their own urb/*ombligo*. Morris writes:

> 'La principal ocupación de los habitantes de la ciudad consiste en mirarse el ombligo. Ellos no se dan cuenta, porque sumergidos en uno de los pliegues más recónditos, que se ramifica en dos, y tiene, además, algunas rugosidades, han olvidado por completo que se encuentran en las profundidades de un ombligo, y no en el mundo' (119).

> [The principal occupation of the city's inhabitants is staring at their navels. However, they are not aware of it: buried in one of its most hidden folds which ramifies and spreads into multiple creases, they have completely forgotten that they are in the depths of a navel and not in the real world at all (121).]

In short, this extreme metropolitanism makes the *ombliguistas* poor world citizens. Morris points this out explicitly in his report: "'By contemplating their navels all day, the city's inhabitants are kept fully occupied and have no time left to worry about what may happen in the world outside" (121). The places in the text where a more utopian vision becomes possible are specifically places devoid of such divisive, binary-based identities. For example, the park where Morris comes across and falls in love with Percival (a nine-year-old boy who has not lost his sense of a primordial relationship with his surroundings) is a place where a heterogeneous harmony reigns— where Percival, for example, is bothered by the flock mentality of the pigeons (138) but is able to contemplate his *own* affinity with the ducks (135). It is significant that the love affair Morris has with the small boy defies duality: he goes with Percival and Percival's mother to live in Africa. Morris writes to Ecks: "Together we three—a magic number full of cabbalistic references—form a rather eccentric group as you may imagine" (146). Indeed, a true intersubjectivity becomes possible precisely where the oppressive dualism of nationalist or metropolitanist identities has been undone. For example, on a distant and unidentified island where foreigners have congregated, where "their speech is a mixture of different tongues which meet in the making of invocations" (97), Ecks is able to find a sense of community with Morris and Graciela, again forming not a duo but a trio.[26] But, of course, as we have seen, even here where everyone seems to be a foreigner, a sense of dualistic identity reasserts itself: the town on the island, Pueblo de Dios, harbors a sense of self-identity that allows a rapist to continue raping in their community as long as he only does it to "outsiders." The utopia of the margins is destroyed as soon as any type of identity begins perpetrating its exclusions and exile of the other. The dilemma thus remains of how to have an identity that would enable community, intersubjectivity, and communication but which would not operate on the violence of the exclusion of difference.

A Dreadful Dissymmetry:
Exile and the Gen(d)eric Condition

So exile is portrayed in *La nave* as sociopolitical condition, which also constitutes, as Ecks tells Gordon, the ex-astronaut, an apt characterization of a generalized social and psychic state: "We have all been exiled from something or someone. . . . I think this is the human condition" (106).[27] Indeed, exile is shown to be a condition of living in a world split, divided, parceled out according to laws and identities that limit and contain human subjects to varying degrees. These identities are parodied in Morris's visit to a publishing company in "the Great Navel." As Morris attempts to fill out a form about a book he wants to publish, he maintains a comical dialogue with the implacably dualistically minded secretary. About the first question as to the genre of his text, he resists the categories offered him: "I don't know whether my work is a short novel, a long story or a narrative essay" (128). The secretary responds, "Either one or the other" (128), insisting on the strict binarism she has been hired to uphold, for, as Morris observes, "There is a secret subtle mechanism which ensures that the more one is oppressed the more repressive one becomes" (129). The form question, *"What predominates in your work? Action? Sex? Politics?"* provokes a lengthy discussion of politics and gender (129–32). Morris observes the lamentable binarism at work in political systems and identities: "The range of political registers of which we seem capable diminishes all the time, like a piano which is losing its keys. Nowadays there are but two politics and the differences between the two are minimal" (132). What he denounces then is the workings of a binary logic that obliterates difference and eventually reduces everything to a "logic of the same." On the "sexuality" of his text, Morris first wants to know: "As for sex . . . the form does not specify. Is there a privileged sex?" (130). The secretary proves an eloquent, no-nonsense spokesperson for the dominant ideology regarding gender and literary production:

> De un modo general . . . le puedo decir que una obra de sexo femenino tiene pocas posibilidades de éxito, salvo, claro está, que sea directamente sentimental. Publicamos pocas obras de sexo femenino, pero no se nota, porque hay pocas escritas en él. El público siempre espera obras masculinas, y los críticos también. Las mujeres que leen prefieren las obras masculinas, es la tendencia de nuestra civilización (128–29).

> [Generally speaking . . . I can tell you that a work of female sex has very little chance of success, unless it is purely and clearly a sentimental story. We publish very few works of female sex, which is not surprising, since there aren't that many written. The public demands masculine works, as do the critics. Women readers also prefer masculine works, such is the trend of our civilization (130).]

Morris, nonetheless, declares the gender of his text as outside of or between the parameters of such a strict binarism: "I think my book is androgynous" (130). The secretary, compassionate but practical, advises him: "You could see a doctor. . . . You mustn't worry too much. Relax and think of other things. I know of many cases like yours. It is not up to me to suggest, but why don't you put down that your book is of masculine sex? Then at least they'll look at it. Sometimes its better to tell a little lie" (131). While the secretary thus suggests a masculine masquerade, Morris, an inadvertent essentialist, worries that such an act would be dishonest: "But this would be betraying the deep essence, the very nature of the work, attributing to it a sex it doesn't have"(129). The secretary, however, in her infinite wisdom about the ways of the world, points out that gender, as Judith Butler would surely agree, mostly amounts to performance:

> —¡Bah!—respondió ella, que ahora parecía mucho más amistosa—. Todo el mundo se atribuye un sexo, ¿no es cierto? Nos pasamos la vida afirmándolo. ¿Se da cuenta? Gastarla así.

La vida entera procurando convencer a los demás y a nosotros mismos de que poseemos un sexo, con identidad propia, y de que lo usamos, lo mimamos, lo blandimos con propiedad.

—Sí —dijo Morris—. Es una preocupación neurótica. Al fin, ¿qué más da?

—Eso mismo. La ambición de un sexo es neurótica. Nos pasamos la vida en esa compulsión. Pero en fin, dado que ésas son las reglas del juego, dejémoslo así. Su obra, desde este momento, es de sexo masculino (129–30).

["And so what?" she asked in a conciliatory voice. "Don't we all attribute ourselves a sex? And spend our lives proving it? Do you realize, we waste our lives trying to convince others— and ourselves—that we have a sex, with its specific identity, which we use and suitably embellish and display."

"Yes," Morris said. "It seems a neurotic preoccupation. What does it matter in the end?"

"That's it; the end of sex is neurosis. It drives our lives. But since those are the rules of the game, let's accept them; from now on your book is of masculine sex" (131).]

There is nothing natural or essential about gender, according to this view; indeed, seen this way, gender—as so many contemporary feminist theorists suggest—is not a "being" at all but a "doing." While the secretary recognizes that one can never really "be" a gender, she does not espouse any sort of challenge to the social order, but rather virtually makes a man of Morris's text with a discursive flourish: "from now on your book is of masculine sex." This conferring of a particular gender on Morris's work by no means stabilizes gender as a category, but rather effectively shows gender to be arbitrarily imposed and ultimately unstable. The stabilization of gender, the claiming one or the other gender as one's own, is revealed to be a social convenience, or even an effective strategy. In addition, what the entire exchange points to is how the unwavering binarism of sexual identities banishes subjects who do not "fit," thus demonstrating how rigid sexual identities also contribute to a sense of alienation. Exile can thus also be a generic condition.

The relationship between sexuality and exile has been addressed by Cristina Peri Rossi in interviews.[28] For her, exile is particularly related to the plight of the woman writer: "It's difficult for me to know the place I occupy in Hispanic American literature because I'm a woman, and there are still few South American women writers, taking into account their problems of distribution for political reasons and *their practice of internal exile* (interview with Camps 44; emphasis added). While she did not expand on women's exile in that context, the concept of exile as a product of gender could have various meanings for women, stemming from the way women have been cut off from access to a desire of their own by the patriarchal sexual economy or the way the place of subjectivity has been appropriated as masculine, thus leaving her silenced and driven inward, without a place from which to speak (homeless, as it were).[29] In short, the alienation of women, theorized by feminists at least since Simone de Beauvoir, can be (and has been) cast as a type of exile. Furthermore, a sort of sexual exile results from the fact that while the subject is multiple, sexual identities are monological and univocal, with strict definitions of "real" masculinity and femininity. Peri Rossi has observed precisely this in another interview that bears a striking resemblance to the views voiced by the secretary in *La nave*: "Attributing to oneself a sex is almost always neurotic. And it is because it creates a tension between the multiplicity of the self and societal demands: there is nothing more ridiculous than a man who thinks he's very much a man; this is always a simplification" (interview with Golano 50). So, while the process of gendering seeks to exacerbate sexual difference and fit all subjects into one or the other gender, the radical failure of a subject to conform to the contours of that identity results in a type of exile, a sense of alienation from self.[30] For women this type of exile is often more acute since the normative representations, or what Judith Butler calls the "regulatory fictions," of woman are even more limiting and alienating than those prescibed for men. Androgyny—a term I use somewhat reluctantly and to which I will return later—would thus seem to provide a positive way of imagining such a sexual exile, a sort of utopia of sexual differences.

Indeed, *La nave de los locos* flirts with androgyny throughout, implying that such a defiance of a determined gender could function as a method of resistance to the rigid binary oppositions of the patriarchal sexual economy. Ecks himself is what I would call equivocally masculine. Peri Rossi chooses a male narrator for, as she herself has said, there is no history to "authorize" a female narrator who confronts the "big" metaphysical and existential questions.[31] So, much like the secretary who simply "declares" Morris's work "masculine," Peri Rossi simply "writes" Ecks as a man, "since those are the rules of the game" (131). Yet that is not to imply that Peri Rossi uses this masculine spokesman simply to reinforce such a hierarchy; she rather puts him in action to suggest a challenge to the "rules of the game" from within the game itself. Indeed, Jean Franco suggests that many women writers use masculine protagonists specifically to question gender hierarchy as it is inscribed in our social and literary relations:

> Estas escritoras [Rosario Ferré, Clarice Lispector y Cristina Peri Rossi] desenmascaran la hegemonía genérica que ubica al narrador masculino en la posición de autoridad y de productor. Las mujeres 'ventrílocuas' se instalan en la posición hegemónica desde la cual se ha pronunciado que la literatura es deicidio, la literatura es fuego, la literatura es revolución, la literatura es para cómplices, a fin de hacer evidente la jerarquía masculina/femenina ("Apuntes sobre la crítica feminista y la literatura hispanoamericana" 42).

> [These women writers (Rosario Ferré, Clarice Lispector, and Cristina Peri Rossi) unmask the gender hegemony that places the masculine narrator in the position of authority and producer. The women "ventriloquists" install themselves in the hegemonic position from which it has been pronounced that literature is deicide, literature is fire, literature is revolution, literature is for accomplices, in order to make evident the masculine/feminine hierarchy.]

Also commenting on this strategy as observed by Franco, Elia Kantaris points out that "Peri Rossi subverts the hegemonic position by making Ecks uncomfortable whenever he is put in the traditional role of the powerful male" (254). I agree and would emphasize that, rather than unequivocally voicing and enforcing the univocal discourse of a patriarch, Ecks's exploits show the "hegemonic position" to be precisely that: a *position*, not a physical, "natural," or essential attribute. Ecks's self-consciously constructed identity, his equivocal and mutable position as perpetual exile, and perhaps most importantly his growing awareness of how alienation and marginalization operate on virtually every level of modern existence, all serve to question and destabilize rather than reinforce the dominant social structure. In fact, the "discomfort" Kantaris talks about is directly related to Ecks's perception and awareness of how marginalization and violent oppression operate, an awareness he owes primarily to female characters.[32] According to the narrator, Ecks (like Morris) espouses androgyny to some degree, believing gender to be irrelevant

(25); and, indeed, the way Ecks takes his name and even his gender draw attention to identity as performance or masquerade. The sense of masquerade is further reinforced by our awareness that the text's author is a woman. This overall strategy has as its effect the denaturalization of genderic identity, of the name, of nationality.

Yet such an espousal of the "irrelevance" and instability of gender does not serve to erase sexual difference nor to foreclose on a denunciation of gender-specific violence in Peri Rossi's narrative. Rather, these strategies serve to point out how identities are always political: how they are constructed and ultimately deployed within systems of power relations. In fact, the text draws much attention to the violence and oppression to which women are subjected; from the pornographic images of the rape of a women on the movie screen to the beaten and disfigured face of a prostitute past her prime who has suffered at the hands of her pimp, Ecks encounters violence against women at almost every turn of his journey. Also included and critiqued are the practices of infibulation in Africa (174–75) and the lack of reproductive freedom in European society (159). The section titled "Eve" provides a tragicomic critique of the ways woman has been used as a scapegoat in patriarchal structure, the ways she is contained by discourses of the feminine, both through ancient mythologies and present day "wisdom." Here Graciela surveys a group of schoolchildren, asking them to describe Adam and Eve and their daily life in paradise. Their responses provide a satirical view of how attitudes about gender and power structures are handed down and assimilated by children at a very young age through such mythologies. A few examples:

Mi padre dise que era como todas las mujeres que se pasan el día conversando con las vecinas y viven fastidiando a los hombres para que les compren cosas, ropas y eso.

Dios sacó a Eva de una costilla de Adán porque el se aburría un poco y tenía ganas de tener a quien mandar .

Adán era muy responsable y muy serio pero Adán no sabía que mientras él andaba por los campos de Dios, ella se dedicaba a charlar con la serpiente que la engaño porque era muy astuta y ese fue un lio de mujeres.

Entonces Adán le dijo: Si quieres estudiar las ciencias del bien y del mal estúdialas, a mí no me importa, pero seguirás limpiando la casa y planchando, que es tu deber (157–60).

[*My dad says that Eve was like all women who spend their time gossiping with their neighbours and are always bothering men to buy them clothes and things.*

God created Eve from one of Adam's ribs because he was bored and he wanted somebody to order about.

Adam was very serious and full of responsibilities and didn't know that while he was walking through God's countryside she had started chatting to the serpent who was very cunning and deceived her. It was all a woman's plot.

And so Adam told her: If you want to acquire the knowledge of good and evil go on, I don't mind, but you must keep on cleaning the house and doing the ironing—that's your job (160–63).]

This section clearly denounces how our predominant mythologies represent women; as Graciela's "study" shows, Eve's "virtues" amount to only one ("beautiful"), while her defects are numerous and varied ("curious," "a gossip," "lazy," "frivolous" etc.). But perhaps what the children's supposed comments show even more precisely is how ideology is transmitted, how both traditional Creation mythology and contemporary constructions of feminine identity— colored by parental admonitions and observations—determine how the children come to see both Eve and women in general. All of this, of course, points to the dissymmetry inherent in a sexual economy that organizes gender, distributes power, and fixes values such that women are relegated to an inferior and negative position.

Masculine Impotence and a New Dream of Symmetry

A response to destructive and dissymmetrical gender identities is somehow demanded of Ecks by the enigma he confronts at the end of the novel. As we shall see, androgyny is taken up as a productive figure that could help imagine a dream of difference without opposition or violence, which could provide a glimpse of what Elia Kantaris has termed "plurality *in* identity."[33] The enigma itself is posed to Ecks in a dream:

En el sueño, había una pregunta que flotaba como un enigma, como aquellos acertijos que los reyes, enamorados de sus hijas, proponían a los pretendientes. Príncipes, caballeros degollados

en el insensato afán de resolver la oscura adivinanza que con-
servaba a las hijas para los padres. En el sueño, Ecks escuchaba
la pregunta: *"¿Cuál es el mayor tributo, el homenaje que un
hombre puede ofrecer a la mujer que ama?"* (183; emphasis in
the original).

[A question floated in the dream, an enigma, the sort of riddle
that kings, in love with their daughters, use to fend off aspiring
suitors.
    Princes and knights go to the scaffold, tempted to solve
the conundrum that keeps the daughters for their fathers alone.
    In his dream Ecks heard this question:
    *"What is the greatest tribute and homage a man can give
to the woman he loves?"* (166).]

The king, the most symbolic and authoritarian of fathers, desires
his daughter but produces all sorts of laws, games, riddles in order to
cover up that prohibited, incestuous desire.[34] Meanwhile, the king's
virtual monopoly on signification, being the only one who has access
to the meaning of his question, makes it impossible for any other to
gain access to his jealously guarded treasure. Pretending to be a game
about a search for the truth (the *right* answer), it is really a game
about the desire and power of the king (the *king's* answer). If the
princes play the game, they automatically submit to its rules,
authored and authorized by the king alone. By putting themselves
into play, the princes both accept the king's law and risk decapita-
tion, a symbolic "castration." What the dream sums up, or indeed
allegorizes,[35] is the patriarchal sexual economy: the way women are
scripted as pawns in ritualistic exchanges among men, the way all
possibilities for signification are controlled by a phallic power, the
way assuming the active subject position in such a structure revolves
around a (male) Oedipal crisis. Ecks searches for an answer to this
riddle that would avoid the violence of the "sacrifice," the multiple
sacrifice where the king alone, the phallic authoritarian par excellence, determines the fate of all involved.[36]
    The dream responds to and eventually finds its "solution" in
Ecks's encounters (in the last three tableaux of the novel) with two
women, each of whom has been victimized and violated by the dominant sexual order. In each of these situations Ecks begins by occupying a traditionally masculine and paternalistic position vis-à-vis
the women involved. Although always sympathetic, he remains
detached from their subaltern position, his masculine identity and

prerogative "intact." But as he listens to them, witnesses the suffering caused ultimately by unequal gender/power relations, and actually falls in love with one of them, his separation from them is threatened and he is transformed in the process.

In the first situation, Ecks has a job leading busloads of women to London so that they can obtain abortions. The women, victimized by their circumstances and by state policies that restrict their access to reproductive control, submit to a range of indignities including the verbal abuse on the part of the owner of the bus company who takes advantage of their desperation. Ecks, far from comfortable with his position, is nonetheless also subject to difficult circumstances due to his status as *extranjero*, observing, "there is not much choice at present" (167). Longing to establish some sort of tie with his charges, he buys cigarettes before each trip just to be able to offer the women some show of goodwill during the grim journey. Ecks reflects on these trips with sadness, finding similarities with mass experiments on pregnant women in Nazi Germany and associating their bus with myriad forms of social marginalization: "Field hospitals for the war-wounded. Military hospitals housing political prisoners. Woods where troublesome opponents disappeared. Ships of fools, the ship as substitutes for the madhouse. Evil-smelling prisons to lock up transgressors. Private clinics" (181). In an almost Foucauldian gesture, Ecks groups these spaces together as all places of stigma and isolation, created especially to receive those exiled from the realm of reason, health, and righteousness.[37] Ecks observes that these women, "accidentally and briefly thrown together in this ghetto-like situation," have as a result much in common with other marginalized groups: "[Ecks] senses that sharing anything, however inconsequential and incidental, that belongs to this humiliating experience makes them hostile toward each other. The fact of being pregnant is in this way like being born with the wrong skin colour, coming from the wrong side of the tracks, being an exile, [a red-head] or amputee: nobody has sympathy to spare for fellow sufferers" (169). Identity is thus portrayed as primarily a means of exclusion and as provoking violence. Furthermore, the marks that are systematically used to marginalize others (e.g., race, national identity) are shown to be as arbitrary and ultimately inconsequential as having red hair or lacking an arm.

It is in this situation that Ecks meets and falls in love with Lucía, a poor woman who becomes a passenger on the abortion bus only because Ecks takes pity on her and lets her ride for free. Feeling she has been victimized by the patriarchal sexual order, Lucía has vowed to never sleep with a man again:

La humillación no es sólo este autobús, el viaje silencioso, la clínica con su rápida intervención. La humillación es saberse víctima del azar, otra opresión. Jamás, jamás volveré a acostarme con un hombre. A través de ellos el azar entra en nuestras vidas, sometiéndonos. Venenosa intromisión. Jamás. Jamás. A través de ellos la esclavitud se propaga, se difunde, nos encadena. Jamás, jamás (176).

[The humiliation is not so much this bus, the silent journey, the clinic with its assembly-line service. The real humiliation is to know that you are the victim of chance, one more form of oppression. I'll never sleep with a man again. Never, never again. Men bring about our slavery, forge the chains. Never again (180).]

After listening to her, Ecks falls silent, powerless to respond: "Ecks was silent. They were now entering a part of the city without trees. Like men without phalluses, he thought" (180). By being part of this journey and empathizing with Lucía, Ecks must deal with the "other" side of the gender hierarchy, thus momentarily experiencing what it would mean to be like "a man without a phallus," to forego his privileged relationship to phallic power. The effect of this immersion in otherness causes Ecks to literally see himself as other: "As if in a dream, Ecks looked at her, saw himself looking at her and, from afar, saw them both" (181). In this way, Ecks becomes a vehicle of perception, a medium for making the reader perceive what is at stake in the hierarchies of the patriarchal sexual economy.

A similar brush with disempowerment occurs when Ecks encounters and tries to help a prostitute, another woman victimized by the unequal power relations in the conventional sexual order. Previously Ecks had briefly entertained the thought that prostitution offered women some escape from the constraints of the sexual oppression Lucía had denounced. After all, "women of the world" (translated from the Spanish "mujer de la vida" meaning prostitute) were among the few women who had the freedom to enter a bar unaccompanied by a man and order a drink alone: "To be a 'woman of the world' meant to be nobody's woman, not the woman of Ecks, nor of the kitchen, nor of the children. It meant to belong to life, to which we all—that is to say men—belong" (182). And yet he realizes that this far from equalizes things, that indeed prostitutes are ultimately at men's disposal, constituting virtual signs of male power: "A sad man enters a bar, asks for a beer . . . he possibly ends the night with some 'woman of the world' ejaculating his semen in her arse, because that's why he has a penis and has money to pay for his pleasure. Where do women turn, in whose arse do they discharge their misery?" (182). Indeed, Ecks comes face to face with the reality of the "women of the world" in the final tableau. The tired and spent prostitute Ecks meets in a public eatery, having been badly beaten by her pimp, convinces him to go up to her room with her so she can at least simulate turning a trick and avoid more violence. As they go up the stairs, Ecks suddenly has the sense that he has stepped over to the "other" side, to the realm of the powerless, the trapped, the impotent: "Ecks experienced a moment of vertigo and his heart jumped with terror; he felt as if he had leapt into the void. He remembered the exiles' stories: simulated executions; hooded figures pushed towards the cliff's edge" (192). So here, as in the case of the women on the abortion bus, Ecks explicitly associates the realm of the abused and denigrated woman with that of others victimized in a similar way by the dominant order: political prisoners who had been tortured, killed, and exiled.

The encounter with the prostitute, rendered utterly powerless by her subaltern position within the sociosexual system, provides Ecks with several lessons about the unequal power relations between the sexes and about how to try to undo some of those inequities. The entire time he is with her he is still questing for the answer to the enigma posed in the dream that begins this last tableau: "What was the answer? The only correct answer which could stop the sacrifice?" (193). The mere giving of a package of cigarettes, the gift of a symbol of (male) power that would only further aggrandize the giver, will not suffice; when Ecks offers a package of cigarettes to her, she rebels and proudly rejects his facile gift, causing him to muse: "Ecks thought at times it is better not to give. Could that be the answer? he asked himself. 'Do not give.'" (194). Unconvinced, he attempts a new strategy: declaring that he is incapable of an erection, he virtually offers her not a symbol of his own power (the cigarettes) but a sign of his own impotence, his own lack of phallic power. He continues: "If you want to know . . . I find that there is a kind of harmony in impotence" (194). Ecks has begun to understand what is required for a new dream of symmetry, the "harmony without sacrifice." What is involved here is not the threat of "castration" but an acceptance of the male body in its materiality, an attempt to disengage the penis from the transcendent and powerful phallus: "He stood naked, the flaccid member between his legs deserving no attention from anyone" (195).[38]

This encounter is the beginning of Ecks's realization and precipitates the end of his quest: "He left her room with the feeling that something had cleared in his mind. Without knowing why, he felt he was nearer the solution of his dream" (195). While still searching for the answer to his riddle, the "solution" that could throw the sacrificial, patriarchal order into question, that would radically undo the oppressive, rigid binary oppositions at work in the patriarchal sexual economy and, by extenstion, the authoritarian political system, Ecks stumbles upon Lucía as a participant in a transvestite porno-show. Witnessing her lesbian pantomime with a (female?) dancing partner, he suddenly begins to see the solution of the enigma through the constructions and deconstructions implicit in transvestism. He sees Lucía's dancing partner as "a man dressed up as a woman, or a woman disguised, someone who had changed identity to assume the identity of a fantasy, someone who had decided to be what s/he wanted to be and not what s/he was programmed to be" (198). Thus, through masquerade and parody, agency becomes possible, offering a model of social subjectivity whereby the individual would be not only subject to cultural norms but also subject of his/her own cultural production.

So, transvestism and a parodic masquerade are here cast as key elements in Ecks's journey to enlightenment. Judith Butler has theorized drag as a subversion and denaturalization of gender identity that has wide-ranging (and sometimes disparate) results. For Butler, "*In imitating gender, drag implicitly reveals the imitative structure of gender itself—as well as its contingency*" (137; emphasis in the original). Of course, as Butler also points out, while parody has plenty of political potential, "parody itself is not subversive" (139). Certainly, at the drag porno show in *La nave*, in the "ring of blood and sand, in which Hemingway would have liked to write, Henry Miller to ejaculate (or vice versa)" (198), where the men present "all members of the same sex . . . jeered and taunted, burst inflated paper bags, belched, whistled, applauded, stamped their feet" (197), the effects of the parody of gender identities is not the same for the other men in the audience as it is for Ecks. The erotic lesbian scene seems to send out disparate signals: while explicitly enacted for the titillation of the male spectators, it also parodies the gender identities and the compulsory heterosexuality of the conventional sexual economy that virtually sponsors the show. Perhaps, then, we can answer Butler's question of "*what performance where* will compel a reconsideration of the place and stability of the masculine and the feminine?" (139) by saying that the possibilities for such a destabilization of gender codes do not lie in the nature or the place of the spectacle alone. Rather such a reconsideration of gender can only occur in the spectator and performers themselves, that is, in the personal and political history each spectator brings to the scene of the spectacle, as well as in what each performer takes to the performance.

In this regard, it is especially significant that the subject Peri Rossi chooses for such a transformation—that is, Ecks—is gendered masculine. For the politics of parody to do its work, it cannot be women's work alone. Indeed, Lucía, as her name attests, is already "enlightened." It remains for the privileged, male subject to "see the light," which Ecks does with considerable enthusiasm, humility, and tenderness.

Indeed, this encounter with drag has subversive and enlightening results for Ecks in the final scenes of the text. Through such a deliberate defiance of univocal sexual identities, such an insistence on bearing a plural identity, the dream for difference without hierarchizing opposition that virtually drives Ecks's quest suddenly comes into view. The full impact of this realization hits Ecks when he sees Lucía after the show, dressed and half undressed as a man, ambiguously feminine and masculine (195). All at once, Ecks glimpses a new dream of symmetry:

> Descubría y se desarrollaban para él, en todo su esplendor, dos mundos simultáneos, dos llamadas distintas, dos mensajes, dos indumentarias, dos percepciones, dos discursos, pero indisolublemente ligados, de modo que el predominio de una hubiera provocado la extinción de los dos. Más aún: era consciente de que la belleza de uno aumentaba la del otro, fuera el que fuera (195).

> [He saw the unfolding of two parallel worlds in all their splendour; two different calls, two messages, two appearances, two perceptions, two languages, yet inseparably connected in such a way that the triumph of one would cause the death of both. He was aware that the beauty of one increased the beauty of the other . . . (202–03).]

Ecks suddenly realizes the possibilities of a doubleness such that difference can be included, incorporated, integrated. This is the quest, as we have seen, that has dominated *La nave* since the first tableau: how to continue to represent in this cultural milieu when "the wheat and the chaff have mixed" (1), how to represent our world without eliminating or exiling all the "chaff," how to find, in other words, "un equilibrio sin sacrificios" (35) ("an equilibrium without sacrifices").

Stunned by this vision, Ecks finally sees how to dream a new ending to his enigmatic dream. Later, when he once again faces the old king, Ecks at last rises up against the patriarch and in his dream announces the answer to the riddle: "The greatest tribute and homage a man can give to the woman he loves is virility" (204). To avoid the "sacrifice"—the killing/castration of the prince and, in more general terms, the violent smothering of one term by the other—man can offer his "virility," his masculine procreative, productive power, to woman, thus unveiling and demystifying the male prerogative, the privileged access to phallic power he enjoys. Ecks's "answer" also suggests that what man can best grant woman is *her* virility, her own sexual ambiguity, her own capacity to have access to a power ordinarily reserved for males. I agree with Elia Kantaris that this is not a question of foreclosure and castration. Kantaris points out that, rather than a univocal destruction of masculinity, the ending is open, implying simultaneously a "giving up of virility and the proffering of virility, the cutting of the cultural bond between authority, power and male sexuality without destroying that sexuality, the creation of a double discourse in which both the male and female can commune in a harmonious, shifting and complementary relation of equality" (262). Indeed, the very ambiguity of "su" (which in Spanish can mean his or hers) in the phrase "su virilidad" ("his/her virility") points to such an openness, doubleness, and lack of closure: neither his virility nor hers alone, the male monopoly over the phallic power of the (re)production of meaning is thus undone, while a gift of anything else would merely maintain his superiority. In this way, since neither one nor the other has a privileged relationship to the phallus, the different and unequal access men and women have to power is deconstructed. This is why as Ecks utters these open-ended and ambiguous yet defiant words, the symbolic father of the king, gatekeeper of our symbolic and sexual orders, dramatically shrivels up and dies, forever losing his power and authority: "the king shrinks, is now no bigger than a toy, a paper-maché puppet, a chocolate king; and he falls to the ground, blends with the mud; overcome, beaten, the poor little king disappears. He dies with a whimper" (204).

The ending to the text seems also to suggest androgyny as a sexual utopia, bringing up interesting questions regarding Cristina Peri Rossi's view of the function of gender differences. While seeming to advocate a certain utopian androgyny, *La nave* does not inscribe a complete erasure of gender difference or a utopia *beyond* gender sometimes implied by androgyny. Peri Rossi's text rather conceives of a coexistence of differences and radical reimagination of the sexual economy. Indeed, she seems to suggest not a complete erasure of gender differences but rather equal access to the diverse manifestations and privileges those differences offer. Her position here seems somewhat aligned with that of certain feminists who consider gender differences as limiting categories that should be eliminated.[39] However, as Margaret Whitford points out in her introductory essay on feminism and utopia, Luce Irigaray espouses a different utopia, one that would not eliminate gender differences but would imagine a "harmonious coexistence of men and women in the fertile conjunction of two sexual economies" (20). Certainly, the androgynous dream at the end of *La nave de los locos* does not contradict that vision either. Rather than, once again, placing these two visions in opposition, Whitford advocates a more dynamic view of utopia as process and prefers to see the similarities between these two versions of the future: "we are standing between two phantasies, two versions of the conditions for the future good life between which we cannot and do not need to arbitrate definitely" (20). My view of Cristina Peri Rossi's text is that her utopia is of this dynamic sort; we are left not with a blueprint for the future but a glimpse of how we can begin to change the mental paradigms that entrap us in the destructive binary gender system we now have. In other words, the final fate of gender differences as we know them is left in *La nave de los locos*, happily, without a "final solution."

The ending of *La nave* not only radically questions the gender system but our systems of representation as well. The diminishing of the representative of the phallic order that we have seen has its corollary in the last installment of the running description of the tapestry of the Creation on the very last page of the novel that reads simply: "The tapestry is missing January, November, December and at least two of the rivers of Paradise" (205). The tapestry—symbol of totality, harmony and wholeness—is left incomplete. Previously, such a lack would have only inspired confidence; since the tapestry followed such a closed system, it could simply be filled in, for the work had "a structure so symmetrical, so dependable that even when incomplete, it is possible to recreate the whole, if not on the cathedral wall, then within *the framework of our imagination*" (14; emphasis added). And, indeed, since almost half of the tapestry is missing, the running description we find interspersed throughout

La nave is an imaginary reconstruction of that harmony according to its own logic: "There [in the imagination] the missing parts unfurl, fragments intimating the larger harmony of the universe" (14). Yet, at the end of the narrative, after Ecks's realization of another possible harmony, the possibility for such reconstruction is undone; Lucía Guerra-Cunningham points out that *La nave de los locos* not only undermines order in its own content and structure but also "destroys the perfection of the structure represented in the tapestry in pointing out that at least two of the four mythical rivers of Paradise are missing" (72). However, it is not that Ecks's journey simply renders impossible or completely deconstructs that other utopia. The ordered world of the tapestry holds its own beauty and fascination, which the novel renders in the twelve tableaux it dedicates to its reconstruction. Yet Ecks's quest has altered his consciousness, has changed the parameters of the "framework of the imagination" where the tapestry was being reconstructed according to its inexorable logic. The open-ended break in the systematic description of the tapestry of Creation is not a facile destruction of that old order (which would ultimately fall into the exclusionary tactics Ecks denounces) but rather suggests new *work to be done*, not according to the "old dream of symmetry" but according to new concerns, according to a new model for a possible harmony that could allow for dynamic identities in/of difference. Those "two rivers of Paradise" that are lacking run toward places yet to be (re)imagined; the "January, November, December" left blank push us toward a future yet to be envisioned. Such a view of utopian vision as dynamic process is in direct contrast with the stasis of the utopia of the tapestry, "una metáfora donde todo el universo está encerrado" (21) ["a metaphor which encloses the whole universe"].

For many feminist theorists, such a dynamic utopia is the kind that can truly move forward: "[Utopia] is not, finally, any one place or time, but the capacity to see afresh—an enlarged, even transformed vision . . . a vital utopia requires change and interaction with alien forces; otherwise it becomes a barren and useless idea."[40] In bringing a static utopian vision into contact with the decentering forces of Ecks's own utopian search, *La nave* is able to enact just such a broadened notion of dynamic utopia. As Olivera-Williams points out: "Peri Rossi . . . looks at the chaotic signs of present reality and, using them as a point of departure, is able to create images of the ideal" (88). I agree: Ecks's contemporary quest attempts to turn disintegration and marginalization into an opportunity for plural identities and new intercommunication. Yet I see this gesture less as a *return* to a lost harmony (as Olivera-Williams suggests) than as an attempt to expand the notion of harmony to a *new* dream of symmetry that would avoid the violence of exclusion that Ecks himself sees in the harmony represented by/in the tapestry, the type of harmony that makes him observe near the beginning of the text that any "harmony assumes the destruction of those aspects of reality which oppose it" (13).

In this way, then, we are confronted with two distinct and interrelated utopian visions in *La nave*, one static (symbolized by the perfect, patriarchal order of the tapestry where "one could live one's life, engaged in a perfectly rational discourse whose meaning cannot be questioned" 14) and one dynamic (symbolized by Ecks's search for community in the midst of the alienation and marginalization in some sense caused by the first vision). Both of these utopias constitute allegorical gestures, attempts at translating the concepts of harmony, plenitude, and symmetry into figural and narrative images. And yet in the translation process itself these concepts are transformed. The concept of harmony operates in both allegorical gestures in *La nave*: the closed, static, and exclusionary harmony of the tapestry, reflecting the social system "whereby all meaning is deferred downwards from the Pantocrator through the man (father, namer) to the woman" (Kantaris 256), and the plural, dynamic, non-hierarchical, and inclusive harmony that is the goal of Ecks's quest, which he momentarily glimpses in Lucía's simultaneously feminine and masculine appearance. At first glance, these two visions would appear to be in radical opposition. On the relationship between the two representations, of the tapestry and of Ecks's journey, Lucía Guerra-Cunningham observes: "The tapestry functions as a symbol of a nucleus of cohesion that is totally absent in Ecks's peregrinations" (65). And yet, while Ecks's perambulations (which, through decentering and fragmentation, contradict the ordered unity usually attributed to traditional allegories) certainly provide a mirror opposite of the ordered world of the tapestry, their goal is also an ideal, an "equilibrium without sacrifices," a new kind of order. What Ecks's allegorical journey does, then, is expand and transform the *idea* of symmetry: turning it from an idea of a closed unity (which forces anything other to it into a "blind spot") into a conception of a multiplicitous and harmonious set of correspondences.[41]

Such a dream has political consequences as well. As Gabriela Mora has shown, the idea of "harmony" in the novel—what I have also termed "symmetry"—is closely bound up with the idea of the "natural." Mora quite rightly observes that the text is marked by "the desire to make *natural* characters and actions which transgress taboos" ("Peri Rossi" 345) and furthermore "the novel . . . proposes that the filth and poverty of the contemporary city, as well as the aggression directed toward the 'disappeared,' the prostitute and the unmarried pregnant woman, disrupt the 'natural' and the 'harmonious' in a world of ideal equilibrium" ("Peri Rossi" 347). Indeed, as the text strives to denaturalize identities (sexual, textual, and national), it is, in effect, denaturalizing what the authoritarian regimes of the Southern Cone attempted to naturalize, that is that "National Security" necessitates the silencing, disappearance, and even murder of any and all opposition (real or perceived), that the need for foreign capital makes it acceptable to neglect the economic exigencies of one's own citizens, and that sexuality should be confined to matrimonial heterosexuality where women's traditional roles are upheld.[42] *La nave*'s radical interrogation of the "natural" versus the "unnatural" seems especially resonant given the Uruguayan military regime's penchant for portraying the nation as well as the military itself as natural and organic (Payne 49). The military sought to characterize its ascent to power as the "natural" solution in the face of the chaos and "artificiality" of the democratic system and leftist opponents.[43] Such appeals to the organic or natural are also common to other authoritarian regimes—witness the Argentine junta's view of "the 'national being' as 'essential, normative base'" and its attempt to portray anything it felt threatening to its power as "alien" or "not ours."[44] Cristina Peri Rossi's text works to transform ideas of what constitutes a "natural" order, undoing—at least in "the framework of the imagination"—the "old dreams" of the National Security State.

Ultimately, Peri Rossi's text demonstrates how the allegorical mode, with all its politicoethical capabilities and linguistic duplicities, can not only simply refer to static abstract concepts but actually transform those very ideas. The concept of harmony, for example, can be given a new allegorical expression that would propose a reevaluation and re-imagining of that abstract value. I realize, of course, that symmetry and harmony seem almost jarring terms to be used regarding a text I have placed in a postmodern context. Indeed, forward-thinking postmodern thought espouses dispersion and fragmentation, declares "war on totality," thus making harmony seem a suspect idea for the "terror" it has left in its wake.[45] But, ultimately, it is not harmony itself that is the culprit but rather the way it has been imagined. The allegory of Ecks's journey in *La nave* attempts to re-imagine a harmony that would not simply suppress and exclude the other but include the marginalized and propose a true intersubjectivity. In this regard, I agree with Chilean critic Lucía Invernizzi Santa Cruz who proclaims this attempt a resounding success: "As a space of communication and dialogue, of exchange between writing and reading . . . *La nave de los locos* is established as an effectively realized utopia: a place of encounter and authentic relation between subjects" (52). And as Invernizzi Santa Cruz indicates, the realization of this utopian project is based on the participation demanded of and offered to the reader, who must construct and create the meaning of the text, thus turning the reader/writer relationship into an intersubjective exercise (51). In this way, Ecks's allegorical journey and *La nave* as a multiply allegorical text belie what has sometimes been called allegory's enactment of a single, conceptual meaning that leaves the reader no interpretative freedom.[46]

In transforming and re-imagining harmony through allegorical technique, *La nave* demonstrates the extent of the ethical possibilities of allegory.[47] This dream of symmetry, because of the way the entire text has been constructed allegorically, has implications for not only the gender system but also the sociopolitical realm and the way representation is carried out. The refusal to merely destroy the tapestry, indeed the refusal to opt for *either* a language of the ideal *or* the real, helps make *La nave de los locos* an example (an allegory, perhaps) of the very textual practice it, in some sense, preaches: it defies the binary "sacrifice" of the other as far as it can and opts instead for a new dream of symmetry where differences could harmoniously coexist. Indeed, Peri Rossi's text, utopian without being programmatic, finds hope in marginalization and dispersion and puts into play the positive possiblities of allegorical dreaming.

CONCLUSION

TRANSGRESSION AND TRANSFORMATION: AESTHETICS, POLITICS AND (POST-) AUTHORITARIAN CONTEXTS

Creo profundamente en la mujer que, al transgredir
pautas atávicas, crea campos de conocimiento y
de apertura para sí y para otros . . . Creo que la mujer
democrática es la que . . . al transgredir
produce verdaderas transformaciones y sustenta
los procesos de cambio que desencadena.

[I believe profoundly in the woman who, in transgressing
atavistic rules, creates fields of knowledge and
of opening for herself and others . . . I believe that the
democratic woman is the one who . . . in transgressing
produces true transformations and sustains
the processes of change that she unleashes.]

—Liliana Mizrahi
La mujer transgresora

Texts are worldly, to some degree they are events,
and, even when they appear to deny it, they are
nevertheless a part of the social world, human life,
and of course the historical moments in which
they are located and interpreted.

—Edward Said
The World, the Text, and the Critic

O que se fizer em minha carne
se estará fazendo no mundo.

[What is done to my flesh
will be done in the world.]

—Nélida Piñon
A Casa da Paixão

Revolution has long been both a sociopolitical reality and a literary theme and practice in Latin America. Certainly, each of the texts I have examined in this study shows some form of *disconformidad*: that is, resistance to the status quo and desire for change. Yet, the model for change in these texts is decidedly not one of revolution but of *transformation*. It is perhaps no coincidence that, as Sonia Alvarez's study shows, in this period in the Southern Cone significant social change is being accomplished not so much by a radical, revolutionary break with old institutions, but rather by a transformation through and against those very institutions.[1] This is also, in effect, the kind of change Argentine writer Liliana Mizrahi imagines for women; she advocates not a total break with old ways but a dialogue with them, thus using current contradictions with old patterns as an opportunity for creative transformation.[2] Such a model of change—working through and against previous forms—is certainly apropos to the fictions included here. Indeed, these fictions pick up the materials bequeathed to them by authoritarian and patriarchal social systems, the symptoms of repression, violence, censorship, terror, and exile, and proceed to transform them—with the aid of allegorical techniques—into sources of resistance and creativity.

The transformations in these texts are concerned with how to produce new meanings, how to alter traditional gender patterns as well as other oppressive social structures. Each text offers a particular, innovative understanding of gender and a refusal of assumptions about women's writing as personal rather than political, or traditional rather than experimental. Not all of these texts, by any means, enact the same transformation, but change is in itself a significant textual trajectory in each case. In *A Casa da Paixão*, for example, the psychosexual transformations of Marta and Jerônimo are of primary importance. But even as Marta is transformed and manages to rescript the gendering process to a degree, her context ultimately remains untransformed, her quest falls into a familiar pattern, and change is frustrated. In this way, the text shows us the perilous path to a feminine erotics and subjectivity, forcing us to reflect on the pitfalls of the quest, the difficulties inherent in our will to make meaning and to transform an old and ingrained social structure. On the other hand, Piñon's text does enact an important degree of change, managing to envision a feminine erotics and, more importantly, the *writing* of that feminine erotics which in itself is a utopian and ground-breaking gesture. The quest for change dominates the narrative trajectory in the other novels as well. In *Por la patria* we saw how Eltit's text manages to articulate and transform the margins from a space of pain and fragmentation into an erotically, politically, and textually vibrant place. In concrete terms, the women are freed, the bar is reopened, collective speech is restored and preserved. Change is also of prime importance in *La rompiente*, which traces the protagonist's transformation from censored silence to writerly subjectivity. As the novel documents her path out of silence, the ending holds promise that, yes, she will find the "splendor of a voice," and indeed this "itinerary of writing" has constituted the first step. Finally, regarding *La nave de los locos* we saw how the very idea of harmony was transformed from an exclusionary representational mode into a generous and tenderhearted acceptance of real differences. Ecks himself, transformed though his quest, is able to dream a new ending to his dream: to recognize and deconstruct the privileges of masculinity and to imagine something different.

In each case, the transformations involved are portrayed, to varying degrees, as functions of the processes of reading and writing. As Teresa De Lauretis points out, views of narrative have recently turned to consider the "transformative effects produced in processes of reading and practices of writing" (*Alice Doesn't* 105). Each of the texts included in this study revolves around the postulation or representation and reproduction of such "transformative effects," in all their contradictions and dissonances. In each case, there is a thematics of writing that draws attention to such transformative properties. In *A Casa da Paixão*, writing as theme appears as Marta's "writing on the wall" that ultimately determines the second half of the novel. As Marta writes quite literally from the body, she expresses her desire as well as her determination to be the author of her own quest. Her writing provides a means of challenging patriarchal authorities and of transforming the process of "becoming a woman." In a very different way, Eltit's protagonist, Coya/Coa, virtually writes herself, her fellow inmates, and collective speech out of imprisonment and into a more viable subjectivity. It is explicitly through her *writing*, produced from within the repression of the prison, that Coya's resistance can take hold. In Roffé's novel, the exercises of reading and writing undertaken by the protagonist are figured as practices that can break through silences imposed by patriarachal and political authorities. And in *La nave de los locos*, "el viaje leído" / "the read journey" provides a structuring principle for the novel, and writers and readers abound (Morris, Graciela, Ecks himself). Each of these characters engages in writing as important ways of interpreting, critiquing, and reimagining our world. Yet, even though in each text writing is cast as a politically and erotically transformative activity, these authors do not therefore necessarily eschew political action of a practical, collective sort. They do, however, recognize the symbolic and cultural spheres as prime battlegrounds for the production of meaning and as where social transformations can begin to be conceptualized.

In sum, the sometimes utopian transformations envisioned by these novels actually offer theories of social and sexual change. First, returning to the point I made at the beginning, these texts theorize change not as a break with the past but a dynamic, deconstructive and reconstructive interaction with it. Second, engaging in an intellectually inflected form of what Beatriz Sarlo has called "politics as passion" ("Women, History, and Ideology" 240–42), these texts show how the political and the sexual are inextricably linked for women subjects, especially for women in acute political situations such as authoritarianism. In insisting on the simultaneity of political and sexual concerns, they refuse the model for change that Sarlo designates "politics as reason," wherein "gender politics and social politics are considered two noncontradictory levels of thought and action" ("Women, History, and Ideology" 238). For these writers, feminist critique cannot take second place to political resistance, but rather must be an integral part of any sociopolitical and cultural resistance. Finally, and perhaps most importantly, the theories of change envisioned here recognize that language is the most basic building block of our social structure and that sociocultural transformation begins by transfiguring our imaginary, our symbolic systems, our modes of expression and ways of seeing. Reading and writing are foregrounded by these texts in recognition of the prime importance of and serious difficulties with representation, particularly for women who write in the face of political oppression. The narratives studied here thus defy any facile dichotomy of the aesthetic and the political, affirming the value and importance of art even in the context of political and national disaster.

Clearly, any kind of change necessarily entails confrontations with authorities of various kinds and, in the case of narrative, these authorities are generic and sociopolitical as well as literary. This is perhaps why transgression is such a principal component of these texts; each text narrates some type of transgression in order to imagine a disarticulation of restrictive discursive boundaries. Indeed, in these novels, transgressive sexuality in particular becomes a means of figuring confrontation with the traditional ways sexuality and gender have been constructed in the cultural imagination, a way of violating the boundaries articulated by dominant discourses, and of breaking through the containment and oppression of authoritarian structures. Along with other forms of defiance—that is, defiance of the father's law (*A Casa da Paixão*), of official history (*Por la patria*), of imposed silence (*La rompiente*), of accepted ways of imagining identity (*La nave de los locos*)—these transgressions all work to resist authorities and social regulations.

While transgression certainly operates on a thematic level, it is also a textual strategy, a strategy that relates very closely to the literary experimentation of these narratives. Experimentation in narrative often entails breaking established norms, whether with regard to genre, narrative structure, character, or language. Indeed, many of the specific techniques found in the texts studied here—allegorical gestures, unconventional and disruptive usage, rupture of syntactic structures, linguistic play with rhyme, rhythm, alliteration, and placement of the words on the page, representing the writing process itself—all constitute marks of experimental writing and most could also be considered types of textual transgression. Such writing is especially transgressive coming from the woman writer who is, we have seen time and again, not expected to write in a highly intellectual, experimental, or symbolic style, if she writes at all. But, beyond defying gender expectations, what is further interesting about this experimentalism is that it has complex political *as well as* aesthetic aspirations and effects.

In the authoritarian context, literary transgression can take on more political functions. The transgressive can be seen as part of the quest to disarticulate dominant conventions and authoritarian modes, as attempts to undo the univocal logic of dictatorship and to question notions of truth. On another level, textual experimentation can also work to disrupt the literary conventions pertaining to politically critical fictions, literary conventions that are often more comfortable with the modes of realism and testimony. Writing on politics and aesthetics, Adorno notes that "committed" art works at the level of "fundamental attitudes" while "tendentious" art is intended to generate particular measures or legislative acts (180). The writings analyzed here are certainly politically "committed" in this way; rather than advocating contextually specific reforms, they propose to change modes of representation and perception. Yet as Adorno also observes, "what gives commitment its aesthetic advantage over tendentiousness also renders the content to which the artist commits himself inherently ambiguous" (180). It is perhaps this ambiguity that makes such politically committed narrative that has complex aesthetic concerns (concerns with language, style, and

modes of representation) suspect and unwelcome in some oppositional political circles. The fact that such an aesthetically complex
narrative practice *also* insists on a radical critique of gender politics makes it even more disruptive.

Yet, aesthetically preoccupied writing is also subversive of
authoritarian modes in another way. It is an intimate resistance, a
passionate refusal of authoritarianism's attempt to be sole source
of meaning. As Diamela Eltit puts it, "I wrote four books under dictatorship and it is social space that I salvage for myself from that
time. But that does not for one instant make amends for the humil-
iations, or the fear, or the pain or impotence for the victims of the
system. To write in that space was something passionate and personal. My secret political resistance" ("Errante, Errática" 18–19).
Reina Roffé also refers to such an intimate resistance and the "luxury" of writing:

> The 'líneas de fuerza' for the protagonist, like the writing of *La
> rompiente* for me, functioned . . . like a form of intimate resis-
> tance, like a secret *power* that no one had the *power* to snatch
> away. The act of reading and writing is always—and much
> more so in limit situations—a type of personal luxury, in which
> the reader or the one who writes appropriates an/other world
> that corrects or opposes the world of reality and where the feel-
> ing that reigns is, or should be, free will. It's like saying: I can,
> in spite of everything.[3]

Writing, especially writing so aesthetically rich, stealthily attacks
authoritarian illusions of control over the hearts and minds of its
citizens. While writing experimental literature in the face of the horror of authoritarianism might seem almost self-indulgent and even
barbaric in the same way that writing lyric poetry after Auschwitz
was said to be barbaric, such writing also refuses to allow the forces of
terror to have their way, responding as only culture can, "with life to
the machinery of silence and death."[4] In reflecting on the crisis of representation in Argentina, Luisa Valenzuela observes: "The madness of
power resides in its idea that it can control fiction, that is to say, the
imaginary expression of desire. The madness of fiction is to believe
that it doesn't" (82). Such fictional "madness" affirms hope and
refuses to surrender whatever transformative powers it can muster.

As we have seen in individual readings, experimental, nonre-
alist forms can be both the product and denunciation of authoritarian regimes. They confront the crisis of representation wreaked by

brutal dictatorship and turn that crisis into an opportunity for creation, a creation that defies and undoes authoritarian dictates. Ultimately, it is style, and most especially allegorical gestures, that can
transform the materials and fallout of repression. On the other hand,
these writings are perhaps also a confrontation with the crisis of
representation implied by postmodern international literary trends,
reconfiguring and repoliticizing that more aesthetic or philosophical
"crisis." In *The Politics of Postmodernism*, Linda Hutcheon notes
that there has been a "two-way involvement of the postmodern with
the feminist" whereby feminism has caused postmodernism to
reconsider the relationships between the public and the private (and
the personal and the political) while postmodern representational
modes have provided feminism with much-needed tools to challenge patriarchy's stranglehold over signifying systems (167). In the
context of fictions critical of authoritarianisms, such a "two-way
involvement" is complicated and enriched such that both feminism
and contestatory politics can lift useful representational strategies
from the postmodern repertoire and, likewise, postmodernism can
thus be conjugated with a new set of political imperatives.

My concluding remarks thus far obviously reflect a narrative
production steeped in power struggles and bent upon a very political
creativity. Reading in context means taking such power relations
into consideration. As Edward Said has pointed out:

> The realities of power and authority—as well as the resistances
> offered by men, women, and social movements to institutions,
> authorities, and orthodoxies—are the realities that make texts
> possible, that deliver them to their readers, that solicit the
> attention of critics. I propose that these realities are what
> should be taken account of by criticism and the critical con-
> sciousness (*The World, the Text, and the Critic* 5).

Certainly, by now it should be clear that I agree with Said that attention to how texts engage with their contextual authorities is a necessary and fruitful focus. My goal in reading each of these novels
has been to look carefully at the power struggles they enact and the
authorities that are addressed by such power struggles. What I hope
my readings have elucidated is how these texts both inscribe and
are marked by their sociopolitical and generic contexts.

The marks of sociopolitical and generic contexts are both similar and different in these narratives, reflecting to a degree the par-

ticular personal and political situation of each author. While I would certainly resist reducing such complex texts to biographical referents, such resistance should not, and ultimately cannot, erase the very real circumstances under which texts are written, cicumstances that are very much a part of reading in context. Nelida Piñon, Diamela Eltit, Reina Roffé, and Cristina Peri Rossi all lived through the experience of dictatorship, although each in a very different way. Some wrote from within dictatorship, others from without (that is, from exile), but all at some point experienced its heavy hand. Certainly the way they experienced authoritarianism marks their writing, as we have seen in individual chapters. But how do they compare? Nelida Piñon, for example, stayed in Brazil and wrote under the burdens of authoritarian political practices. During a time of strict state censorship, she wrote a supple, linguistically transgressive denunciation of patriarchal law, which, if read in context, calls into question the authoritarian text. But while in *A Casa da Paixão* she wrote from within authoritarian conditions, her engagement with language bespeaks a concern with power and limitations on freedom which goes far beyond her immediate sociohistorical milieu. Her approach in this novel was to focus on one of the most repressed and controlled realms: feminine sexuality and its relationship to language. Piñon's concern with form and language, and with the politics of sexuality, is shared by Diamela Eltit, who also remained in an authoritarian context, of Pinochet's Chile. Yet in other ways, their writing is in sharp contrast. While Piñon's text never refers directly to Brazil and seems to touch only tangentially upon the issues raised by the authoritarian context, in *Por la patria* Eltit virtually wrote *through* the materials provided by the dictatorship. Eltit takes up the violence, terror, social fragmentation, torture, and guilt wreaked on the margins of Chilean society and turns them into a political poetics. Her referents, as overcoded as they may be, ultimately have to do the reign of terror in Chile during the most repressive and violent years of Pinochet's regime.

The other two writers included in this study both wrote from outside dictatorship, although the fallout from authoritarianism is still very much present in their narratives. Reina Roffé was silenced by the Argentine regime in a very direct way when her novel *Monte de Venus* was banned. She wrote *La rompiente* from outside the regime, in exile in the aftermath of her silencing. But through the complex narrative structure of her text, she is able to re-produce her writing under authoritarianism such that she can read (and we, as readers, can read with her) the traces that censorship and terror have left in her unconscious, in her dreams, and in the "text" within her text. In spite of its ambiguity and multiple narrative voices, her novel is, as her other writings attest, highly autobiographical. Peri Rossi on the other hand, even though she also writes from the experience of exile, writes from considerably more emotional distance than does Roffé. While her experience was certainly painful, she wrote *La nave de los locos* after many years in exile when she was able to approach her subject in a less directly autobiographical and more humorous mode. She explains: "I was already starting to feel de-exiled when I wrote *La nave de los locos*, I had separated myself quite a bit from the image of the exile, . . . For that very reason I could write the novel of exile not in first person and with a certain irony" (Interview with Camps 43). In this sense, of the four writers, she is, at the time of writing *La nave de los locos*, the most "outside" the authoritarian regime. But it is precisely this distance that allows her a unique vantage point: she can see authoritarianism as not peculiar to Latin American or even developing nations but as a political system operating in many parts of the world and as resonant with other authoritarianisms—textual and sexual as well as political.

So the texts I have examined variously provide a vision from outside or from inside, from within censorship and terror or in its aftermath, from the perspective of different degrees of exile. In representing authoritarian conditions from diverse perspectives and positions, they provide compelling examples of the different ways experimental, aesthetically preoccupied writings by women engage their political contexts.

But, pursuing the question of readerly and writerly contexts even further, why study "writings by women" as a separate entity at all? As Reina Roffé's imagined gentleman interlocutor objects: "How is it possible to make such a division, was a masculine literature per chance ever spoken about?" ("Qué escribimos" 206). Roffé's response to his challenge is revealing:

"If masculine literature was never spoken about it was because it wasn't necessary, there was only one literature, the one made by men. And it was precisely when the literary production by women began growing in quantity and quality that critics began calling it 'feminine literature.' It was used as a pejorative term, disqualifying, in order to indicate that it was a minor literature. It was believed, and you demonstrate that it is still believed, that the author, the authority, was masculine and the ones authorized to write were men. Now it seems that they want to have us come in through the front door," I said, remembering some of the participants of the round tables. "They don't miss the opportunity to authorize us, to give us permission, to permit us to have access to the univocal and grandiose field of Literature" ("Qué escribimos" 207).

As Roffé points out, "women's writing" as a category is in the process of being transformed. Originally used in a disparaging way, it has been appropriated and revalorized by feminists—much in the way of Eltit's gesture of occupying and rearticulating the margins, or other similar revalorizations and resemanticizations.[5] But what Roffé's response also reveals is that the issue is not only inclusion or exclusion but also who is opening and closing the door. Roffé's comments ultimately exemplify women's real and perceived unequal access to authority and processes of authorization. This different relationship to power is, in part, why I have enacted a strategic separatism for this project. As Marta Traba suggests in referring to women's writing as "a different writing": "If we became aware of our marginalization and, in addition, our place in the counterculture, it would be easy for us to reject *being spoken* by others" (26). Indeed, it seems urgent to me, at the present moment, to see how women writers work out their own relation to cultural and political authorities, how they incorporate their context and write from their own somatic and social experience as women, how they speak for themselves and refuse the ways women have been "spoken" by traditional models. Luce Irigaray's meditations on the practical, positive possibilities of a temporary, strategic separatism for women are worth repeating:

> For women to undertake tactical strikes, to keep themselves apart from men long enough to learn to defend their desire, especially through speech, to discover the love of other women while sheltered from men's imperious choices that put them in the position of rival commodities, to forge for themselves a social status that compels recognition, to earn their living in order to escape from the condition of prostitute . . . these are certainly indispensable stages in the escape from their proletarization on the exchange market. But if their aim were simply to reverse the order of things, even supposing this to be possible, history would repeat itself in the long run, would revert to sameness . . . (*This Sex* 33).

In a sense, the separatism operant in such configurations as women's studies or women's writing provides benefits similar to the ones Irigaray describes. Yet Irigaray's warning about the danger of separatism is well taken. Furthermore, imagining women's writing as different, as Traba proposes, entails risks of its own due to women's precarious inclusion in literary circles. Diamela Eltit points out these risks in an interview:

> What the system would seek would be to put women in competition and leave the literary space open and protected for the masculine. This bothers me very much since even though I conceive of the feminine as specificity and difference it seems to me that this attitude reiterates, and in a dangerous way, the same ideological conditions that mold the tactics of omission (interview with Ortega 237).

It is thus crucial to recognize that to embrace the "difference" of women's writing is ultimately no more than a strategy, a tactical redeployment of a difference that has a long and ingrained history of marginalizing the feminine on so many levels.[6] Nonetheless, as a strategy, it continues to have value.

All things considered, it is perhaps the context of these texts (political, social, generic, Latin American) that most drew my attention as I began this project. As U.S. feminists struggle to deal with gender issues in conjugation with class and race, we have much to learn from Latin American women who must often confront these multiplicities simultaneously, as inhabitants of dependent capitalist nations and as inheritors of a cultural context that has been heavily marked by colonialism and neocolonialism. The authoritarian context, furthermore, marks a place where generic and political oppressions are most acute, most intertwined, and most mutually supporting. The literary interventions reflect this confluence and thus provide rich ground for analysis regarding how feminism and liberational politics are both the same and different struggles, how sexuality and politics are neither neatly separate nor merely an exact reflection of one another. If nothing else, these texts teach important lessons about what I view as a complex, primarily metonymic relationship between sexuality and politics.

That said, what are the lessons that can be drawn from these texts? What theories of gender do they enact? Perhaps the most obvious lesson, and the one consistently explored in individual chapters, is that gender cannot be isolated from the sociopolitical context.

These texts provide eloquent testimony of how women are censored, exiled, and limited by patriarchal authorities long before an explicitly authoritarian government steps in. Other lessons also emerge again and again. While these texts all flirt with androgyny at times, it is mostly used as a trope to denaturalize gender, not as an end in itself. Ultimately, comparing the representations of gender in these texts, we can see that difference is reiterated, not obliterated. Piñon's Marta, for example, is not striving toward an androgyny that would flatten differences, but rather wants both genders to have access to the privileges and insights of the other. Although sexual undecidability is a prime feature of the narrative voices of *La rompiente*, Roffé ends her text with menstruation as signifier of feminine difference and also as a component of a new female imaginary. Eltit's Coya is perhaps strategically *andrógina* but as the very gender of that adjective shows, she always maintains a certain degree of femininity. And even though Peri Rossi's narrative ends with a virtual spectacle of androgyny, she proposes not the sheer erasure of difference, but the possible complementarity of genders and the coexistence of differences such that "the triumph of one would cause the death of both" (*The Ship of Fools* 202). In all of these texts, difference is desirable, accepted, and even celebrated. Yet, drawing from Marta's "misfortune" in *A Casa da Paixão*, essentializing difference can make imagining social change difficult. Femininity as difference, like the "difference" of women's writing, is most productive when conceived dynamically as strategy not essence. For the most part, gender *is* portrayed as dynamic in these writings, as both product and process at once. Furthermore, in casting gender and the process of gendering as places of political contention, these texts all attempt to envision changes in the way gender and power have been organized, in the way gender relations have been imagined and practiced. A simultaneous transgressive critique of the status quo and utopian vision for transformation are common to these fictions. In perhaps the most utopian text of all, *La nave de los locos*, the denunciation is relentless and change is brilliantly realized. But what that novel shows us is that it will take a realization the likes of Ecks's to truly turn things around, to incapacitate the murderous king, to loosen the patriarchal order's stranglehold on social relations. Ultimately, as Ecks so clearly sees, for women to become truly empowered, men must forego some of their power and their privileged relationship to the production of meaning. Certainly, with her utopian narrative, Peri Rossi sets in motion a theory for such a transformation. Putting her theory into practice is another story.

But in the meantime, in the wake of the "redemocratization" of the Southern Cone, when certain military leaders of Uruguay and Argentina are attempting a belated and somewhat suspect *mea culpa* in order to "clean the slate," and when many are attempting to forget and somehow erase the dictatorships' crimes, one of the most important legacies of the texts studied here is their inscription of their political context and how that political context was experienced by women who write. Correspondingly, one of our most important tasks as readers is not to forget what they tell us.

NOTES

All translations from the Spanish and Portuguese throughout the book are my own unless otherwise noted.

Introduction

1. The development and implementation of this doctrine—which was influenced by "counterinsurgency" practices developed by the French and the United States during the Cold War—is discussed by Armand Mattelart in "Ideología, información y estado militar" (Ideology, Information and Military State) in Michele and Armand Mattelart, *Comunicación e ideologías de la seguridad* (Communication and Ideology of Security). See especially pages 51–83. Also see "The Doctrine Behind the Repression" in *Nunca Más* (442–45), which provides insight into the doctrine of National Security as implemented in Argentina.

2. Pinochet, cited in Munizaga and Ochsenius (80). René Jara analyzes how the cancer metaphor was used in Southern Cone authoritarian discourse in order to justify the radical, "surgical," techniques of the regimes (32–34).

3. In many ways, the reign of Brazil's military (1964–85) served as a "model" for the other countries mentioned (Alvarez 7; see also Armand Mattelart). While the general trend I describe was followed in the authoritarian regimes of Argentina (1976–83), Chile (1973–89), and Uruguay (1973–85), the course of events and the functioning of the military regime in each country was also quite different. It is not my goal to launch into an extended discussion of the differences between the political environments of each country nor the distinct relationships between culture and social and political institutions in each case. I merely want to note the similarities among these regimes in order to clarify the consequential plight of cultural production and the correlation seen by women between authoritarianism and gender politics in their respective countries.

4. This is not to say that the violent circumstances of the Southern Cone are entirely autochtonous or isolated from the international arena. They very much form part of the cold war scenario, predominant from the 1950s to the late 1980s. Indeed, the (at least initial) U.S. support for these regimes is well-known. Foreign investment, furthermore, was encouraged as

these regimes espoused "free market" economic policies; and the concern for foreign capital often took precedence over more national interests. That said, the insider/outsider configuration is a complex one, worthy of further exploration.

5. Masiello "La argentina" (11–12); Sarlo ("Política" 40); Jara (29).

6. Marily Martínez de Richter has also pointed out that Sarlo's article completely ignores narrative produced by women that relates to the sociopolitical context of the authoritarian regime. See her article on Marta Lynch and Reina Roffé (90).

7. The term is Gayle Rubin's. In her seminal essay "The Traffic in Women," she defines the sex/gender system as "the set of arrangements by which a society transforms biological sexuality into products of human activity, and in which these transformed sexual needs are satisfied" (159). For a rich and lucid analysis of the particular issues at stake in using such a conceptual model vis-à-vis Latin American texts, see the chapter entitled "Translating Gender" in Amy Kaminsky's *Reading the Body Politic*. I certainly agree with Kaminsky's observations on the untranslatability of the English term "gender." Yet, as Kaminsky's own arguments show, while "gender" may frustrate the translator, it is far more successfully handled by the interpreter. For my part, I employ the term throughout this study as it is currently used in U.S. feminist criticism, albeit always trying to draw my theoretical observations out of the Latin American texts themselves, as I will explain shortly.

8. For the process of "othering" see Simone de Beauvoir, *The Second Sex* (157–253). The alienating effects of this mirroring process are described by Luce Irigaray in *Speculum of the Other Woman* as well as in *This Sex Which Is Not One*. In "The Laugh of the Medusa," Hélène Cixous also shows how woman's body "has been more than confiscated from her," and suggests that only writing her self "will give her back her goods, her pleasures, her organs, her immense bodily territories which have been kept under seal" (250). In the North American context, these ideas have been developed by Catharine MacKinnon in "Feminism, Marxism, Method, and the State," to cite just one example.

9. For example, as Chilean writer Diamela Eltit sees it, the dictatorship in her country constitutes a virtual caricature of patriarchy: "Beyond feminist theory, it is a fact of current society that it is the man who holds power. It is also unarguably his failure. Chile is an example of this, extreme and caricatural. Here, the failure of patriarchal power is so severe that it needs a father/dictator to administer it" (interview with Ríos 31). Clearly, for this writer, the political concerns of authoritarianism are inevitably bound up with issues of gender.

10. See Andrés Avellaneda (*Censura* 20–21), Munizaga and Ochsensius (74–76), and Sonia Alvarez (27–36). Yet to say that the authoritarian dis-

course on the sex/gender system is univocal is *by no means* to suggest that it is not without its dissonances, contradictions, and real failures as evidenced by the movements that led to its downfall.

11. See Sonia E. Alvarez (especially pages 5–14) for an overview of women and the authoritarian regimes of the Southern Cone and Brazil. In the rest of this chapter, I have frequently used the term Southern Cone alone to refer to these countries as a group.

12. That is *not* to say that the regime accomplished such a division or that it in any way abdicated its (public) authority with regard to private matters. We will return to the complexities of the relationship between the public and private spheres later in this chapter.

13. *Nunca Más* (286–332); Jacobo Timerman (30–31); Ximena Bunster-Burotto "Surviving Beyond Fear: *Women and Torture in Latin America*"; Lea Fletcher "La tortura genéricamente específica" (Gender Specific Torture) paper given at the conference "Mujeres y escritura" (Women and Writing) organized by *Puro Cuento* in Buenos Aires, August 1991. In Argentina and Uruguay, at least, the effects of these atrocities are still being felt as is evidenced by the recent, highly publicized cases of "adopted" children who have been identified by the Abuelas de la Plaza de Mayo as their grandchildren, born to imprisoned mothers and then "adopted" by friends of the authoritarian regime.

14. "Beyond" 513. As Franco observes, "By attacking them [the family and the Church] and by appealing to more deterritorialized forms of domination . . . the military governments have also unwittingly contributed to the subversion of these formerly 'sacred' categories" ("Beyond" 513).

15. On the Madres de la Plaza de Mayo see Laura Rossi's "¿Cómo pensar a las Madres de la Plaza de Mayo?" (How to Think About the Mothers of the Plaza de Mayo), Debra Castillo (16–18), María del Carmen Feijoó's "Women and Democracy in Argentina" (76–78), Masiello's "Cuerpo/presencia" (Body/Presence) (156) as well as Franco's "Beyond" (513–14).

16. The difference between Woman and women, as I use them in this study, is between a discursive model or regulatory fiction (Woman) and real social subjects (women). Such a distinction (which I borrow from recent North American feminist theory by such thinkers as Teresa de Lauretis, Sally Robinson, and Judith Butler) suggests that the reflections of Woman that women see in discursive representations authored by men are often quite at odds both with women's real situation and their possibilities for authoring their own self-representations.

17. On this topic see the first part of Francine Masiello's excellent article "Cuerpo/presencia" (Body/Presence) (especially 156–60), Mario Cesareo's "Cuerpo Humano e Historia en la Novela del Proceso" (Human

Body and History in the Novel of the Process) and Hernán Vidal's "La Declaración de Principios de la Junta Militar Chilena Como Sistema Literario: La Lucha Antifascista y el Cuerpo Humano" (The Chilean Junta's Declaration of Principles as Literary System: The Anti-Fascist Struggle and the Human Body).

18. The term subjectivity as used throughout this study refers to the ways social entities actively engage with language, simultaneously subject to discursive conventions and subject of their own linguistic (re)productions. I borrow this formulation of subjectivity from Sally Robinson, Paul Smith, and Julian Henriques, et al. I will elaborate further on this concept in chapter 1.

19. The only one of these works currently available in English translation is *La nave de los locos* (*Ship of Fools*) by Cristina Peri Rossi. Through the rest of this study, I have referred to the works using only their original Spanish titles.

20. See Munizaga and Ochsensius, Avellaneda, and Alvarez for further analyses on the gender-specific policies of the authoritarian regimes.

21. It is, in fact, this self-consciousness regarding language and narrative that causes me to refer to these texts as experimental, an issue I will return to in the next section.

22. "Apuntes" 41. This is obviously a complex issue, worthy of an essay in itself. Clearly, a big part of such resistance to the term "women's writing" has to do with the fact that nobody, as Franco observes, likes to be pigeon-holed: women writers understandably prefer *not* to join the "poetisas" (poetesses) in the last paragraphs of literary histories, in the last sessions at conferences, etc. (41). I would also add that there has been a virtual "boom" in attention to women's writing, which could perhaps be located, as Brazilian Hispanist Marcia Roppe Navarro recently suggested, as beginning with Allende's *La casa de los espíritus* (*The House of the Spirits*), which has now gone into more than twenty printings. This turn of events has caused male writers in Mexico, for example, to complain bitterly that to be published now, one must be a woman (Elena Poniatowska, "Hispanic Women Writers," talk given at Brown University, Spring 1992). Ironically enough, after being marginalized from the publishing world for centuries because of their sex, women have finally attained a degree of freedom and attention in the literary world only to be told that it is *because* they are women. It is thus perhaps not surprising that many women would prefer not to be seen as opportunistically "taking advantage of their sex." I suggest, however, that female privilege still pales in comparison to male privilege, which has been so naturalized as to be made virtually invisible, much the way white privilege has. In this state of affairs, any female and/or minority advantage is seen as unfair, while male and/or white advantage is rarely even *seen* at all.

23. It is only fair to point out that the writers of the "Boom" have had to wrest their own authority from a metropolitan tradition, which had previously subordinated third world literary production. For a discussion of these issues see Jean Franco "Beyond Ethnocentrism: Gender, Power, and the Third-World Intelligensia" (503–09).

24. These are, necessarily, generalizations. Nonetheless, they do have an undeniable psychological weight. As Reina Roffé points out in the preface to *La rompiente*, women's writing is "supposed" to be nonsymbolic, referential, repetitive, too detailed, and characterized by a tone of anger and resentment; and as a woman who writes, she continually struggles under these assumptions. We will return to this issue of experimental writing by women later in the chapter.

25. I use the term ideology in this study to refer to the realm of naturalized meanings or what often passes for common sense within a particular class or community. I have gleaned this understanding of ideology and its implementation or deployment in narrative from Rachel Blau DuPlessis's work which in turn draws on Louis Althusser for whom ideology is a "system of representations by which we imagine the world as it is" (cited in Blau DuPlessis *Writing Beyond the Ending* 3).

26. I should point out at once that when I suggest that these writers' experimentalism involves a certain critical stance I am placing them not in opposition to the writers of the "Boom" (most of whom are considered experimentalists of a sort) but against the univocal discourse of authoritarianism and expectations about women's writing (namely that it is not structurally or linguistically innovative or experimental). I do, however, think that some of these writers contend with the "Boom" in a critical way, most notably Roffé. This would be the subject of another study, however.

27. For Robinson, Simone de Beauvoir's original claim that "one is not born, but becomes a woman" is the grounding for most feminist theory, even though there is much contention as to how that "becoming" actually proceeds. Robinson points out, though, that in the wake of poststructuralist critiques of the "subject" and "identity" as convenient, ideological fictions, feminists have been able to to rethink social subjectivity as discursively produced, that is that "bodies sexed female are produced as 'women' by their placement in systems of signification and social practices" (1). In this study, such "production" is generally referred to as the gendering process.

28. Munizaga's and Ochsensius's work provides an invaluable resource in this regard, as we shall see.

29. In an interterview with Clarice Lispector, Nélida Piñon explicitly states her views on the literary avant-garde, noting its politicoethical implications: "Within the current Brazilian framework, the avant-garde for me is the permanent critique of the social and linguistic system. . . . And, above

all, an intransigent ethical attitude in the exercise of the means of expression" (interview with Lispector 189).

30. I have interpolated these general formulations from Beatriz Sarlo's article in which she discusses the political function of what she calls "figuration." I will return to these ideas in the next section.

31. Experimental and politically contentious women writers do have a history in Latin America. But, as Diamela Eltit has suggested in the case of Chile, canonical women writers (such as Gabriela Mistral and Marta Brunet) have often been misrepresented in literary history in ways that demobilize their more critical or contentious aspects. See Eltit's interview with Luisa Ulibarri.

32. Angus Fletcher simply states that in the most general terms, "allegory says one thing and means another" (2). For a slightly different take on the etymology, see Craig Owens for whom the allegorist confiscates images in order to make them "other," to turn them into something different (69). Northrop Frye sees allegory as when an author indicates that "by this [he] *also (allos)* mean[s] that" (90).

33. Barbara Johnson puts this quite simply: "Normally, allegory presents a narrative of concrete events, which, upon interpretation, yields a second narrative that is figurative and abstract" (16).

34. Fletcher notes that allegories are most often symbolic power struggles (23) and he draws extensive parallels between psychoanalysis and allegory (especially chapter 6). There is a certain amount of resonance among the theorists of allegory about these traditional features. Gay Clifford, for example, notes that allegorical elements most notably include personification, personified abstractions, and the incorporation of commentary and interpretation (5–6).

35. Joel Fineman (28), Angus Fletcher (324–28), Mihai Spariosu (60–61), to name a few, all dwell to some extent on allegory's political possibilities. Fredric Jameson's controversial article "Third World Literature" offers a broad sketch of how "third world" literature can be read as national allegory. Stephen Slemon's piece, "Monuments of Empire," analyzes the political uses of allegory in colonialization as well as how allegorical procedures have been put to work in post-colonial, anti-imperialist texts.

36. In a volume of *Ideologies and Literature* devoted to fascism and literary experience in Hispanic and Lusophone literatures, there are several references to concrete uses of allegory. See Hernán Vidal, "Hacia un Modelo General de la Sensibilidad Social Literaturizable Bajo el Fascismo" (Toward a General Model of Literaturizable Social Sensibility Under Fascism); Flora Süssekind, "Polêmicas, Retratos & Diarios (Reflexões Parciais Sobre a Literatura e a vida Cultural no Brasil Pós-64)" (Polemics, Portraits and Journals:

Partial Reflections on Literature and Cultural Life in Post-64 Brazil); and Viviana Plotnik: "Alegoría y Proceso de Reorganización Nacional: Propuesta de una Categoría de Mediación Socio-Histórica para el Análisis Discursivo" (Allegory and Process of National Reorganization: Proposal for a Category of Socio-Historical Mediation for Discursive Analysis). Allegory is seen in these analyses as almost excessively referential, as denotative, and as reductionist. Yet these critics, especially Plotnik and Süssekind, are addressing allegory in what Süssekind calls "neonaturalistas romances-reportagem" (neo-naturalist journalistic novels) which do not call into question identities, nationalities, or the act of writing itself (Süssekind 282–86). For this reason, we cannot extend such judgments to more complex allegorical texts (such as the ones I have chosen), which give rigorous attention to language, which *do* question national and sexual identities, and which reflect on the very possibility of representation. Also the allegories these critics refer to are often set up as one-to-one correspondences where one character, for example, becomes a personification of the nation. As we shall see, the texts included here do not employ a method of simple analogy.

37. According to Lacanian analysis, the phallus, signifier of the "Law of the Father," serves as a guarantee of authority and meaning. As Jane Gallop reiterates: "The Lacanian phallus is . . . a linguistic concept. Discourse is phallocentric. Therefore, to have the phallus would mean to be at the center of discourse, to generate meaning, to have mastery of language, to control rather than conform to that which comes from outside, from the Other" (*Thinking Through the Body* 126).

38. Decree 2038, cited in Avellaneda (200). See Avellaneda's introductory essay (especially 25–26) for a fascinating discussion on how the regime saw the multiplication of meanings as a primary military concern. Such a view is apparently not exclusive to dictatorship in the Latin American context. In a recently published article on women's writing during and after the dictatorship in Greece (1967–74), Karen Van Dyck notes that the Greek regime similarly attempted to control meaning, viewing "undecidability" as threatening. She notes that "any kind of undecidability, textual or sexual, was considered subversive" (48). Her article contains interesting parallels with the situation in the Southern Cone.

39. On the intensification of alienation during these regimes, see Neil Larsen's introduction to *The Discourse of Power: Culture, Hegemony and the Authoritarian State in Latin America*, René Jara's article in the same volume, and Beatriz Sarlo's article "Política, ideología y figuración literaria" (Politics, Ideology, and Literary Figuration).

40. Sarlo finally points out that even texts still inclined toward realism end up being read allegorically in such a sociopolitical climate ("Política" 45). Allegory is, as many theorists note, both a question of writing and reading, functioning "as a rhetorical figure and as an exegetic instrument" (Spar-

iosu 60). Consequently, the line between allegorical production and allegorical reception is, at best, a blurred one.

41. Skepticism about the possiblities of representation is a key element of what has come to be called postmodernism and, indeed, the texts I have chosen to include in this study could all be read as in dialogue with a postmodern context. But the postmodern project, which, according to contemporary thinkers, includes the undoing of master narratives, the death of the author as ultimate signified of a text, the endless play of the signifier, and the indeterminacy and plurality of meanings, develops in a specifically critical way in Latin America; indeed, Latin American postmodern texts "go beyond existing definitions and frameworks by giving their postmodernity an even more critical accentuation, voicing emerging social and aesthetic exigencies" (Julio Ortega, "Postmodernism in Latin America," unpub. ms.). In the authoritarian context of the Southern Cone, the nature of such "exigencies" includes a crisis of representation that is related both to postmodernism and to the more sociopolitical situation described earlier.

42. My dictionary, for example, lists as one of the definitions of "value": "precise meaning, as of a word" (*Webster's New Twentieth Century Dictionary*).

43. In his "The Will to Allegory in Postmodernism," Smith is specifically responding to a set of articles by Craig Owens who alludes to allegory's relinquishment of mastery and its appropriation of images to then "empty them of their resonance, their significance, their authoritative claim to meaning" ("The Allegorical Impulse" 69).

44. In this regard, see Dilnot and García-Padilla (52). I thank Luis Avilés for drawing my attention to this article. While these critics deal specifically with paintings by Vermeer, the overall goal of their article is to explore the epistemological, aesthetic, political, and ethical issues involved in allegorical procedures.

45. Bernard Cowan, "Walter Benjamin's Theory of Allegory," cited by Dilnot and García-Padilla (49). The previous assertion is not unlike Lukács's assessment of allegory as "that aesthetic genre which lends itself par excellence to a description of man's alienation from objective reality" (40). Lukács, however, thought realism to be superior to allegory.

46. See Angus Fletcher (326). Also Michael Holquist makes the following comment on the politics of representation in the Russian context: "For Russians, utterance has ever been a contest, a struggle. The need to speak indirectly has resulted in a Russian discourse that is always fabular precisely when it is fueled by the most intense desire to mean. Such indirection has resulted in an allegorical mode known as 'Aesopic language.'" (181).

47. See Nancy K. Miller's "Changing the Subject: Authorship, Writing and the Reader," in *Feminist Studies/Critical Studies*, Teresa De Lauretis ed. (especially 108–09). In many respects, Gilbert and Gubar's well-known study *Madwomen in the Attic* addresses the problem of assuming authorship (or subjectivity for that matter) for nineteenth-century woman writers who had to think through and against the images of Woman in patriarchal cultural production.

48. In his well-known article, "Third World Literature in the Era of Multinational Capital," Fredric Jameson has gone so far as to suggest that the abstract "other" story that "third world" texts *always* tell is that of national oppression. Jameson universalizes this formulation to propose that all "third world" texts—evidently those texts produced in countries "which have suffered the experience of colonialism and imperialism" (67)—are always necessarily national allegories (69). This is an intriguing formulation that has, of course, drawn much criticism for its excessive generalization and misleading homogenization. One of Jameson's most convincing critics, Aijaz Ahmad, argues, first off, that there is no such thing as a unified "third world literature" and furthermore suggests that the allegorization that occurs is not only of a national sort but is an attempt to conflate public and private spheres, to relate personal experience to a collectivity, such as race, class, and gender among others (4; 15). Such a gesture is clearly not specific to the "third world." Ahmad points out that many Black and feminist writings in "these postmodernist United States" could be considered allegories of collectivities in this way (15).

49. It is significant that during such marches the square virtually emptied, the only occupants being the marchers themselves, called "locas" by the press and government officials. In the official response to such transgression of the public/private separation, the public space is effectively privatized and the mothers who had taken their private concerns to the very heart of public life discursively remarginalized as madwomen.

50. Indeed, in general terms, Amy Kaminsky notes that especially in Latin America, not only is the personal the political but vice versa. She writes: "In much of Latin America, the official and unofficial policies of the state are played out on the bodies of its citizens, thus becoming the intimate personal experience and shaping the unique vision of the individual that gets expressed in what we recognize as the writer's particular voice" (*Reading the Body Politic* xv).

51. See Sarlo "Política" (35–39); Brunner *La cultura autoritaria en Chile*; Neil Larsen (5–6).

52. As Ahmad points out, the whole issue of the public/private separation—which subtends Jameson's argument on the "first world"-"third world" opposition—is of major concern to "first-world" feminists of the United States and Europe (24).

53. See Julieta Kirkwood, *Feminario* (126–27). See also Kirkwood's article "Feministas y políticas" where she makes the statement included as epigraph to this introduction, "the concrete, everyday experience of women is authoritarianism" (64), and proposes that the traditionally private sphere be considered "politically" (65).

54. See Salvaggio's article on space and feminist theory (especially pages 274–75) for details on these transformative effects.

55. Each of these authors has discussed gender concerns in interviews or in critical essays. In addition, several of them have expressed their opposition to authoritarianism in specifically generic terms. I will refer to these comments in my discussions of the individual authors.

Chapter 1

1. See *Folha da Tarde*, 11 de agosto de 1981 and *Jornal do Brasil* de 26 de julho de 1981.

2. See the interview with Geneton Moraes Neto, *Jornal do Brasil*, 5 de Dez., 1987, (8–9) where he explicitly refers to her as a "militant" writer. In her discussion with Moraes Neto on her political position, Piñon refers to her militancy as a "militancy of passion," having to do with writing, with the struggle to forge new meanings through linguistic innovation.

3. See the interview with Geneton Moraes Neto in the *Jornal do Brasil*, December 5, 1987.

4. Her "difficulty" is brought up in many journalistic articles and interviews. See, for example, Cremilda Medina's article in *O Estado de São Paulo*, April 9, 1978, or her interview with Clarice Lispector. Her "difficulty" is also noted by Naomi Hoki Moniz, who specifically relates it to her experimentation with language (*As Viagens de Nélida* 83).

5. In her book on Piñon's narrative, Naomi Hoki Moniz has pointed out the use of allegory in *A Casa da Paixão*. According to this critic, Piñón "presents a rare, allegorical image of the search for the psychological essence of the masculine and the feminine" (*As Viagens de Nélida* 130).

6. "Note, however, that, contrary to many women writers who look for the androgynous ideal in the fusion of the opposites masculine/feminine, Piñon presents her characters as attaining the realization of self-liberation through their individual situations. [. . .] The author shows the necessity of maintaining the equilibrium of the masculine/feminine polarity in such a way that their identities are not reduced to a common denominator" (Moniz "Ética, Estética" 139). This observation, in a somewhat revised form, is included in Moniz's book as well (*As Viagens de Nélida* 84–85).

7. "Marta, in preparing her body for the weight of this knowledge (the weight of the cross), permits Jerônimo, the sacred name, to be able to disseminate himself though the signs of that consecration. And between the perpetual flame of passion and the baptismal water of the river, she initiates the 'new birth,' conscious that 'to change the state of the body was to change all thinking'" (Régis 143). As we shall see, Régis's omission of the final phrase of this citation from the text—it reads "to change the state of the body was to change all thinking, *she saw her misfortune*" elides the ambiguities and irony of the final outcome of the novel.

8. In the conclusion of *The Political Unconscious*, Fredric Jameson asks how it is possible for one text to legitimate, for example, a certain form of class domination while simultaneously proposing a utopian impulse that contradicts its "ideological vocation" (288). Revealing the inevitable dialectic between the ideological and the utopian, Jameson proposes that readings of the ideological functions of texts must be brought in alongside readings of their utopian projections. See pages 291–99.

9. Jameson declares in no uncertain terms that marxist cultural analysis is "the only current critical method" to assume a negative hermeneutic function (*The Political Unconscious* 291).

10. I am referring, here, to the way woman has been symbolically cast as man's other, hence functioning as the mediator between man and his world. I explain this conceptualization more fully in the coming pages, especially when I turn to Simone de Beauvoir's explication of the process of "othering."

11. The phrase "One is not born, but becomes a woman" belongs, as I noted in the Introduction, to Simone de Beauvoir. I have borrowed the term "script" as it is used by Rachel Blau DuPlessis in *Writing Beyond the Ending*. Following several social scientists, DuPlessis points out that "any social convention is like a 'script,' which suggests sequences of action and response, the meaning we give these, and ways of organizing experience by choices, emphases, priorities" (2). Furthermore, literature is itself organized by many "ideological scripts," by many dominant narrative patterns or master plots that serve to produce and disseminate, legitimate, and sustain, certain values and attitudes (2–3). DuPlessis's book basically examines how women's writing of the twentieth century works to delegitimate and undo such "scripts" in order to tell the "other" side of that oft-repeated story.

12. Narrative, Webster's dictionary tells us, is the "act or process of telling the particulars of an act, occurrence, or course of events." But my use of the term in this study also takes into account the driving forces behind such an account of a "course of events," whether those events be historical happenings or psychosexual occurrences. For Sally Robinson, for example, narrative is driven by a desire to mark out boundaries. She defines narrative

as "any discourse that is mobilized by a desire to construct a history, an accounting of the limits and boundaries of gender, subjectivity, and knowledge" (*Engendering the Subject* 17). Consequently, we could say that narratives often are enacted to both construct and account for what usually passes for "common sense" regarding who we are and why. As Rachel Blau DuPlessis puts it: "Narrative . . . is a version of, or a special expression of, ideology: representations by which we construct and accept values and institutions" (*Writing Beyond the Ending* x). Regarding the different narratives I mentioned, I will, in due course, return to each of these "plots" and explain them a bit more fully. In a preliminary way, we could say, however, that they are interlocking narratives that serve a common function: engendering female docility and compliance.

13. Joan Dassin explains that the 1968 decree known as Institutional Act No. 5, which authorized censorship and other "coercive measures" with no proof of "state of siege," constituted a "coup within a coup" by the hard-line military (156). In describing the chronology of state censorship, Dassin notes that it is only with the beginning of General Ernesto Geisel's presidency in 1975 that a relaxation of censorship occurred (170).

14. For an excellent discussion on the function of the ethical and the aesthetic during what she has called Piñon's avant-garde phase, see Naomi Hoki Moniz's book *As Viagens de Nélida* (18–23). Unfortunately, this first book-length study of Piñon's work came to my attention when I was already making the final revisions on my manuscript.

15. For an analysis of *O Calor das Coisas* [The Heat of Things] and *A República dos Sonhos* [The Republic of Dreams] with regard to the dictatorship, see Lúcia Helena Costigan's article, "Literatura e Ditadura: Aspectos da Ficção Brasileira Pós-64 em Alguns Dos Escritos de Lygia Fagundes Telles e de Nélida Piñon" [Literature and Dictatorship: Aspects of Post-64 Brazilian Fiction in Some of the Works of Lygia Fagundes Telles and Nélida Piñon]. Similar to the way I read Piñon's work as an allegory of Brazil's authoritarian context, Costigan reads the rooming house in Lygia Fagundes Telles's *As Meninas* (1973) as a metaphor for Brazil itself (144).

16. *A Casa* 14–15. Moniz describes the interdependent relationship between Marta and the father thus: "The relationship between the Father and Marta is tense and dependent since there was a pact 'established between them, for one to be the shadow of the other.' His figure is authoritarian, omnipresent, and possessive. Only the appearance of another masculine element could help Marta develop herself completely" ("Ética, Estética" 134). I should note that this observation bespeaks a positive reading of the role of Jerônimo in the narrative as the "savior" of Marta. While he certainly conceives of his role that way and Marta finally accepts him in that capacity, there is considerable ambivalence and ambiguity in the text as to what it finally means that he is indeed her only salvation.

17. See "Any Theory of the 'Subject' Has Always Been Appropriated by the 'Masculine'" in *Speculum* 133–46.

18. Robinson draws on such theorists as Teresa DeLauretis, Denise Riley, and Diana Fuss. See specifically pages 4–9.

19. "Sexuality is to feminism what work is to marxism: that which is most one's own, yet most taken away"(MacKinnon 1). MacKinnon goes on to reiterate woman's historical alienation from her own sexuality: "A woman is a being who identifies and is indentified as one whose sexuality exists for someone else, who is socially male. Woman's sexuality is the capacity to arouse desire in that someone. . . . Considering women's sexuality in this way forces confrontation with whether there is any such thing" (19). It would seem that it is in these terms that Piñon's text is revolutionary: Marta's sexuality is very much hers to enjoy, especially at the beginning of the novel. What is less clear is whether the resolution of the novel, the mythic union between Marta and Jerónimo, reinscribes sexual alienation for the woman.

20. Regarding the conflict of quest plots, Sally Robinson cites Peter Brooks on the female plot of ambition, which is often "in resistance to the overt and violating male plots of ambition" (Robinson 31; *Reading for the Plot* Brooks 39).

21. This theme is taken up again by Piñon in even more explicit (or "realistic") terms in her recently translated novel *Republic of Dreams* where Esperança's bitter realization that she is to be excluded from public life because of her femaleness leads her to wage battle with her father and her brother, Miguel. In fact, the relationship between Esperança and Madruga (the novel's patriarch) bears a marked resemblance to that between Marta and the father in *A Casa*. This description of Esperança, for example, reveals that Madruga's strategies for controlling her are identical to those employed by Marta's father: "Her proud bearing, even in the portrait, seemed to be resisting fulfilling the father's demands. Madruga's orders were firm ones, even though he lined his words with soft down so that his daughter would follow them as though she herself had issued them" (188). The paternal fear at seeing himself reproduced too closely by his daughter similarly recurs in the Esperança/Madruga relationship: "she had stolen his blue eyes from him. A genetic theft that at times made him feel uneasy" (188). It would be interesting to compare more in depth these two father/daughter relationships, especially in terms of an "unseemly" mimeticism.

22. The rituals of this scene seem to deal head on with the social scripts, explained by Claude Lévi-Strauss, which place women in circulation as commodities to be exchanged among men. Many feminists have done critical readings of this economy. For example, as I mentioned in the Introduction, Gayle Rubin critically examines the exchange rituals as set forth by

Levi-Strauss in her essay, "The Traffic in Women: Notes on the 'Political Economy' of Sex." She examines how the exchange of women is used basically to form kinship structures and social relationships among men and shows how the Oedipal complex serves to reinforce patriarchal social structures. In a similar if more poetic vein, Luce Irigaray explores the implications of what she terms this "hommosexual economy" her essay "When the Goods Get Together" in *This Sex*.

23. Clearly Moniz is right when she suggests that a Jungian or archetypal approach seems called for in reading this novel. The egg as a symbol of original and originary perfection and as of prime importance in creation and fertility myths is explored by Jungian scholar Erich Neumann in *The Origins and History of Consciousness* (8). Using Jungian models, Antônia could be analyzed according to the archetype of the Great Mother.

24. Luce Irigaray speculates on the disruption that could be caused by women, the commodities of the exchange rituals of patriarchy, getting together in "Commodities Among Themselves" in *This Sex Which Is Not One* (196–97).

25. Annis Pratt has analyzed the role of nature in contemporary women's literature finding that a relationship to nature often serves to augment women's self-sufficiency, an autonomy that is often threatening to patriarchal, social norms ("Spinning Among Fields" 112). Specifically regarding women's quest literature, Pratt observes: "To the young hero of women's fiction, nature is a home from which she is forced into society. Nature is therefore less of a staging ground for initiation into culture than a world in itself where she, like the ancient virgins, can freely enjoy her own body" ("Spinning Among Fields" 112). In *A Casa*, Marta's communing with the natural world represents just such sexual freedom and autonomy.

26. In addition to associating him with the natural world, that Jerônimo has "the hand of a tree" also gives his figure a certain resonance with the Egyptian god Osiris whose lover, Isis, recognizes him in the form of a tree and whose symbol is thus the *djed*, or sacred pillar. We shall return to this correspondence later.

27. Moniz reports: "The publishing house that came out with this book had problems with the censorship because of the unconventional sexual episodes" ("Ética, Estética" 138, n. 21).

28. This, in a sense, reveals the dilemma of masculinization: how to obey the father's law, how to identify with power, and yet also attain the freedom and autonomy necessary to form a viable male subjectivity.

29. For a discussion of what is at stake in the complex notion of "writing the body," a concept usually associated with the French feminists such as Hélène Cixous and Luce Irigaray but also with male theorists such as

Roland Barthes, see Trinh T. Minh-ha, *Woman Native Other*, especially pages 36–44. For Minh-ha this activity occupies the very border between the personal and the political: "'Writing the body' is that abstract-concrete, personal-political realm of excess not fully contained by writing's unifying structural forces. Its physicality (vocality, tactility, touch, resonance), or edgeing and margin, exceeds the rational 'clarity' of communicative structures and cannot be fully explained by any analysis" (44).

30. There are many examples of the importance of the invisibility of the male body. In my opinion, the prohibition of male frontal nudity in mainstream film is one such example. Lacan also reveals invisibility to be a necessary element for transcendence in his observation that in order to function as transcendent signifier the phallus and the operations of its power must remain "veiled." Ultimately, many types of power work best undercover. As Foucault has stressed, the effective operations of the technologies of power virtually depend on invisibility (*The History of Sexuality* 86).

31. For this study, I have found Sally Robinson's conceptualizations of subjectivity (in many ways a reading of various recent formulations by Paul Smith, Teresa de Lauretis, and Diana Fuss, among others) to be especially useful in that she foregrounds the ways subjectivity always involves a dynamic process of negotiating with subject positions already available in the social field. As she most cogently puts it regarding women's writing: "The woman writing within patriarchal culture is subject *to* the discursive and social practices that require her silence and repression, but also, and undeniably, subject *of* her own cultural productions" (12). Thus, subjectivity marks the place of active engagement with previous cultural representations, neither entirely determined by nor free to ignore such representations. Ultimately, agency lies in the dynamic and reversible nature of that engagement; that is, if subjective representations can affect social constructions then agency is possible (see Robinson 56 and De Lauretis *Technologies of Gender* 9).

32. Significantly, Marta's writing is not a permanent inscription but is in the process of vanishing just as Jerônimo reads it. Perhaps her writing, transitory as it is, refuses the more permanent writing of the proverbial writing in stone of patriarchal law.

33. A fascinating confluence of pedagogy and menstruation is worked out by Jane Gallop in "The Student Body." Following Irigaray, she explains that menstrual blood messes up the phallic structure upon which our pedagogical system is based (i.e., the system where "the student is empty, a receptacle for the phallus; the teacher is the phallic fullness of knowledge" 43): "Irigaray, in her reading of *Philosophy in the Bedroom*, suggests that Sadian libertines like only the blood they cause to flow. Like menstruation, defloration includes bleeding, but in the latter blood is a sign of some penetration of interiority from without, while in the former it flows from interior

to exterior without the necessity of a penetrating agent. Just as pedagogical tests seek to draw out from the student what was implanted there by the teacher; so the Sadian surgeon wishes to examine an interiority devoid of any sexuality, any carnal knowledge originating within" (43). Thus, desire in this order must be implanted in the student by the teacher and the only blood to be seen is the blood resulting from the penetration of the virginal body by his instrumentation. Clearly, *A Casa* undoes this order and Jerônimo's resistance to Marta's menstrual writing corresponds to the phallic logic that finds any sign of feminine sexuality not bound up with male desire to be a threat. In addition, Marta's pedagogical order virtually reverses the phallic pedagogical system.

34. The roles of Orpheus and Eurydice are both reinscribed and undone in *A Casa* and merit further study. While Marta sees herself as Eurydice, she also becomes like a female Orpheus, enchanting others with her music. Jerônimo meanwhile still casts *himself* as Orpheus: "Eu sou o homen desta mulher. Eu decido por ela. Jerônimo cheirou as árvores proximas, corria como lebre, imitava lebre, liberava-se. A mulher, haveria de encontrá-la no inferno, Orfeu também" (99). Marta's performing the role of Orpheus, her occupying the role of heroine, ultimately conflicts with Jerônimo's own attempts at heroism, his own self-representation as Orpheus.

35. See *The Birth of Tragedy* for Nietzsche's characterization of the Dionysian (as differentiated from the Apollinian).

36. Fuss is basing herself on Althusser's assertion that "when we speak of ideology we should know that ideology slides into all human activity, that it is identical with the 'lived' experience of human existence itself" (from Althusser's "A Letter on Art in Reply to André Daspre" quoted in Fuss 114).

37. See Bataille's *Erotism* for a complete explanation of these relationships.

38. Indeed, there are many parallels with Christ's incarnation, the idea of the word made flesh, and the concepts of transformation, of conversion and of death and rebirth that are key to Christianity. The mythological imagery has to do with the sun as masculine deity, the wood and sacred pillar of Osiris, and the cycle of death and rebirth common to many myths.

39. The wood of the cross also being the wood of the *djed*, the sacred pillar, symbol of Osiris (see Erich Neumann 229–32). The cross itself is also a conflation of both vertical/immortal divine associations and horizontal/mortal/earthly associations.

40. Benjamin "Sado-Masochism?" (296). She is following Georges Bataille's work on religion and eroticism as both allowing for a transgression of the boundary between life and death.

41. See Annis Pratt "Spinning Among Fields" (101–02) and Erich Neumann (253).

42. It is worth noting that Osiris also attains his transcendence through joining with the sun god, Ra (Neumann 234–35). This synthesis signifies, according to Neumann, the hero's achieving a "higher order" of masculinity (see pages 240–56).

43. As to whether "feminist" as a label could or should be applied to Piñon's narrative is debatable. She definitely does, however, consider *herself* a feminist, telling Clarice Lispector in an interview: "Feminism is a consequence of my [condition of] being a woman. The more I enable myself to interpret the world, the better I comprehend the necessity of conquering an identity, that only an active and alert conscience can confer upon us. I am naturally a feminist, and I aspire for women, independently developed, capable of integrating themselves in the center of decisions of which they have been forever excluded, to help make possible and better the communal life of our times" (193).

44. On either/or thinking versus the (feminist) both/and mode see Pratt (94); and Blau DuPlessis in "For the Etruscans" (276).

45. See Rachel Blau DuPlessis's first chapter, "Endings and Contradictions" in *Writing Beyond the Ending.*

46. See Michel Foucault, "We Other Victorians" in *The History of Sexuality.*

47. Utopian sexuality is fraught with difficulty for, as Michel Foucault has shown, the search for truth and freedom in sex is bound to fail since the very idea of salvation through sex is a social construction that scripts sexuality as the origin of our mystery and the keeper of our secrets, rather than as historically produced and determined. The utopian sexual union enacted at the end of *A Casa* operates on such a notion of unchanging sexuality that can hardly be used to break the sequence of gender patterns or to denounce the status quo.

48. See Moniz's article page 131. While I agree with Moniz's description of the protagonists as expressions of certain abstract formulations, I ultimately differ in my view of the ramifications of the ethic of union engendered in *A Casa.*

49. Such a distinction and dilemma, in a sense, provides an illustration of the basic critique of Jungian psychology from a feminist perspective. As Demaris S. Wehr puts it: "The central problem is: Jung ontologizes what is more accurately and more usefully seen as socially constructed reality" in *Feminist Archetypal Theory* (28).

50. See Sonia Alvarez, especially the introduction and chapter 1.

Chapter 2

1. See the introduction of the present study for an extended quotation from Eltit's essay "Cultura, poder y frontera" (Culture, Power, and Boundary) where she explicitly states the importance of working on the level of language and discourse in order to accomplish any social change.

2. Diamela Eltit, "Cultura, poder y frontera" (2).

3. Eugenia Brito explains the primarily negative reaction to Eltit's first novel, *Lumpérica* (1983), as dual ("fascination, on the one hand; horror, denoted as 'obscurity,' 'crypticism'" (*Campos minados* 173) and goes on to point out that such rejection was not only on the part of the Right but also the Left, which, according to this critic, showed little interest "in being receptive to any dissident system that did not fit in with the habitual modes of propagating an ideology critical of the military system" (*Campos minados* 174). Rodrigo Cánovas also addresses the reception of Eltit's narrative in his article on *Por la patria*, observing that the resistance to her work could be seen as related to the persistence in Chilean letters of a "naturalist" model, which Eltit's literary project obviously defies (147). Cánovas sums up the reaction to her work: "it is said that her books are 'difficult to follow' (read: they are incomprehensible), and that they 'speak of things of little interest' (read: they are not edifying, moral judgement included)" (147). Obviously, neither of these two critics share such a negative view and Eltit does have an ever-growing readership that recognizes the importance of her contribution, as evidenced by the publication in 1993 of an entire volume of essays dedicated to her work (Juan Carlos Lértora, *Una poética de literatura menor: la narrativa de Diamela Eltit*).

4. Gligo observes: "the novelistic work produced by Diamela Eltit would perhaps have received a much larger acceptance if the innovation that she offers and the ruptures she produces had come from some 'masculine hand'" (interview with Guillermo Blanco in *Hoy*). Rodrigo Cánovas expressed a similar view in a seminar on Chilean literature and authoritarianism given at Brown University in the spring of 1992. Eltit says as much herself in her essay "Errante, Errática" included in Juan Carlos Lértora's *Una poética de literatura menor* (see pages 23–24).

5. She states, "I consider literature to be my militancy . . . writing, that is my battle, my personal epic" (interview with Julio Ortega 240). In spite of market forces and what Eltit describes as her initial feelings of guilt at the negative reaction to her work (i.e., that it is "incomprehensible"), she remains committed to a writing that is critical of dominant social structures and symbolic systems.

6. According to Lacan's psychoanalytic model, it is the "law of the father," the psychosexual and social authoritative prohibitions, which force

the child from its imaginary unity with the maternal body. This separation is intimately tied up with the child's acquisition of language and entry into the "symbolic" since language ultimately signals and represents the absence of the object of desire. For Eltit, the "law of the father," borrowed from the Lacanian model, relates to the masculine authority upon which symbolic systems are based (see her comments in "Cultura," especially page 1).

7. Such a poetic transformation of the margins is, in fact, one of the predominant tropes of the avant-garde artistic movement with which Eltit's work is intimately associated. Known as the *avanzada*, this group advocated an avant-garde artistic practice combining aesthetic and philosophical concerns with a desire to provoke social change. The *avanzada* espoused a politics of difference rather than of identity, hoping to disarticulate the oppressive regulatory fictions encumbering the social movements that invoke a unified, revolutionary or proletarian subject. A reappropriation of the margins is key to such a politics, as Nelly Richard explains: "To move from marginality suffered as a result of an overdetermination of power to the productivization of the margin as aesthetic code of neighboring itinerancies, has been the adventure of a scene that knew how to convert exclusion into an enunciative posture" ("Estéticas de la oblicuidad" 8). For an excellent introduction to the artistic practices and theoretical underpinnings of the *avanzada*, see Nelly Richard's book *Margins and Institutions: Art in Chile since 1973*. Her more recent essay "Estéticas de la oblicuidad" also offers a systematic exposition of the *avanzada's* political aesthetics. Also quite helpful in this regard is the FLACSO document "Arte en Chile desde 1973." Rodrigo Cánovas's article on *Por la patria* also contains a good synopsis of this movement.

8. As Eltit explains in an essay, what has been historically assigned to the masculine has to do with the power of the center, relegating to the feminine what falls through the cracks: the more private and marginal realms ("Cultura, poder y frontera" 1). Eltit is, obviously, not alone in such an understanding of the feminine. Indeed, many feminists express similar views. In the context of French feminism, one of the most illustrative representations of the gendering of symbolic structures occurs in Hélène Cixous's "Sorties" where she sets up series of binary oppositions in order to show how culture's "dual *hierarchized* oppositions" are conceptually related to "'the' couple man/woman," that is, to sexual difference (90–91).

9. As she has asserted on numerous occasions in interviews (see, for example, Patricio Ríos's interview with her,"Chile: ni desprecio ni puro amor"), Eltit's own self-proclaimed concern is to write an epic of the margins. Epic is, perhaps, the most hegemonic of genres, essentially working to exult and consolidate the power of a group through the literary enactment of heroic deeds and accomplishments. An epic of the margins might seem, then, almost an oxymoron: after all, epic usually works to construct the *center*. Yet epic empowers its subject in a very direct way. Indeed, we could

say that it is *through* epic that the Cid, upstart that he is, can *become* a national hero. This lesson is not lost on Eltit, avid reader and teacher of the Spanish classics, who wishes to claim these hegemonic possibilities for the marginalized and disempowered of Chile and Latin America.

10. The term is from Giselle Munizaga's and Carlos Ochsenius's article, "El Discurso Público de Pinochet (1973–76)," in which they compile Pinochet's public speeches and read his discourse as an attempted foundational narrative with mythic characteristics.

11. Cited from Pinochet's speeches in Munizaga and Ochsensius, 71.

12. This protagonist is doubly named Coya and Coa, symbolizing both a collective memory ("Coya," the original queen of the Inca empire, refers to a noble indigenous past, vindicating a now suppressed racial and cultural identity) and collective language ("Coa," meaning slang or "jerga," refers to the language of the delinquent marginalized classes—the "hampa"). Eltit herself has explained this nomenclature in various interviews.

13. Munizaga and Ochsensius describe how the official disourse worked to establish this "Great Chilean Family" (75) and how "any change into an alternative meaning constitutes, like madness or sin, a transgression, a perversion" (97).

14. In "La *Declaración de Principios* de la Junta Militar Chilena Como Sistema Literario," Hernán Vidal convincingly argues that the resurgence of the body in Chilean narrative of resistance directly responds to the attempted obliteration of corporality in the official discourse, exemplified by the political document, *La Declaración de Principios / Declaration of Principles*. Vidal notes that in this political manifesto, "the human totality is reduced to an animated spirituality, dignified by the divine. . . . The human body, as concrete reality of needs and work, does not appear on this ideological horizon" (65). The cover design of *Por la patria* is the work of *avanzada* visual artist, Lotty Rosenfeld.

15. Eltit has indicated that one of the events that most affected her emotionally while writing *Por la patria* was this action by the government; and consequently, references to Pisagua appear throughout the text. About this phenomenon, Eltit observes, "I understood delinquency to be very tied to the political . . . what was happening was that in [Chile] the boundaries between the legal and the illegal were very blurred" (Ortega 234). Clearly, this erasure of boundaries between political militancy, delinquency, and other forms of marginalization is represented in *Por la patria*.

16. Nelly Richard has referred to the use of allegorical gestures in the *avanzada*'s artistic practice: "an entire allegorical chain of figures that name itinerancy (the journey, the exiles) or decentering (the feminine, the periphery) runs through the Chilean productions" ("Estética de la oblicuidad" 8). In

this way, allegorical gestures are used to mobilize conceptualizations that defy mimetic representation ("itinerancy" or "descentering"). Within the text itself, the episodes in the *barrio* are later explicitly referred to (read or understood) as "the allegory of the *barrio*" (185) by Coya, and are also written by her as a simulacrum of the margins "It will be a great copy, a substitute, a collective recording of speech" (199).

17. Such violent sieges, including the use of tanks and other weaponry, were part of the Chilean military's method for demobilizing, terrorizing, and controlling the marginal neighborhoods. For actual testimonials of such roundups, recorded through interviews with residents of marginal neighborhoods in Santiago, see Cathy Lisa Schneider's book, *Shantytown Protest in Pinochet's Chile* (especially pages 73–76).

18. Eugenia Brito has also noted that Juan is a representative of "la historia oficial" / "the official (hi)story" (*Campos minados*).

19. Cánovas 158. See his essay on *Por la patria*, especially pages 157–60, for more details on the linguistic experimentalism of this text.

20. In her review of the novel, Agata Gligo has suggested that the broken language Eltit employs is "a stylization of Mapuche speech" pointing out also that the diverse elements of classical and popular language reflect a *mestizaje* of language in *Por la patria*. (See note 23 for an explanation of the term *mestizaje*.)

21. Regarding the aesthetic of the margins, Eltit specifically states, "My project was to restore the *aesthetic* that pertains to and mobilizes those spaces" (interview with Ortega 232; emphasis added). On the issue of desire, see, for example, the interview with Claudia Donoso, 47.

22. Kristeva develops her idea of the Semiotic in *Revolution in Poetic Language* (1974) and in *Desire in Language* (1977), excerpts of which are included in the *Kristeva Reader*. I have found Judith Butler's explication of the evolution of Kristeva's use of the term to be one of the clearest and most helpful (*Gender Trouble* 79–93).

23. *Mestizo* (of mixed parentage) and *mestizaje* (miscegenation) are terms in Spanish used to refer to the mingling of races and cultures which began with the arrival of the Spanish and Portuguese in what is now known as Latin America. I will explore this problematic of the indigenous mother and *mestizo* cultural identity shortly.

24. Rodrigo Cánovas has convincingly analyzed the neo-baroque aspect of Eltit's work in his article "Apuntes sobre la novela *Por la patria* (1986), de Diamela Eltit" cited earlier.

25. Kristeva goes so far as to say in *Desire in Language*: "Carnivalesque discourse breaks through the laws of a language censored by grammar

and semantics and, at the same time, is a social and political protest. There is no equivalence, but rather identity between challenging official linguistic codes and challenging official law" (65; cited in Stallybrass and White 201).

26. Eltit observes, "After 1973 a political as well as a linguistic rupture becomes operant. For that very reason, all literary production was altered. The distinctive feature of the emerging literary generation as I see it has to do with that torturous way of naming reality to be found in daily life" (interview with Ríos 30).

27. In her article "The Traffic in Women," Gayle Rubin does a feminist reading of Freud, Lacan, Lévi-Strauss, and Marx, showing Freud's Oedipal crisis and Lévi-Strauss's kinship systems as necessarily intertwined and mutually enforcing. Indeed, Rubin argues that the Oedipal phase and kinship structures work hand in hand to divide the sexes and institute the rules and taboos necessary for the cultural reproduction of heterosexuality. The incest trope is also central in Eltit's later novel *El cuarto mundo*.

28. The function of ritual in Eltit's work is an interesting one, worthy of further exploration. For an analysis of ritual in Eltit's novel *Lumpérica*, see Sara Castro Klarén, "Escritura y cuerpo en *Lumpérica*," in Juan Carlos Lértora's *Una poética de literatura menor*.

The ritualistic use of the body I have alluded to in my analysis here is not confined to her written texts. Between 1980 and 1983, Eltit staged several art actions in Santiago, one of which included cutting and burning her own flesh before reading a part of her first novel, *Lumpérica*, in a brothel. As Nelly Richard points out, these acts, as well as those of Raúl Zurita, belong to a sacrificial tradition that aims to purge both the individual and society of the violence it suffers: "The acts of mortification used by Zurita and Eltit belong to that primitive tradition of communal sacrifice, or the *ritual exorcism of violence*. Even though not every manifestation of marginality need pass through a process of self-torture, it still enables one to purge oneself through the mystical experience of going beyond the self" (*Margins* 68). We can certainly see a similar function of communal "ritual exorcism of violence" as well as a desire for bodily transcendence in Eltit's ritualistic portrayal of erotic scenes with the father. Incest here functions as a transgression that, represented in a cathartic way, strives toward expiation and transcendence. Furthermore, in this case, the desire to go beyond the body is transformed, through the sacred, ritualistic aspect of this incestuous union, from a personal, bodily desire into a collective, politically significant transgression with a social function.

29. As Judith Butler points out: "What remains 'unthinkable' and 'unsayable' within the terms of an existing cultural possibility is not necessarily what is excluded from the matrix of intelligibility within that form; on the contrary, it is the marginalized, not the excluded, . . . that calls for dread or, minimally, the loss of sanctions" (77).

30. *La época*, 28 julio de 1987; cited as an epigraph by Antonio Ostornol in his recent novel *Los años de la serpiente* 1991; cited as epigraph to this chapter as well.

31. I am thinking specifically of *La casa de los espíritus* by Isabel Allende, *Los años de la serpiente* by Antonio Ostornol, *Santiago Cero* by Carlos Franz and *El anfitrión* by Jorge Edwards. In all of these texts betrayal (la traición) plays a central role.

32. René Girard explains how ritual often simultaneously enacts a representation and an exorcism. See his *Violence and the Sacred*.

33. The "law of the father" can be seen to reign supreme in traditional models of subjectivity (whereby the psychosocial prohibitions of the father's law intervene in separating the child from the mother's body, forcing the entry into the symbolic realm and the acquisition of language), in the conceptualization of the foundation of Latin American culture (which symbolically elides the indigenous mother), as well as in the structure of the authoritarian political system (which Eltit herself characterizes as paternally coded: "Here, the failure of patriarchal power is so acute that it needs a dictator/father in order to administrate it. [. . .] It is no accident that it is precisely in this period of dictatorship and catastrophe that numerous organized women's movements appear" [interview with Ríos]).

34. Montecino suggests that the profound ambivalence toward cultural *mestizaje* has been one of the reasons for the Mariana cult: in adopting the (white) Virgin as "common Mater," the *mestizo* subject solves and obliterates the ambivalence-producing ties to the indigenous mother. See *Madres y huachos: Alegorías del mestizaje chileno*, especially page 29.

35. Cited in Munizaga and Ochsensius.

36. As Rodrigo Cánovas points out: "The mothers are figures that enact a role designed beforehand; they are actresses that follow a script. There is a theatricality of the sign that marks the false (literary, artistic) character of the representation" (150).

37. Irigaray's reading of "Femininity" can be found in "The Blind Spot of an Old Dream of Symmetry" in *Speculum* 13–129; the comment quoted above is specifically found on page 80 (emphasis added).

38. As Cánovas points out regarding the second "visión," "The relationships here are complex: abused fatherland, abused mother; national lack and maternal lack; against social lacks, auto-erotic gratifications, writerly transgressions" (151).

39. In the Argentine context, Lea Fletcher has begun a study on rape as a gender-specific torture and its lack of representation in literature that deals with the Process. As Fletcher observes, the "algo habrán hecho" /

"they must have done something" used to justify and silence the violations committed by the authoritarian regime are part of the same rhetoric used to justify and erase the rape of a woman, blaming her for having transgressed the norms, for having been raped. The woman raped while detained as a political prisoner is thus doubly silenced for having disobeyed the Law of the Father carried to its extreme in a military dictatorship" (2). For Fletcher the lack of literary representation of political rape reflects this double silencing. Eltit's representation of rape certainly defies this socio-sexual taboo.

40. *Por la patria* (91); the phrases in italics are what Rodrigo Cánovas has highlighted as "lexicon related to the national anthem" (151).

41. The list of female characters whose supposed promiscuity has been portrayed as generating social disorder and destruction is long, including, in the Hispanic context, La Cava and La Malinche. In traditional mythological formulations, the chaotic realm of the Great Mother is dominated by the most earthy, bodily, sexually active aspect of femininity; "civilization" must thus work to suppress this side of femininity if it is to prevail. See Erich Neumann's work, *The History of Consciousness*, for example.

42. This exact dream is also described on page 217.

43. For a compelling analysis of Eltit's work, particularly *Lumpérica* and *Por la patria*, see Djelal Kadir's "A Woman's Place: Gendered Histories of the Subaltern" in *The Other Writing*, a work that unfortunately only came to my attention once the present study was already in press.

Chapter 3

1. The perceived "subversive" nature of Roffé's text has to do not only with its social critique but surely also with the fact that the main character is a lesbian. For more on this aspect of *Monte de Venus* see David William Foster, "The Demythification of Buenos Aires" and O. Uribe "Literary Experience/Social Experience."

2. For another testimony of this period in Roffé's life, and more details on the aftermath of the banning of *Monte de Venus*, see her article appropriately titled "Omnipresencia de la censura en la escritora argentina" ("Omnipresence of Censorship in the Argentine Woman Writer").

3. This paper provides special insight into the various writers and feminist theorists that have influenced Reina Roffé's thinking. Besides Djuna Barnes, she mentions several writers familiar to U.S. feminists (including Virginia Woolf, Patricia Meyer Spacks, Julia Kristeva, and Luce Irigaray) as well as many Latin American writers and critics (Marta Traba, Ana María Shúa, Liliana Mizrahi, and Noemí Ulla among others too numer-

ous to mention here). Significantly, after her talk Roffé was verbally attacked by some of the male writers attending the symposium. The editor, evidently somewhat embarrassed by such a hysterical display, felt obliged to be selective in the comments he transcribed, noting: "Of the interventions provoked by Roffé's talk, I select those that go beyond the mere aggressiveness that characterized some contributions" (*Literatura argentina de hoy* 293).

4. From Dennis Lee's article, "Cadence, Country, Silence: Writing in Colonial Space," cited in *The Empire Writes Back*, 141.

5. Subjectivity, according to Sally Robinson, is not an essential thing but an active engagement with social discourses; hence, she points out that subjectivity is most usefully conceived of as a "doing" not a "being": subjectivity "is not constructed, once and for all, at some locatable point in the individual's history; rather, it is a continuous process of production and transformation. Subjectivity, like gender, is a 'doing,' rather than a being" (11). These comments seem particularly apropos to the construction of subjectivity in *La rompiente*.

6. Paul Smith introduces the terms "actor" and "agent" in his book, *Discerning the Subject*: "A person is not simply the *actor* who follows ideological scripts, but is also an *agent* who reads them in order to insert him/herself into them—or not" (xxxiv–xxxv; emphasis added). The distinction between "actor" and "agent" is similar to the distinction Robinson makes, in her comments on subjectivity, between being *subject to* certain normative discursive and social practices and *subject of* other, new interventions. The point is that subjectivity involves both passive and active modes.

7. Such multiplicity of voices is a common feature in narrative of this time period. Beatriz Sarlo observes: "In the face of the monologue practiced by authoritarianism, a communicative model appears that tends toward the perspectivization and the framing of discourses" ("Política" 43).

8. Roffé made these comments to me in a letter, March 10, 1993, in response to my questions to her about her views on reading and writing under dictatorship. Her comments in Spanish are perhaps even more resonant: "*poder* secreto que nadie iba a *poder* arrebatar. . . . Como decir: puedo, a pesar de todo" (emphasis in the original).

9. "Líneas de fuerza" translated literally would be "lines of force" or "lines of strength," neither of which seem to me to capture the particular resonance of the original Spanish.

10. As this first quotation from the body of the text reveals, *La rompiente* is exceedingly complex in terms of narrative voice and ambiguity. As the story progresses, it becomes clear that the third person singular form refers generally to "usted" or the formal "you." The "usted" is not, however,

reiterated frequently, thus preserving to a degree that dizzying sense of not being sure who is speaking or being spoken to.

11. While in Argentina I had the opportunity to talk about this issue with Argentine literary critic and scholar, Cristina Piña, who included *La rompiente* in a seminar she taught in the university there. She agreed that there is no gendered adjective or construction that determines the gender of the narrator/interlocutor, but told me that in her class there was almost complete agreement that the interlocutor was a woman, due to the level of "intimacy" of the "conversation." I, on the other hand, had imagined the interlocutor as male, perhaps because of associations with the traditional male analyst/female patient relationship, perhaps because of his/her rather distant and controlling tone, perhaps because of similarities between the situation in this novel and that in Carmen Martín Gaite's *El cuarto de atrás* where the interlocutor is most definitely a man. The interesting thing here, it seems to me, is that each reader ultimately brings his/her own history (personal, cultural, and otherwise) and his/her own reading *to* the narrative. As such, in an even more marked way than is usually the case, the reading tells as much about the reader as it does about the text. In addition, the fact that each reader stubbornly imagines this narrative voice as gendered even when deliberately deprived of clues perhaps proves Freud's observation that when meeting someone "the first distinction you make is 'male or female?' and you are accustomed to make the distinctions with unhesitating certainty" ("Femininity" 100). Such a custom evidently extends, as well, to narrative voice.

12. Note that in the Spanish the "old friend" is nuanced feminine while the "postponed love" is nuanced masculine due to the gender of the nouns.

13. The idea that this (possible) lover might be a woman would be even especially enhanced for those who had read Roffé's second novel, *Monte de Venus*, which foregrounds a lesbian relationship. In her article, Marily Martínez de Richter also refers to the possibility that the potential lover is a woman and further points out that the woman friend who sends the protagonist letters from abroad in the third section of the novel gives the reader another clue as to the sexual identity of this friend and/or lover (104).

14. *This Sex* 30. Later, as we shall see, the protagonist explicitly denounces this phenomenon of othering when she tells her male lover: "deseas que . . . me convierta en tu doble" / "you want . . . me to turn into your double" (66).

15. For the discursive boundaries of "us" and "them" during authoritarian rule, see Andrés Avellaneda, volume I, 20. For the way these limits were constructed (i.e., in secret and not negotiated), see Beatriz Sarlo "Política" (37).

16. Cited by Susana Zanetti, "'Brechas del muro'. Exilio interior y censura," in Kohut, *Literatura argentina de hoy*, 276.

17. See the introduction of this chapter for Roffé's comments to this effect.

18. See Andrés Avalleneda volume 1, page 20 for a discussion of these terms.

19. In part 3 (105–07), fashion returns as this type of force-fed happiness, feminine ritual, and imposition of standards (what's "in," what's "out") without regard for subjective preferences.

20. As Andrés Avellaneda also suggests, that which was most prohibited through the discourse of censorship in Argentina was anything that questioned the status quo: quoting an Argentine writer, he notes that "en Argentina se reprimen sobre todo las obras 'que cuestionen con mayor o menor hondura los sistemas de vida y de poder'" / "in Argentina the works that are repressed are those 'that question to a greater or lesser degree systems of life and power'" (51).

21. For example, abortion, prostitution, homosexuality, promiscuity, adultery, or anything seen to assault the institution of matrimony are deemed unfit for public consumption for, after all, according to the logic of the regime, "Great economic, political and social plans in favor of the family and the community will be worthless if we do not combat immorality in other terrains, banishing eroticism, pornography and violence from the means of social communication" (cited in Avellaneda from the "Comunicado de las Ligas de Padres y Madres de Familia en ocasión del 25 aniversario de su creación por el Episcopado Argentino en 1951" volume 1, 143). For details on the designation of the "nuestro" and the "ajeno" in terms of sexuality see Avellaneda's introduction, especially page 20, volume 1.

22. An Argentine military official, the Vice Admiral Lambruschini, makes this clear in a speech in 1976: "En el teatro doctrinario se lucha por impedir la utilización del armamento ideológico del enemigo, que se propone objetivos muy concretos . . . [Uno de ellos es] minar la fe de los argentinos en su sistema de vida democrático y pluralista. Para ello atacan en la célula inicial, en la relación padres e hijos y *llegan hasta cuestionar la relación hombre-mujer*, en aquellos elementos que hacen a su dignidad esencial" / "In the dogmatic arena the fight is against the utilization of the enemy's ideological weapon, which proposes very concrete objectives . . . [One of them is] to undermine the Argentines' faith in their democratic and pluralist way of life. In order to accomplish that they attack the most basic component, the relationship between parents and children and *they even question the relationship between man and woman*, in those elements that lend it its essential dignity" (cited by Avellaneda 1; 143; emphasis added).

23. Andrés Avellaneda explains that one of the authoritarian regime's methods was "la represión ejercida de modo indiscriminado y sin fundamento claro para internalizar masivamente el concepto de castigo y *paralizar de tal manera el mayor número de reacciones posibles*" / "exercising repression in an indiscriminate and groundless way in order to internalize en masse the concept of punishment and *in this way paralyze the largest number of possible reactions*" (I, 14; emphasis added).

24. See John Mowitt's introduction to Paul Smith's *Discerning the Subject* (xxi). Of course, key to such a procedure is not only reading but "reading resistantly" (xxi). The source of such resistance can be the reading subject's own history and resultant class and generic interests. Agency is the explicit concern of Paul Smith in *Discerning the Subject*. His project, as eloquently summed up by Mowitt in the introduction, is to establish a "coherent account of political resistance that neither resorts to a metaphysics of voluntarism, nor appeals to a teleologically designated subject of history" (xv). Agency, thus, is used by Smith to designate the "activating dynamic that exceeds individuals at the point where this dynamic nevertheless empowers them to oppose that which confronts them, as individuals, from without" (xv). Clearly, for any model or theoretical account of the social subject that hopes to provide a means for imagining change, agency is a key ingredient.

25. The scene is from *Mrs. Dalloway* and seems to be an explicit reference to Clarissa Dalloway's remembering her love for Sally and her ecstasy when Sally kissed her on the lips in the woods (48–53). It is worth pointing out that the passage in *La rompiente* begins with a reference to Woolf's *A Room of One's Own*. The protagonist remembers her feelings of exclusion while waiting for a friend outside a library that she is not authorized to enter, a scene reminiscent of Woolf's meditations on her own outsider status as she looks into a library from which she is excluded because of her gender (*A Room* 5–10; 24). The exile Roffé's text inscribes is even more complex, involving exclusion on account of her foreignness ("su destino particular y sudamericano" 26) as well as her age. The resonance with Woolf, the various levels of exile, and the exploration of a forbidden but nonetheless glimpsed sexual desire between women—all remarkably condensed into this short passage—would be worth further analysis.

26. Letters also constitute, in their very writing and reading, a certain act of faith in the possibility of communication. As Johnny Payne shows in his excellent analysis of Ricardo Piglia's *Respiración artificial*, epistolary fiction and letters in general become attempts at maintaining hope and the possibilities of dialogue in the face of the discommunication and isolation reigning among Argentine intellectuals during the military regime. See especially pages 101–09 of *Conquest of the New Word: Experimental Fiction and Translation in the Americas*.

27. In her essay "Visual Pleasure and Narrative Cinema," Laura Mulvey analyzes the scopofilic instinct (that is, "pleasure in looking at another person as an erotic object" 426) and the sexual politics involved in an economy in which "Woman displayed as sexual object is the leitmotiv of erotic spectacle: from pinups to striptease, from Ziegfeld to Busby Berkeley, she holds the look, plays to, and signifies male desire" (418). While Mulvey holds that "in a world ordered by sexual imbalance, pleasure in looking has been split between active/male and passive/female" (418), Roffé's protagonist shows that while that may well be the "sexual order," defiance can still be productively and transgressively imagined.

28. The term "subject positions" has been adopted by many critics and theorists from Foucault who conceived of subjectivity as "not the speaking consciousness, not the author of the formulation, but a position that may be filled in certain conditions by various individuals" (from *The Archaeology of Knowledge* 115; cited in Fuss 32).

29. See, for example, Hollway (252); Smith (xxxv); Robinson (15, 56–57).

30. Indeed, I agree with Mónica Szurmuk who has called *La rompiente* "the textualization of repression." She sums up Roffé's narrative project thus: "In *La rompiente*, Reffé explores the possibilities of finding a voice that can speak of the dictatorship's repression, but that can also point to other types of repression—sexist sexual repression, the internalized repression of those who lived under a regimen of death, 'dirty wars and the laundering of souls' (23), self-repression" (125). As I pointed out in the previous section, while "finding" such a voice is the protagonist's self-proclaimed project, I propose that the author virtually *produces* this voice as a function of the textual search itself.

31. From here on, I refer to the text within the text as the protagonist's "novel"; the "protagonist" refers to the heroine of the "novel"; finally, I here put "real events" in quotations since they are also textualized within the protagonist's narrative, but are deliberately plotted as the "real story" vis-à-vis the "novel."

32. As we saw in the introduction, this type of challenge was common to the literature of the Proceso. According to Sarlo, while the authoritarian regime was characterized by its univocality, its attempts to be the sole source of meaning, the discourses produced by literature of the period primarily sought to open paths of signification and to generate multiple points of view ("Política" 40).

33. Play and gaming are key activities in the "novel" that would be worth exploring further. From the first, it seems that sex has been replaced with gaming with its set protocols, its climax of winning. The "protago-

nist's" participation in card games is a complex combination of escape from the unbearable paralysis and guilt of being among the survivors of a brutal "dirty war" as well as a tentative exorcism of that paralysis, a simulated foray into action, power, agency. The game ultimately has to do with simulation, with playing a role, with beating the other and not revealing emotions. With its rigid protocol, its rules and formulas, the game offers the protagonist a chance to *act* according to a set script. Yet, the game also provides an "instancing of agency," offering as it does the opportunity for making decisions, taking the initiative, and ultimately wielding a certain power, however illusory, temporary, or meaningless. For a somewhat different view of play and gambling in the novel, especially with regard to feminism, see the excellent article by Marily Martínez de Richter, "Textualización de la violencia: *Informe bajo llave* de Marta Lynch y *La rompiente* de Reina Roffé" (113–14).

34. It should be noted that in both cases (whether gamblers or literati) there is a similar sensation of passion, conspiracy, and secrecy. See Gramuglio, especially pages 130–32, for her comments in this regard.

35. By censorship I mean that these literary expectations form, like more explicit censorships, a discursive and social injunction determining suitability or acceptability. As I pointed out in the introduction to this chapter, Roffé makes clear in the preface to *La rompiente* how such literary expectations involve a type of censorship of their own.

36. That is to say, one story told as another that, as I explained in the introduction, is one way of conceptualizing the modus operandi of allegorical procedures. Szurmuk has also referred, in passing, to the use of allegory here: "the novel of the second part, narrated, criticized, commented upon, is the product of a repressive state, it is the attempt to tell— between the lines and on the basis of an allegory—an experience of terror and silence" (126).

37. The critic with whom the protagonist has an affair (in part 3 we learn she is divorcing him as her husband) is ironically named Boomer, ludicrous participant in the "Boom" and its accompanying masculinist malaise. In fact, we could read *La rompiente* as resisting the silent place assigned to women (both as representations and as writers) in the "Boom." Another irony is that "Boomer is lacking something" (41); incomplete, inadequate, Boomer is written as castrated on many levels. Indeed, he is missing a hand, a lack that the protagonist feels as her own, and that pushes her to play her hand, as it were, "por las manos del otro" / "for the hands of the other" (44). Thus, undoing the idea that it is the woman who is always "missing" something, whose lack the male writer explores, "plays," and writes (Onetti's *La vida breve* being a prime example on that score), *La rompiente* re-imagines lack as a male condition. In one of her essays, Roffé draws critical, feminist attention to the Boom: "The classic places that

woman occupied in masculine writing were . . . that of the muse (not only in antiquity but also in our century for the surrealists), that of unattainable object of passion (the poetics of Pablo Neruda), that of the eternal mystery of the feminine (Ibsen, Flaubert), that of prostitute, of adulteress, and of witch *even for the acclaimed writers of the Latin American boom*" ("Qué escribimos" 208; emphasis added).

38. The mirror plays an important role in *La rompiente* from the beginning; indeed the cover of the book portrays two images of the same woman, one in profile wearing sunglasses, the other reflected in a cracked mirror. In her essay "Qué escribimos," Roffé makes clear that the narcissism her interlocutor cites as a flaw in women's writing actually has a productive function: "Look upon [the narcissism] in them as a necessity of recognizing themselves, of discovering themselves, of looking at themselves though the mirror of writing. . . . The narcissism that you point to as sick could indicate, furthermore, a quest for singularity, . . . a battle against the shame of looking at oneself in order to preserve the integrity of an 'I,' in order to affirm the omnipotence that the external world negates; for that reason women talk more about themselves than about their characters, because they still have a lot to say to themselves" (206). Not only do these comments elucidate the importance of the mirror for the protagonist's resistance, they also reflect on the narrative project of *La rompiente* at large.

39. Masquerade, a feminine forté if we are to give Irigaray any credit, is evidently not Piglia's cup of tea. To hear him tell it, censorship doesn't affect his literary production in the least: "es que no escribo para el censor, y que por lo tanto no tengo presente al censor cuando construyo mi obra, y no acomodo mis textos a las posibilidades de admisión que me permite la censura" / "it's that I don't write for the censor, and so as such I don't take the censor into account when I construct my work, and I don't accommodate my texts to the possibilities of admission that censorship permits me" (Kohut *Literatura argentina hoy* 291). He, it would seem, "writes like a man," never *subject to* external constraints, always *subject of* whatever he might want to write. His comments are in stark contrast with Roffé's reaction to censorship. She concludes that she had always been censored and that political oppression was just the most explicit form of censorship she faced.

40. See Sarlo, who likewise observes that allegory is a function of reading as well as writing (45).

41. See Mowitt's comments on these properties of reading (Smith *Discerning the Subject* xxi).

42. See Diana Fuss who observes that for Irigaray: "women are engaged in the process of both constructing and deconstructing their identities, their *essences*, simultaneously" (70).

43. The title of Roffé's text similarly inscribes a doubleness of process and product: *rompiente* is both an action or a doing (*rompiente* from the verb to break, *romper*) as well as a reified place or product (a *rompiente* as the place where waves break). Mónica Szurmuk also alludes to this doubleness, stressing the way the title as well as Roffé's text itself defy any simplistic binarism (124; 130 n. 9).

44. As I noted, Sarlo has described how authoritarianism strips individuals and groups of a viable subjectivity, noting that they, like Roffé's protagonist in this instance, "son pensados por ellos (los valores impuestos)" / "are thought by them (the imposed values)" (38).

45. Mónica Szurmuk's reading of Roffé's text provides some very insightful comments on the feminine spaces at the end of the novel. See pages 128–29 of her article. To my mind, the spaces articulated at the end of the text are very much like the fluid, marginal spaces of feminist theory that Ruth Salvaggio talks about in her essay "Theory and Space," and would be worth further analysis.

46. See the end of Irigary's essay "This Sex Which Is Not One" in the volume by the same title.

47. The body here provides, as Mónica Szurmuk notes, a temporarily utopian space (129). I would especially emphasize that it is utopic in the fullest sense of utopia (*ou*—not; *topos*—place), stressing constant deferral of any realization or arrival at a definitive or essential Body, and yet always pushing forward in a drive to actively re-imagine the female body.

48. Mizrahi 88. Mizrahi's formulations are particularly appropriate to Roffé's text; see especially her description of "el ser proyecto" (88). I suggest that Roffé's protagonist becomes, through *La rompiente*, sum total of her disparate voices and contradictory narratives, the textual counterpart of just such a "being in process."

Chapter Four

1. This novel has been very ably translated by Psiche Hughes as *The Ship of Fools*. All English quotations from the novel in this chapter are from that translation except where otherwise indicated. All other translations from the Spanish, including critical articles and interviews, are my own.

2. Interview with Montserrat Ordóñez 198. The protagonist in *La nave* expresses a similar sentiment; when asked if he is a foreigner he replies: "Only in some countries . . . and hopefully I will not be one forever. I was not born a foreigner . . . it is a condition one acquires through force of circumstances. You could become one too, if you chose . . ." (24).

3. With the term "postmodern condition" I refer specifically here to Lyotard's "diagnosis" of the contemporary demise of what he calls the "grand récits" or master narratives. The characteristics of postmodern literary texts as well as theoretical/philosophical interventions are often described as including a decentering of the subject, a self-conscious fragmentation (i.e., of subjectivity, of narrative time and space), heterogeneity (i.e., mixing of discourses), pronounced linguistic play, and acute skepticism regarding traditional ideas of Truth. As we shall see, several of these characteristics are present in *La nave de los locos* and the exile portrayed in this text is intimately bound up with such conditions.

4. Mabel Moraña does an excellent job in documenting the ways Cristina Peri Rossi's fiction uses allegorical procedures (see the section entitled "La estructura alegórica" pp. 39–44). In her article on Cristina Peri Rossi's collection of short stories, *El museo de los esfuerzos inútiles* (The Museum of Useless Efforts), Mercedes M. de Rodríguez also examines the uses of allegory, especially as pertaining to exile (see "Variaciones").

5. On allegory as commentary see Fletcher (8), Frye (89–91), Clifford (5).

6. For more on the most common characteristics of allegorical texts including the often-used structure of the journey see Clifford's account of allegory and Fletcher's introduction.

7. While I have aligned Peri Rossi's work with the "postmodern condition" due to its marked fragmentation and reflexivity and its grappling with the crisis of legitimation Lyotard addresses (xxiv), this does not invalidate Ana Rueda's suggestion that Peri's work should be considered within a romantic tradition due to her attempt to recuperate a mythical connection to the natural world (See Rueda 202, 204). Postmodernism and romanticism are neither mutually exclusive nor as far removed from one another as they might seem. Paul Smith, for example, sees certain postmodern texts as marked by romantic tendencies, often manifested as "an almost overdetermined nostalgia for the primordial" ("The Will to Allegory" 112). Indeed, it is precisely in postmodernism's "will to allegory" that Smith finds a romantic gesture.

8. Peri Rossi's comments in an interview indicate that she views allegory as a response to censorship that can then go beyond that immediate function. Responding to a question by Eileen Zeitz about censorship she says: "In my case, the existence of censorship functions like an incentive to elaborate the metaphor capable of surpassing it. . . . That constitutes a challenge in my work. I would never not approach a theme because I knew ahead of time that it was censored; I would do everything possible to refer to that theme allegorically, and this game would be very fruitful" (81). Peri Rossi also sees fantastic literature allegorically: "I find [fantastic literature] fascinating, although I realize that its codes and allegories are sometimes obscure for an uninitiated reader" (84).

9. Indeed, Cristina Peri Rossi has explicitly pointed to her allegorical use of exile in this text: "*La nave de los locos* attempted to be a novel about exile as a metaphor or allegory, as the condition of man" (interview with Susana Camps 40).

10. My translation. Ecks refers to an image of Venice that he finds comforting in that it provides an "equilibrio sin sacrificios" (*La nave* 35). The English translation reads only "the existence of a possible order and equilibrium" (30), omitting the key phrase (for my purposes, at least) "without sacrifice."

11. Dreams play a key role in *La nave*, frequently providing a revelatory knowledge that cannot often be assimilated into the waking state, "Like all revelations, those which come in dreams are given to people unable to understand them, much less act on them. For in dreams one is always naïve, inadequate and lacking discernment. Therefore one either forgets or ignores their content" (42). Nonetheless, the quest at the end of *La nave* involves Equis's attempt to comprehend and solve an enigmatic dream. For more on the role of dreams in the text see Rodríguez article, "Oneiric Riddles in Peri Rossi's *La nave de los locos*." She bases her analysis on Freudian and, to some degree, Irigarayan theories.

12. Craig Owens, in keeping with Heidegger's formulation of the modern age as the age of the master narrative as well as the age of representation, points to the possibility of representation as precisely what is simultaneously in crisis and under fire in postmodernism ("The Discourse of Others: Feminists and Postmodernism" 58–59; 64–67).

13. For example, as Roland Barthes points out: "The tableau (pictorial, theatrical, literary) is a pure cut-out segment with clearly defined edges, irreversible and incorruptible; everything that surrounds it is banished into nothingness, remains unnamed, while everything that it admits within its field is promoted into essence, into light, into view" (*Image-Music-Text* 70). As we shall see, Equis is well aware of this violent exile when he considers the harmony of a traditional representation. Later in the narrative he contemplates the medieval tapestry (which is described in short sections of text interspersed between the accounts of Equis's travels): "cualquier armonía supone la destrucción de los elementos reales que se le oponen, por eso es casi siempre simbólica" (20).

14. In his article "The Discourse of Others," Owens cites the following from Paul Ricoeur's "Universal Civilization and National Cultures" in *History and Truth* (278), which bears an uncanny resemblance to the situation we have in *La nave de los locos*: "When we discover that there are several cultures instead of just one and consequently at the time when we acknowledge the end of a sort of cultural monopoly, be it illusory or real, we are threatened with the destruction of our own discovery. Suddenly it

becomes possible that there are just others, that we ourselves are *an 'other' among others*. All meaning and every goal having disappeared, it becomes possible to wander through civilizations as if through vestiges and ruins. The whole of mankind becomes an imaginary museum [. . .] *We can very easily imagine a time close at hand when any fairly well-to-do person will be able to leave his country indefinitely in order to taste his own national death in an interminable, aimless voyage*" (cited in Owens 57–58; emphasis added). Owens sums up, "Lately, we have come to regard this condition as postmodern" and then points out that the advent of the postmodern entails a loss of mastery and a collapse of the claims of authority of works of art as based on universal aesthetic standards (57–59), a state of affairs Ricoeur bemoans while Owens, Lyotard, and many feminists, for example, celebrate. In addition to describing the traits of postmodernism, Ricoeur's description portrays almost exactly the state of exile in *La nave*, further marking the resonance between Peri Rossi's text and the postmodern condition.

15. Lucía Guerra-Cunningham also points out that this initial confusion and ambiguity is the motivating force of the text: "It is from this ambiguity that annuls the hierarchizations of the androcentric epic that one must understand Ecks's trajectory, significantly initiated in the first section by a dream in which the significant and insignificant, the wheat and the chaff, are mixed" (71). "The androcentric epic" is precisely the type of masculine "master narrative" thrown into question by the text as well as by postmodernism at large.

16. Equis is at once victim and volunteer of exile. As Cristina Peri Rossi herself describes his character: "the protagonist is the symbolic exile, one that voluntarily exiles himself from all possible types of violence" (Interview with Ordóñez 198). Equis himself also emphasizes, however, that his travels are not entirely of his own choosing: he travels aimlessly, he says, "due to special circumstances having more to do with the way the world turns than with my personal wishes" (76). While Equis is certainly subject *to* exile, victim of his social circumstances, he also becomes subject *of* his exile, making his exile into an opportunity for creative production.

17. Olivera-Williams discusses the critical advantage of exile (120), which we will return to later.

18. Others have noted this quest for harmony in *La nave*. See Olivera-Williams, Guerra-Cunningham (especially 71), and Mora, for example. Mora's articles are primarily concerned with this topic. In one she uses Deleuze and Guattari's model of the "rhizome" to account for the seemingly contrary textual impulses of a search for harmony and a desire for change ("Peri Rossi: *La nave de los locos* y la búsqueda de la armonía"). In another version of this article, translated into English, she shows how the desire for harmony is the unifying theme that underlies the apparently disparate frag-

ments of the novel ("Enigmas and Subversions in Cristina Peri Rossi's *La nave de los locos*").

19. Owens "The Discourse of Others" 62; emphasis added. Such a task, as Owens explicitly states, is not only key to postmodernism but also a top priority for many feminist thinkers. One of the most well-known feminist critique of binarism as the lynchpin of phallogocentrism is Hélène Cixous' "Sorties," translated and included in Marks and Courtivron, *New French Feminisms* (90–98).

20. We will turn to the sociopolitical context in the next section. Meanwhile, the methodology for imposing such an "old dream of symmetry" on the societies of the Southern Cone is well-documented, operating on a cultural level by virtually "encarcelando, asesinando o exiliando a quienes se desvían del criterio canónico impuesto" (Avellaneda "Realismo" 578). In the particular case of Uruguay, Juan Rial has described the development of a social imaginary that aimed at unifying the nation and subsuming any "other," alternative imaginaries or ideologies by installing four primary myths (Uruguay as middle class, as "different" from the rest of Latin America, as democratic, and as composed of cultured citizens). As this social imaginary was thrown into crisis by pressures from within demanding social change, it was actually further fractionalized by the military dictatorship (1973–85) which paradoxically tried to restore that "old dream" of unity by using methods that virtually contradicted the myths themselves (See Rial 82–85; Carina Perelli 125).

21. The letter "X" also stands for Christ (since 1100 A.D.; see for example *Webster's New Twentieth Century Dictionary*, or any unabridged dictionary), so the lack of restriction of a proper name implied by "X" simultaneously suggests an expansiveness capable of signifying the identity of the "Son of Man," redeemer of the world. Mercedes M. de Rodríguez points out other indications of Equis's similarity to Christ: he is thirty-three years old (78), he is identified with the Creator of the Universe (cited earlier), and he carries a dove with him wherever he travels (34) [see "Oneiric" 523]. This critic likewise reads the "X" as a reference to "any man, unnamed to establish his universality" (521), pointing out as well that Irigaray "refers to the 'all' of X as the 'symbol of universality' and the 'universal quantifier' in 'The Mechanics of Fluids' in *This Sex*, 108" (521).

22. Indeed, as María Rosa Olivera-Williams points out *La nave* "condemns the individualism that reigns in the world. As such, to expand on the tragedy caused by South American militarism—Argentine, Brazilian, Chilean, Uruguayan—would be, in part, to become enclosed in one of the folds of the 'Great Navel'" (87).

23. For documentation of this horrific practice, see Frank Graziano's *Divine Violence* (40; 245 n. 106, n. 107).

24. The impossibility of return is also related to the relationship drawn in the novel between sociopolitical/national exile and exile from the maternal body. The narrator specifically suggests such a resonance, describing "la ternura que inspira un hombre *sin patria*, es decir, *sin madre*" ["the tenderness inspired by a man without *country*, that is, without *mother*"] (38; emphasis and translation mine). Mercedes M. de Rodríguez has explored how this correspondence surfaces in *La nave*, noting that for Freud the womb can be understood as the former home of all human beings and that the narrator casts Equis as "Expelled from the womb of the earth. Eviscerated: once more to give birth (2)" (521).

25. What the Argentine film, *La historia oficial* [The Official Story], represents is precisely how this type of division operated and finally crumbled. The female protagonist manages to remain oblivious to the disappeared and the sociopolitical crisis, esconced in her affluent homelife and her job as a high school history teacher. It is only when her students plaster the classroom with pictures of the disappeared that she begins to question the origins of her adopted daughter and her husband's role in the terrifying tactics of the regime. As she becomes increasingly aware of her political surroundings, the neat categorizations and divisions that had allowed her to ignore the fallout from the "dirty war" begin to dissolve.

26. Ironically, "la isla" is also the name given by prisoners to the building used for punishment and solitary confinement in the notorious Libertad Prison, a military prison located outside of Montevideo (*Uruguay: Nunca Más* 123, 151).

27. It is worth noting that the original Spanish version of "the human condition" reads "la verdadera condición del *hombre*" (106; my emphasis). Peri Rossi frequently uses "hombre" ("man") to refer generically to the human subject, a usage that seems discordant with the author's general denunciation of genderic dissymmetry. I would suggest that this is, however, in keeping with her consistent use of male protagonists, an issue I discuss more at length in the next few pages.

28. In one interview, for example, she points out that exile fascinates her not only on a poetic level but also in terms of sociology, observing that "in the Nordic countries they are studying the relationship between sexuality and exile," and that exile disrupts identity to such a degree that sexual relationships are ultimately affected (interview with Montserrat Ordóñez 197).

29. For a discussion of woman's "homelessness" in this sense see Whitford on Irigaray (125; 135–36). Mercedes M. de Rodríguez has also noted regarding exile in *La nave* that Peri portrays two kinds of exile, one a banishment from one's homeland, the other "a more subtle form of exile, ascribing to the word the meaning of marginality to refer to the position adjudicated by men to women in the history of civilization" ("Oneiric Riddles" 521).

30. Judith Butler's comments help clarify this phenomenon: "The injunction to *be* a given gender produces necessary failures, a variety of incoherent configurations that in their multiplicity exceed and defy the injunction by which they are gendered" (145). And for Butler, such "failures" to "be" a given gender ultimately have positive, political potential.

31. Peri Rossi states: "The Western reader is accustomed to the idea that intimate and sentimental themes have a woman as a protagonist; metaphysical themes and psychological complications are masculine. Anyone who wants to utilize a feminine protagonist with metaphysical vacillations or existential problems has to invent her from scratch because as a character, she doesn't have sufficient bibliography; so one would have to do a character novel. The writer works based on certain assumptions; you can't fight against all of them" (interview with Golano 49). These comments and the fact that in most of Cristina Peri Rossi's narrative the main character is masculine, effectively draw attention to what she views as the difficulty for women to intervene *as women* in the more philosophical fields of fiction.

32. For example, in the first tableau it is "she" who draws his attention to the excluded "chaff"; later an abused prostitute exposes him to the pathetic conditions and violence of her trade and challenges him to see a certain harmony implicit in male impotence, and Graciela informs him about the varied oppressions to which women are subjected. Guerra-Cunningham has also noted the primacy of the female character in the final episode: "Contradicting the phallogocentric paradigms of the fairy tale that exalt masculine intelligence and wisdom, Ecks obtains the answer to the enigma from feminine motivating forces" (69). It is, indeed, Lucía's escape to a transvestite club and her cross-dressing that bring him to a final epiphany in the last tableau. I turn my attention to this ending in the next section of this chapter.

33. Kantaris suggests, quite correctly I think, that what Peri Rossi's text primarily grapples with is how to maintain "plurality *in* identity" (257).

34. Interestingly, Irigaray similarly unveils the law as a "cover" for the father's desire for his daughter. Reversing Freud's assertion of the little girl's seduction by the father as sheer fantasy, Irigaray points out that the father indeed might desire his daughter, but because "he refuses to recognize and live out his desire, *he lays down a law that prohibits him from doing so.* That said, it is his desire, which, come what may, prescribes the force, the shape, the modes, etc., of the law he lays down or passes on" (38; emphasis in the original). This is precisely the sexual economy worked out in the enigma in *La nave de los locos*: the king desires his daughter but "not daring to call her by her name" (203); he thus devises a law that covers over his desire and yet keeps the daughter for himself.

35. Indeed, Fletcher points out that the *aenigma* or riddle is actually one of the oldest types of allegory, citing Henry Peacham's sixteenth-century

definition: "Aenigma: a kind of Allegorie, differing only in obscuritie, for Aenigma is a sentence or forme of speech, which for the darknesse, the sense may hardly be gathered" (Fletcher 6, 8).

36. Ecks specifically uses the term "sacrifice" here as well as when referring to his dream of harmony as he contemplates the etching of Venice. In both cases, I suggest, he draws attention to the "sacrifice" of the "other" in the binarism of Western logic as it operates in representation, in national and political identities, and in sexuality.

37. Ecks is evidently an avid reader of Foucault, suggesting his works to others during the "literacy campaign" he undertakes by trying to get people to read over his shoulder in buses (66–67 in the English version; 69 in the Spanish).

38. As we saw in chapter 1, there is a similar preoccupation with disengaging the penis and the symbolically transcendent phallus in Piñon's *A Casa da Paixão*.

39. See Whitford 15–16 for an overview of the socialist feminist position that she sums up: "gender differences are a product of patriarchy and . . . we should fight for their elimination as part of the fight against the patriarchal order" (15).

40. From Lee Cullen Khanna's "Change and Art in Women's Worlds: Doris Lessing's *Canopus in Argos: Archives,*" (273–75), cited in Whitford (19).

41. Another idea transformed by the novel, in all its allegorical dreaming, is the notion of the *natural* which can help point to the way the novel radically questions political systems as well.

42. See the introduction of this study.

43. I am indebted for this insight on the Uruguayan regime's self-legitimation to Johnny Payne's analysis in *Conquest of the New Word.* See the beginning of his chapter on Nelson Marra's "El guardaespalda" (especially 46–49).

44. See Avellaneda 20–21.

45. Lyotard, for example, ends his answer to the question "What is Postmodernism?" with the following call to arms: "We have paid a high enough price for the nostalgia of the whole and one, for the reconciliation of the concept and the sensible, of the transparent and the communicable experience. [. . .] Let us wage a war on totality; let us be witnesses to the unpresentable; let us activate the differences and save the honor of the name" (81–82).

46. The supposed constrictions of the allegorical mode are often alluded to in allegory theory. Frye observes, for example, that "The com-

menting critic is often prejudiced against allegory without knowing the real reason, which is that continuous allegory prescribes the direction of his commentary, and so restricts its freedom" (90).

47. The advantages of such an ethical function of allegory, especially for the disenfranchised, are missed by Paul Smith ("The Will to Allegory in Postmodernism"). Smith denounces the will to power and meaning in post-modern allegory, taking issue with its tendency to fall back into the very repressive moralizing it tries to escape. But I suggest that there is a difference between morality and ethics, between attempts to contain and attempts to free. The "truth" *La nave* proposes at the end of Ecks's journey is not the same as the "truth" proposed in the closed system of the tapestry. Smith neglects the ways the will to power he sees as universally evil can have very different registers when used in an oppositional context. For Smith, "Post-modernism is the era of inflated truth, when The Author *reappears*, speaking allegory about/to himself" (118). Smith thus criticizes what he sees as post-modern allegory's tyranny: without the consensus that enabled the allegories of yore, the postmodern allegorist alone constructs the value system that subtends his allegory, leaving the reader more at his mercy than ever (see especially pages 115–19). Such a generalized pronouncement on allegory as an ultimately conservative gesture and on authorial, authoritative *reappear-ance* takes no account of the differences among the individuals occupying that authorial position. All the "Authors" Smith refers to are men (primarily Barth, Coover, Barthelme, Borges, and Beckett); he never pauses to consider what such a powerful tool might be capable of in the hands of other types of authors, those making perhaps not a *re*appearance but a debut.

Conclusion

1. This view of the process of change in Southern Cone countries has been observed and articulated by social scientists of the region. These scholars point out that social movements rather than enacting a radical break with former conditions, as being completely innovative, autonomous, and discontinuous must involve some sort of institutional mediation to be effective, even if that restricts some of their innovative potential (34–35). Alvarez quotes various scholars on this point including Renato Raul Boschi on Brazil and Jane S. Jaquette on Latin America in general. In addition, pro-cesses of sociopolitical change and their effects on women have also been characterized as transformational rather than revolutionary: "The democ-ratization processes still under way in Brazil and other South American nations fall far short of even the most restricted concept of 'revolutionary.' They nevertheless significantly transformed women's social, economic, and political roles in these societies" (Alvarez 14).

2. See her essay, especially pages 75–86.

3. This is from a letter dated 10 March 1993 in which Roffé responded to several of my questions about her work. Her original comments read: "Las 'líneas de fuerza' para la protagonista, como la escritura de *La rompiente* para mí, funcionaban como una puesta en orden interior frente a la incertidumbre exterior, como una forma de resistencia íntima, como un *poder* secreto que nadie iba a *poder* arrebatar. El acto de la lectura y de la escritura siempre es—y mucho más en situaciones límites—una especie de lujo personal, en el que el lector o el que escribe se apropian de 'otro mundo' que corrige o se opone al mundo de la realidad y donde el sentimiento que impera es o debería ser de libre albedrío. Como decir: puedo, a pesar de todo."

4. Eduardo Galeano 255; in his essay on commitment, Adorno refers to the saying that "to write lyric poetry after Auschwitz is barbaric" (188).

5. Similar gestures, as I have noted elsewhere, include the revalorization of "Black" in the civil rights movement in the United States or, in the Latin American context, the re-vision of the character of "Calibán" as per Fernández Retamar's essay. In the feminist context, these revalorizations or resemanticizations are prevalent, one example being Gilbert and Gubar's reappropriation of the portrayal of the woman writer as "madwoman in the attic."

6. This is the position Mary Ann Doane takes in her essay "Post-Utopian Difference." As she puts it, "the elaboration of a feminine specificity or sexuality has only tactical or strategic value—but this 'only' is not a 'merely.' This strategy is necessitated by a history of discourses which are indifferent and in their indifference erect and maintain a standard of masculinity, effectively effacing the woman. The history cannot be undone by reinserting indifference at another level" (77). See her discussion 77–78.

BIBLIOGRAPHY

Adorno, Theodor. "Commitment." In *Aesthetics and Politics*. Fredric Jameson, afterword. [First published in *Noten zur Literatur* Frankfurt 1965.] London: Verso, 1986.

Agosín, Marjorie. *La literatura y los derechos humanos: Aproximaciones, lecturas y encuentros.* Costa Rica: Editorial Universitaria Centroamericana, 1989.

―――. *Zones of Pain/Las zonas del dolor.* Cola Franzen, trans. New York: White Pine Press, 1988.

Ahmad, Aijaz. "Jameson's Rhetoric of Otherness and the 'National Allegory.'" *Social Text.* 17, 1987.

Althusser, Louis. "Ideology and Ideological State Apparatuses." *Lenin and Philosophy and Other Essays.* Trans. Ben Brewster. New York: Monthly Review Press, 1972.

Alvarez, Sonia. *Engendering Democracy in Brazil: Women's Movements in Transition Politics.* Princeton, N.J.: Princeton University Press, 1990.

Arrate, Marina. "Los significados de la escritura y su relación con la identidad femenina latinoamericana en *Por la patria*, de Diamela Eltit." In *Una poética de literatura menor: La narrativa de Diamela Eltit.* Juan Carlos Lértora, ed. and intro. Santiago: Editorial Cuarto Propio, 1993.

Ashcroft, Bill and Gareth Griffiths and Helen Tiffin. *The Empire Writes Back: Theory and Practice in Post-Colonial Literatures.* London and New York: Routledge, 1989.

Avellaneda, Andrés. *Censura, autoritarismo y cultura: Argentina 1960–1983.* Vol. 1–2. Buenos Aires: Centro Editor de América Latina, 1986.

―――. "Realismo, antirrealismo, territorios canónicos: Argentina literaria después de los militares." In *Fascismo y experiencia literaria: Reflexiones para una recanonización.* Hernán Vidal, ed. Minneapolis, Minn.: University of Minnesota, Institute for the Study of Ideologies and Literature, 1985; 578–88.

Balderston, Daniel, et al. *Ficción y política: La narrativa argentina durante el proceso militar.* René Jara y Hernán Vidal, presentación. Buenos Aires: Alianza Editorial, 1987.

Barthes, Roland. *Image-Music-Text*. Stephen Heath, trans. New York: Hill and Wang, 1977.

Bataille, Georges. *Erotism: Death & Sensuality*. Mary Dalwood, trans. Orig. published: *L'Erotisme*, 1957. San Francisco: City Lights Books, 1986.

Benjamin, Jessica. "Sado-Masoquism?" In *Powers of Desire: The Politics of Sexuality*. New York: Monthly Review Press, 1983.

———. *The Bonds of Love: Psychoanalysis, Feminism, and the Problem of Domination*. New York: Pantheon, 1988.

Benjamin, Walter. *The Origin of German Tragic Drama*. John Osborne, trans. London: NLB, 1977.

Blanco, Guillermo. "Las mujeres se interrogan." *Hoy*. 10 (August 1987): 49–50.

Brasil, nunca mais. See Dassin, *Torture in Brazil*.

Brito, Eugenia. "La narrativa de Diamela Eltit: un nuevo paradigma socio-literario de lectura." In *Campos minados (literatura post-golpe en Chile)*. Santiago: Editorial Cuarto Propio, 1990.

Brunner, José Joaquín. "Campo artístico, escena de avanzada y autoritarismo en Chile." In *Arte en Chile desde 1973. Escena de Avanzada y Sociedad*. Nelly Richard, coordinator. Santiago: FLACSO, 1987.

———, Alicia Barros, and Carlos Catalán. *Chile: Transformaciones culturales y modernidad*. Santiago: FLACSO, 1989.

———. *La Cultura Autoritaria en Chile*. Santiago: FLACSO, 1981.

Bunster-Burotto, Ximena. "Surviving Beyond Fear: *Women and Torture in Latin America*." In *Women and Change in Latin America*. June Nash and Helen Safa, eds. South Hadley, Massachusetts: Bergin & Garvey, 1986.

Bürger, Peter. *Theory of the Avant-Garde*. Michael Shaw, trans. Jochen Schulte-Sasse, foreword. Minneapolis: University of Minnesota Press, 1984.

Burkert, Walter. *Ancient Mystery Cults*. Cambridge and London: Harvard University Press, 1987.

Butler, Judith. *Gender Trouble: Feminism and the Subversion of Identity*. New York and London: Routledge, 1990.

Campbell, Joseph. *The Masks of God: Primitive Mythology*. New York: Viking, 1959.

Camps, Susana. "La pasión desde la pasión: Entrevista con Cristina Peri-Rossi." *Quimera: Revista de Literatura* 81 (September 1988): 40–49.

Cánovas, Rodrigo. "Apuntes sobre la novela *Por la patria* (1986), de Diamela Eltit." Acta Literaria. 15 (1990): 147–60.

Castillo, Debra A. *Talking Back: Toward a Latin American Feminist Literary Criticism.* Ithaca and London: Cornell University Press, 1992.

Castro-Klarén, Sara. "Escritura y Cuerpo en *Lumpérica.*" In *Una poética de literatura menor: la narrativa de Diamela Eltit.* Juan Carlos Lértora, ed. and intro. Santiago: Editorial Cuarto Propio, 1993.

––––––. "La crítica literaria feminista la escritora en América Latina." In *La sartén por el mango.* Patricia Elena González and Eliana Ortega, eds. Río Piedras, Puerto Rico: Huracán, 1985.

––––––, Sylvia Molloy, and Beatriz Sarlo, eds. *Women's Writing in Latin America.* Boulder: Westview Press, 1991.

Cesareo, Mario. "Cuerpo humano e historia en la novela del proceso." In *Fascismo y experiencia literaria: Reflexiones para una recanonización.* Hernán Vidal, ed. Minneapolis: Ideologies & Literature, 1985.

Chanady, Amaryll B. "Cristina Peri Rossi and the Other Side of Reality." *The Antigonish Review.* 54 (summer 1983): 44–48.

Cixous, Hélène. "Sorties." Ann Liddle, trans. In *New French Feminisms: An Anthology.* Elaine Marks and Isabelle de Courtivron, eds. New York: Schocken Books, 1981; first published in *La jeune née,* 1975.

Clifford, Gay. *The Transformations of Allegory.* London and Boston: Routledge & Kegan Paul, 1974.

Corradi, Juan E., et al. *Fear at the Edge: State Terror and Resistance in Latin America.* Berkeley: University of California Press, 1992.

Costigan, Lúcia Helena. "Litertura e Ditadura: Aspectos da Ficção Brasileira Pós-64 em Alguns Dos Escritos de Lygia Fagundes Telles e de Nélida Piñon." *Hispanic Journal.* 13, no. 1 (spring 1992): 141–51.

Dassin, Joan. "Press Censorship and the Military State in Brazil." In *Press Control Around the World.* Jane Leftwich Curry and Joan R. Dassin, eds. New York: Praeger, 1982.

––––––, ed. *Torture in Brazil: A Report by the Archdiocese of São Paulo.* Translation of *Brasil, nunca mais,* published in 1985. Jaime Wright, trans. New York: Random House, 1986.

de Lauretis, Teresa. *Alice Doesn't: Feminism, Semiotics, Cinema.* Bloomington: Indiana University Press, 1984.

———, ed. *Feminist Studies/Critical Studies.* Bloomington: Indiana University Press, 1984.

———. *Technologies of Gender: Essays on Theory, Film, and Fiction.* Bloomington: Indiana University Press, 1987.

De Man, Paul. *Allegories of Reading: Figural Language in Rousseau, Nietzsche, Rilke, and Proust.* New Haven: Yale University Press, 1979.

———. "Rhetoric of Temporality." In *Interpretation: Theory and Practice.* C. S. Singleton, ed. Baltimore: Johns Hopkins University Press, 1969.

Dilnot, Clive and Maruja García-Padilla. "The Difference of Allegory." *Journal of Philosophy and the Visual Arts.* 1:1 (1989): 40–53.

Doane, Mary Ann. "Commentary: Post-Utopian Difference." In *Coming to Terms: Feminism, Theory, Politics.* Elizabeth Weed, ed. New York: Routledge, 1989.

Donoso, Claudia. "Tenemos puesto el espejo para el otro lado." (interview with Eltit). *Apsi.* (26 de enero al 8 de febrero, 1987): 47–48.

DuPlessis, Rachel Blau. "For the Etruscans." In *The New Feminist Criticism: Essays on Women, Literature, and Theory.* Elaine Showalter, ed. New York: Pantheon, 1985.

———. *Writing Beyond the Ending: Narrative Strategies of Twentieth-Century Women Writers.* Bloomington: Indiana University Press, 1985.

Eltit, Diamela. "Cultura, poder y frontera." *La Época.* 3:113 (10 de junio de 1990): 1–2.

———. *El cuarto mundo.* Santiago: Planeta/Biblioteca del Sur, 1988.

———. "Errante, Errática." In *Una poética de literatura menor: la narrativa de Diamela Eltit.* Juan Carlos Lértora, ed. Santiago: Editorial Cuarto Propio, 1993.

———. "Experiencia literaria y palabra en duelo." In *Duelo y creatividad.* Eleonora Casaula, Edmundo Covarrubias, Diamela Eltit, eds. Santiago: Editorial Cuarto Propio, 1989.

———. *Por la patria.* Santiago: Ediciones Ornitorrinco, 1986.

Fares, Gustavo and Eliana Hermann. "Exilios Internos: El viaje en cinco escritoras argentinas." *Hispanic Journal.* 15, no. 1 (spring 1994): 21–29.

Feijoó, María del Carmen and Mónica Gogna. "Las mujeres en la transición a la democracia." in *Los nuevos movimientos sociales.* Vol. 1. Ed. Elizabeth Jelin. Buenos Aires, Centro Editor, 1985.

———. "The Challenge of Constructing Civilian Peace: Women and Democracy in Argentina." In *The Women's Movement in Latin America*. Jane S. Jaquette, ed. Boston: Unwin Hyman, 1989.

Fineman, Joel. "The Structure of Allegorical Desire." *Allegory and Representation*. Stephen J. Greenblatt, ed. Baltimore and London: Johns Hopkins Press, 1981.

Fletcher, Angus. *Allegory: Theory of a Symbolic Mode*. Ithaca: Cornell University Press, 1964.

Foster, David William. "Los parámetros de la narrativa argentina durante el 'Proceso de Reorganización Nacional.'" In *Ficción y política: La narrativa argentina durante el proceso militar*. Daniel Balderston, et al. René Jara y Hernán Vidal, presentación. Buenos Aires and Minneapolis: Institute for the Study of Ideologies & Literature and Alianza Editorial, 1987: 96–108.

———. "The Demythification of Buenos Aires in Selected Argentine Novels of the Seventies." *Chasqui*. 10:1 (noviembre 1980): 4–25.

Foster, Hal. *The Anti-Aesthetic: Essays on Postmodern Culture*. Port Townsend, Washington: Bay Press, 1983.

Foucault, Michel. *Madness and Civilization: A History of Insanity in the Age of Reason*. Richard Howard, trans. New York: Vintage, 1973.

———. *The Foucault Reader*. Ed. Paul Rabinow. New York: Pantheon, 1984.

———. *The History of Sexuality*. Trans. R. Hurley. New York: Vintage, 1979.

Franco, Jean. "Apuntes sobre la crítica feminista y la literatura hispanoamericana." *Hispamérica*. 4–5 (1986): 31–43.

———. "Beyond Ethnocentrism: Gender, Power, and the Third-World Intelligentsia." In *Marxism and the Interpretation of Culture*. Cary Nelson and Lawrence Grossberg, eds. Urbana: University of Illinois Press, 1988: 503–13.

Friedman, Ellen G., and Miriam Fuchs, intro. and eds. *Breaking the Sequence: Women's Experimental Fiction*. Princeton: Princeton University Press, 1989.

Freud, Sigmund. *The Ego and the Id*. Joan Riviere, trans. James Strachey, ed. New York and London: Norton, 1960.

———. "Feminity." In *New Introductory Lectures on Psychoanalysis*. 1933. James Strachey, trans. New York: Norton & Co., 1965.

Frye, Northrop. *Anatomy of Criticism*. Princeton: Princeton University Press, 1957.

Fuss, Diana. *Essentially Speaking: Feminism, Nature, and Difference*. New York and London: Routledge, 1989.

Galeano, Eduardo. "The Dictatorship and Its Aftermath: The Secret Wounds." In *Critical Fictions: The Politics of Imaginative Writing*. Philomena Mariani, ed. Seattle: Bay Press, 1991.

Gallop, Jane. "*Quand nos lèvres s'écrivent*: Irigaray's Body Politic." *Romanic Review* 74:1 (January 1983): 77–83.

———. *Thinking Through the Body*. New York: Columbia University Press, 1988.

Gligo, Agata. "*Por la patria*, de Diamela Eltit." *Mensaje*. 355 (diciembre 1986): 524–25.

Godwin, Joscelyn. *Mystery Religions in the Ancient World*. San Francisco: Harper & Row, 1981.

Golano, Elena. "Soñar para seducir: entrevista con Cristina Peri Rossi." *Quimera*. 25 (November 1982): 47–50.

Gramuglio, María Teresa. "Aproximaciones a *La rompiente*." Estudio posliminar. *La rompiente*. Buenos Aires: Puntosur Editores, 1987.

Graziano, Frank. *Divine Violence: Spectacle, Psychosexuality, & Radical Christianity in the Argentine "Dirty War."* Boulder: Westview Press, 1992.

Greenblatt, Stephen J, ed. *Allegory and Representation*. Baltimore: Johns Hopkins University Press, 1981.

Guerra-Cunningham, Lucía. "La referencialidad como negación del paraíso: Exilio y excentrismo en *La nave de los locos* de Cristina Peri Rossi." *Revista de Estudios Hispánicos*. 23:2 (May 1989): 63–74.

Henriques, Julian, Wendy Holway, et al. *Changing the Subject: Psychology, Social Regulation, and Subjectivity*. London and New York: Methuen, 1984.

Holquist, Michael. "The Politics of Representation." In *Allegory and Representation*. Stephen J. Greenblatt, ed. Baltimore and London: Johns Hopkins University Press, 1981.

Honig, Edwin. *Dark Conceit: The Making of Allegory*. Evanston, Ill.: Northwestern University Press, 1959.

hooks, bel. "marginality as a site of resistance." In *Out There: Marginalization and Contemporary Cultures*. Russell Ferguson, et al., eds. Cambridge: MIT Press, 1990 (341–43).

Hutcheon, Linda. *The Politics of Postmodernism*. London and New York: Routledge, 1989.

Invernizzi Santa Cruz, Lucía. "Entre el tapiz de la expulsión y el tapiz de la creación: Múltiples sentidos del viaje a bordo de *La nave de los locos* de Cristina Peri Rossi." *Revista chilena de literatura* 30 (November 1987): 29–53.

Irigaray, Luce. *Speculum of the Other Woman*. Gillian C. Gill, trans. Ithaca: Cornell University Press, 1985.

———. *This Sex Which Is Not One*. Catherine Porter, trans. Ithaca: Cornell University Press, 1985.

James, E. O. *The Tree of Life: An Archaeological Study*. Leiden: Brill, 1966.

Jameson, Fredric. *The Political Unconscious: Narrative as a Socially Symbolic Act*. Ithaca: Cornell University Press, 1981.

———. "Third-World Literature in the Era of Multinational Capital." *Social Text*. 15:3 (fall 1986): 65–88.

Jaquette, Jane S. *The Women's Movement in Latin America*. Boston: Unwin Hyman, 1989.

Jara, René. "Arqueología de un paradigma de negación: El discurso del jefe del estado." In *The Discourse of Power: Culture, Hegemony, and the Authoritarian State*. Neil Larsen, ed. Minneapolis: Ideologies & Literature, 1983.

Jardine, Alice. *Gynesis: Configurations of Woman and Modernity*. Ithaca: Cornell University Press, 1985.

Jofré, Manuel Alcides. "La novela en Chile: 1973–1983." In *Fascismo y experiencia literaria: Reflexiones para una recanonización*. Hernán Vidal, ed. Minneapolis: Ideologies & Literature, 1985.

Johnson, Barbara. *The Critical Difference: Essays on the Contemporary Rhetoric of Reading*. Baltimore: Johns Hopkins University Press: 1980.

Kadir, Djelal. *The Other Writing: Postcolonial Essays in Latin America's Writing Culture*. W. Lafayette, Indiana: Purdue University Press, 1993.

Kaminsky, Amy. "Gender and Exile in Cristina Peri Rossi." In *Continental, Latin-American and Francophone Women Writers*. Lanham, Md.: University Press of America, 1987.

————. *Reading the Body Politic: Feminist Criticism and Latin American Women Writers*. Minneapolis: University of Minnesota Press, 1993.

Kantaris, Elia. "The Politics of Desire: Alienation and Identity in the Work of Marta Traba and Cristina Peri Rossi." *Forum for Modern Language Studies*. 25:3 (July 1989): 248–64.

Kirkwood, Julieta. *Feminario*. Santiago: Ediciones Documentos, 1987.

————. "Feministas y políticas." *Nueva Sociedad*. (julio/agosto 1985): 62–70.

Kohut, Karl, y Andrea Pagni, eds. *Literatura argentina de hoy: De la dictadura a la democracia*. Frankfurt: Vervuert Verlag, 1989.

Kristeva, Julia. *The Kristeva Reader*. Toril Moi, ed. New York: Columbia University Press, 1986.

Lacan, Jacques. *Écrit: A Selection*. Alan Sheridan, trans. New York and London: Norton, 1977.

Lértora, Juan Carlos. *Una poética de literatura menor: la narrativa de Diamela Eltit*. Santiago: Editorial Cuarto Propio, 1993.

Lewis, C. S. *The Allegory of Love: A Study in Medieval Tradition*. London: Oxford University Press, 1936.

Lispector, Clarice. "Nélida Piñon" (interview). *De Corpo Inteiro*. Rio de Janeiro: Editora Artenova, 1975.

Lukin, Liliana. *Descomposición*. Buenos Aires: Ediciones de la flor, 1986.

Lyotard, Jean-Francois. *The Postmodern Condition: A Report on Knowledge*. Minneapolis: University of Minnesota Press, 1984.

MacKinnon, Catharine A. "Feminism, Marxism, Method, and the State: An Agenda for Theory." In *Feminist Theory: A Critique of Ideology*. Nannerl O. Keohane, Michelle Z. Rosaldo, and Barbara C. Gelpi, eds. Chicago: University of Chicago Press, 1982.

Malloy, Sylvia. "Sylvia Molloy." In *Historias íntimas: Conversaciones con diez escritoras latinoamericanas*. García Pinto, comp. Hanover, N.H.: Ediciones del Norte, 1988.

Mariani, Philomena, ed. *Critical Fictions: The Politics of Imaginative Writing*. Seattle: Bay Press, 1991.

Marks, Elaine, and Isabelle de Courtivron, eds. *New French Feminisms*. New York: Schoken Books, 1981.

Martínez de Richter, Marily. "Textualizaciones de la violencia: *Informe bajo llave* de Marta Lynch y *La rompiente* de Reina Roffé." *Siglo XX/Twentieth Century*. 11, no. 1–2 (1993): 89–117.

Masiello, Francine. "Cuerpo/presencia: Mujer y estado social en la narrativa argentina durante el Proceso Militar." *Nuevo texto crítico.* 4:2 (Segundo Semestre, 1989): 155–71.

———. "Discurso de mujeres, lenguaje del poder: reflexiones sobre la crítica feminista a mediados de la década del 80." *Hispamérica* 45 (1986): 53–60.

———. "La Argentina durante el Proceso: las múltiples resistencias de la cultura." In *Ficción y política: La narrativa argentina durante el proceso militar.* Daniel Balderston, et al. René Jara y Hernán Vidal, presentación. Buenos Aires and Minneapolis: Institute for the Study of Ideologies and Literature and Alianza Editorial (1987): 11–29.

Mattelart, Michele, and Armand Mattelart. *Comunicación e ideologías de la seguridad.* Barcelona: Anagrama, 1978.

Medina, Cremilda. "Nélida Piñon, resistente, preserva o direito de narrar o humano." *O Estado de São Paolo,* April 9, 1978.

Minh-ha, Trinh T. *Woman Native Other: Writing Postcoloniality and Feminism.* Bloomington: Indiana University Press, 1989.

Mizrahi, Liliana. *La mujer transgresora: Acerca del cambio y la ambivalencia.* Buenos Aires: Grupo Editor Latinoamericano, 1987.

Moi, Toril. *Sexual/Textual Politics: Feminist Literary Theory.* London and New York: Routledge, 1985.

Moniz, Naomi Hoki. "*A Casa da Paixão*: Ética, Estética e a Condição Feminina," *Revista Iberoamericana* Jan.–Mar. 1984 v50: 126–40.

———. *As Viagens de Nélida, A Escritora.* Campinas Brazil: Editora da UNICAMP, 1993.

Montecino, Sonia. *Madres y huachos: alegorías del mestizaje chileno.* Santiago: Editorial Cuarto Propio, 1991.

Mora, Gabriela. "Peri Rossi: *La nave de los locos* y la búsqueda de la armonía." *Nuevo Texto Crítico.* 1:2 (1988): 343–52.

———. "Enigmas and Subversions in Cristina Peri Rossi's *La nave de los locos.*" In *Splintering Darkness: Latin American Women Writers in Search of Themselves.* Lucía Guerra-Cunningham, ed. Pittsburgh: Latin American Literary Review Press, 1990.

Moraes Neto, Geneton. Interview with Nélida Piñon. *Jornal do Brasil.* (5 de Dez. 1987): 8–9.

Moraña, Mabel. "Hacia una crítica de la nueva narrativa hispanoamericana: Alegoría y realismo en Cristina Peri Rossi." *Revista de estudios hispánicos.* 21:3 (October 1987): 33–48.

————. "*La nave de los locos* de Cristina Peri Rossi." *Texto crítico* 12:34–35 (1986): 204–13.

Mulvey, Laura. "Visual Pleasure and Narrative Cinema." In *Women and the Cinema: A Critical Anthology*. Karyn Kay and Gerald Peary, eds. New York: Dutton, 1977.

Munizaga, Giselle and Carlos Ochsensius. "El Discurso Público de Pinochet (1973–1976)." *The Discourse of Power: Culture, Hegemony and the Authoritarian State in Latin America*. Neil Larsen, ed. Minneapolis: Ideologies & Literature, 1983.

Nietzsche, Friedrich. *Basic Writings of Nietzsche*. Walter Kaufmann, ed. and trans. New York: The Modern Library, 1968.

Neumann, Erich. *The Origins and History of Consciousness*. F. C. Hull, trans. Bollingen Series XLII. New York: Pantheon, 1954.

Newman, Kathleen. "Cultural Redemocratization: Argentina, 1978–89." In *On Edge: The Crisis of Contemporary Latin American Culture*. George Yúdice, et al., eds. Minneapolis: University of Minnesota Press, 1992.

Nunca Más: The Report of the Argentine National Commission on the Disappeared. Ronald Dworkin, intro. New York: Farrar, Straus & Giroux, 1986.

Olivera-Williams, María Rosa. "*La nave de los locos* de Cristina Peri Rossi." *Revista de crítica literaria latinoamericana*. 7(23): (1986): 81–89.

Ordóñez, Montserrat. "Cristina Peri-Rossi: Asociaciones." *Eco: Revista de la cultura de occidente*. 41(2): (Junio 1982): 196–205.

Ortega, Julio. "Resistencia y sujeto femenino: entrevista con Diamela Eltit." *La Torre*. 4(14): (abril–junio 1990): 229–41.

————. "Postmodernism in Latin America." (unpub. ms.).

Owens, Craig. "The Allegorical Impulse: Toward a Theory of Postmodernism" Part I. *October*. 12 Spring 1980; and Part II. *October*. 13 Summer 1980.

"The Discourse of Others: Feminists and Postmodernism" In *The Anti-Aesthetic: Essays on Postmodern Culture*. Hal Foster, ed. Port Townsend, Washington: Bay Press, 1983.

Payne, Johnny. *Conquest of the New Word: Experimental Fiction and Translation in the Americas*. Austin: University of Texas Press, 1993.

Perelli, Carina. "El poder de la memoria. La memoria del poder." *Represión, exilio y democracia: La cultura uruguaya*. Saúl Sosnowski, comp. Montevideo: Ediciones de la Banda Oriental/Universidad de Maryland, 1987: 319–33.

Peri Rossi, Cristina. *Indicios pánicos*. Barcelona: Editorial Bruguera, 1981; Montevideo: Nuestra América, 1970.

——. "Genesis de 'Europa después de la lluvia.'" *Studi di Letteratura ispano-americana*. 13–14: (1983): 63–78.

——. *La nave de los locos*. Barcelona: Seix Barral/Biblioteca Breve, 1984.

——. *The Ship of Fools*. Psiche Hughes, trans. London: Readers International, 1989.

Piglia, Ricardo. "Ficción y política en la literatura argentina." *Literatura argentina hoy: De la dictadura a la democracia*. Frankfurt: Vervuert Verlag, 1989.

Piñon, Nélida. *A Casa de Paixão*. 4a edição. Rio de Janeiro: Editora nova fronteira, 1972.

——. *The Republic of Dreams*. Helen Lane, trans. *A República dos Sonhos*, 1984. New York: Knopf, 1989.

Plotnik, Viviana. "Alegoría y proceso de reorganización nacional: propuesta de una categoría de mediación socio-histórica para el análisis discursivo." In *Fascismo y experiencia literaria*. Vidal, ed. Minneapolis: Ideologies & Literature, 1985, 532–77.

Pomeroy, Sarah B. *Goddesses, Whores, Wives, and Slaves: Women in Classical Antiquity*. New York: Schocken, 1975.

Pratt, Annis. *Archetypal Patterns in Women's Fiction*. Bloomington: Indiana University Press, 1981.

——. "Spinning Among Fields: Jung, Frye, Lévi-Strauss and Feminist Archetypal Theory." In *Feminist Archetypal Theory: Interdisciplinary Re-visions of Jungian Thought*. Estella Lauter and Carol Schreier Rupprecht, eds. Knoxville: University of Tennessee Press, 1985.

Rial, Juan. "El imaginario social: Los mitos políticos y utopías en el Uruguay/ Cambios y permanencias durante y después del autoritarismo." *Represión, exilio y democracia: La cultura uruguaya*. Saúl Sosnowski, comp. Montevideo: Ediciones de la Banda Oriental/Universidad de Maryland, 1987; 63–89.

Rich, Adrienne. *Of Woman Born: Motherhood as Experience and Institution*. Tenth Anniversary Edition. New York: Norton, 1986.

Richard, Nelly. *Margins and Institutions: Art in Chile since 1973*. Melbourne: Art & Text, 1986.

——. "Estéticas de la oblicuidad." *Revista Cultural de Crítica*. 1(1): (Mayo 1990): 6–8.

Ricoeur, Paul. *Freud and Philosophy: An Essay on Interpretation.* Denis Savage, trans. New Haven: Yale University Press, 1970.

Ríos, Patricio. "Chile: ni desprecio ni puro amor." Interview with Diamela Eltit. *Cauce 100* (23 de marzo de 1987) 30.

Robinson, Sally. *Engendering the Subject: Gender and Self-Representation in Contemporary Women's Fiction.* Albany: SUNY Press, 1991.

Rodríguez, Mercedes M. de. "Variaciones del tema del exilio en el mundo alegórico de *El museo de los esfuerzos inútiles.*" *Mongraphic Review/Revista Monográfica.* 4 (1988): 69–77.

———. "Oneiric Riddles in Peri Rossi's *La nave de los locos.*" *RLA: Romance Languages Annual.* 1 (1989): 521–27.

Roffé, Reina. *La rompiente.* Buenos Aires: Punto Sur, 1987.

———. "Ominpresencia de la censura en la escritora argentina." *Revista iberoamericana.* I:132–33 (julio–diciembre 1985): 909–15.

———. "Qué escribimos las mujeres en la Argentina de hoy." In *Literatura argentina de hoy: De la dictadura a la democracia.* Karl Kohut y Andrea Pagni, eds. Frankfurt: Vervuert Verlag, 1989: 205–13.

Rojo, Grinor and John J. Hassett, eds. *Chile: Dictatorship and the Struggle for Democracy.* Gaithersburg, Md.: Ediciones Hispamérica, 1988.

Rossi, Laura. "¿Cómo pensar a las Madres de la Plaza de Mayo?" *Nuevo texto crítico.* 4:2 (Segundo Semestre, 1989): 145–53.

Rubin, Gayle. "The Traffic in Women: Notes on the 'Political Economy' of Sex." In *Toward an Anthropology of Women.* Rayna R. Reiter, ed. New York: Monthly Review Press, 1975.

Rueda, Ana. "Cristina Peri Rossi: El esfuerzo inútil de erigir un museo natural." *Nuevo Texto Crítico.* 4:11 (1989): 197–204.

Said, Edward. *The World, the Text, and the Critic.* Cambridge: Harvard University Press, 1983.

———. "The Mind of Winter: Reflections on Life in Exile." *Harper's.* (September 1984): 49–55.

Salvaggio, Ruth. "Theory and Space, Space and Woman." *Tulsa Studies of Literature.* 7: 2 (fall 1988) 261–82.

Sarduy, Severo. "El barroco y el neobarroco." In *América Latina en su literatura.* César Fernández Moreno, ed. México, 1977: 167–84.

Sarlo, Beatriz. "Política, ideología y figuración literaria." In *Ficción y política: La narrativa argentina durante el proceso militar.* René Jara y

Hernán Vidal, presentación. Buenos Aires and Minneapolis: Institute for the Study of Ideologies and Literature and Alianza Editorial, 1987: 30–59.

———. "Women, History, and Ideology." In *Women's Writing in Latin America*. Sara Castro-Klarén, Sylvia Molloy, and Beatriz Sarlo, eds. Boulder: Westview Press, 1991.

Schneider, Cathy Lisa. *Shantytown Protest in Pinochet's Chile*. Philadelphia: Temple University Press, 1995.

Slemon, Stephen. "Monuments of Empire: Allegory/Counter-Discourse/Post-Colonial Writing." *Kunapipi* 9(3): (1987): 1–16.

Smith, Paul Julian. *The Body Hispanic: Gender and Sexuality in Hispanic Literature*. Oxford: Clarendon Press, 1989.

Smith, Paul. *Discerning the Subject*. Minneapolis: University of Minnesota Press, 1988.

———. "The Will to Allegory in Postmodernism." *Dalhousie Review* 62:1 (spring 1982): 105–22.

Sosnowski, Saúl, comp. *Represión, exilio y democracia: La cultura uruguaya*. Montevideo: Ediciones de la Banda Oriental/Universidad de Maryland, 1987.

———, comp. *Represión y reconstrucción de una cultura: el caso argentino*. Buenos Aires: Editorial Universitaria de Buenos Aires, 1988.

Spariosu, Mihai. "Allegory, Hermeneutics, and Postmodernism." In *Exploring Postmodernism*. Matei Calinescu and Douwe Fokkema, eds. Amsterdam: Benjamins, 1987.

Spivak, Gayatri Chakravorty. "Can the Subaltern Speak?" In *Marxism and the Interpretation of Culture*, pp. 271–313, eds. Cary Nelson and Lawrence Grossberg. Urbana: University of Illinois Press, 1988.

———. *In Other Worlds: Essays in Cultural Politics*. Routledge: New York, 1988.

Stallybrass, Peter, and Allon White. *The Politics and Poetics of Transgression*. Ithaca: Cornell University Press, 1986.

Sturrock, John, ed. *Structuralism and Since: From Lévi Strauss to Derrida*. New York and Oxford: Oxford University Press, 1979.

Suleiman, Susan Rubin. *Subversive Intent: Gender, Politics, and the Avant-Garde*. Cambridge: Harvard University Press, 1990.

Szurmuk, Mónica. "La textualización de la represión en *La rompiente* de Reina Roffé." *Nuevo Texto Crítico*. III:5 (primer semestre, 1990): 123–31.

Timerman, Jacobo. *Chile: Death in the South*. New York: Knopf, 1987.

Traba, Marta. "Hipotesis sobre un escritura diferente." *La sartén por el mango*. Patricia Elena González and Eliana Ortega, eds. Río Piedras: Ediciones Huracán, 1985.

Ulibarri, Luisa. "Cien mujeres y cinco días de preguntas" (entrevista con Diamela Eltit). *La época*. Sábado 15 de agosto de 1987.

Uribe, O. "Literary Experience/Social Experience and the Creation of a New Subjectivity in Monte de Venus by Reina Roffé." *Linea plural* (spring 1988): 37–39.

Uruguay Nunca Más: Human Rights Violations, 1972–1985. Servicio Paz y Justicia, Uruguay, 1989. Elizabeth Hampsten, trans. Lawrence Weschler, intro. Philadelphia: Temple University Press, 1992.

Van Dyck, Karen. "Reading Between Worlds: Contemporary Greek Women's Writing and Censorship." PMLA. 109: 1 (1994): 45–60.

Valenzuela, Luisa. "The Writer, the Crisis, and a Form of Representation." In *Critical Fictions: The Politics of Imaginative Writing*. Philomena Mariani, ed. Seattle: Bay Press, 1991.

Velasco, Mavel. "Cristina Peri Rossi y la ansiedad de la influencia." *Monographic Review/Revista Monográfica*. 4 (1988): 207–20.

Verani, Hugo J. "Una experiencia de límites: La narrativa de Cristina Peri Rossi." *Revista Iberoamericana* 48: 118–19 (Jan.–June, 1982): 303–16.

Vidal, Hernán, ed. *Fascismo y experiencia literaria: Reflexiones para un recanonización*. Institute for the Study of Ideologies and Literature. Minneapolis: Monographic Series of the Society for the Study of Contemporary Hispanic and Lusophone Revolutionary Literature, 1985.

———. "Hacia un Modelo General de la Sensibilidad Social Literaturizable Bajo el Fascismo." *Fascismo y Experiencia Literaria: Reflexiones para una recanonización*. Hernán Vidal, ed. Institute for the Study of Ideologies and Literature. Minneapolis: Monographic Series of the Society for the Study of Contemporary Hispanic and Lusophone Revolutionary Literature, 1985.

———. "La declaración de principios de la junta militar chilena como sistema literario: La lucha antifacista y el cuerpo humano." *Casa de las Américas*. 119 (1980): 63–78.

Weed, Elizabeth, ed. *Coming to Terms: Feminism, Theory, Politics*. New York and London: Routledge, 1989.

Wehr, Demaris, S. "Religious and Social Dimensions of Jung's Concept of the Archetype: A Feminist Perspective." In *Feminist Archetypal Theory: Interdisciplinary Re-Visions of Jungian Thought*. Estella Lauter and Carol Schreier Rupprecht, eds. Knoxville: University of Tennessee Press, 1985.

Whitford, Margaret. *Luce Irigaray: Philosophy in the Feminine*. New York and London: Routledge, 1991.

Williams, Raymond. *Marxism and Literature*. Oxford and New York: Oxford University Press, 1977.

Woolf, Virginia. *Mrs. Dalloway*. New York: Harvest/HBJ Books, 1925.

———. *A Room of One's Own*. New York: Harvest/HBJ Books, 1929.

Zeitz, Eileen. "Tres escritores uruguayos en el exilio: Cristina Peri Rossi: El desafío de la alegoría; Eduardo Galeano: El oficio de la revelación desafiante; Saúl Ibargoyen Islas: El nosotros allá." *Chasqui: Revista de literatura latinoamericana*. 9:1 (November 1979): 79–101.

INDEX